Post-Treaty Politics

D0910481

Earth System Governance

Frank Biermann and Oran R. Young, series editors

Related books from Institutional Dimensions of Global Environmental Change: A Core Research Project of the International Human Dimensions Programme on Global Environmental Change

Post-Treaty Politics

Secretariat Influence in Global Environmental Governance

Sikina Jinnah

The MIT Press
Cambridge, Massachusetts
London, England

MIT Press books may be purchased at special quantity discounts for business or sales promotional use. For information, please email special_sales@mitpress.mit.edu.

This book was set in Sabon LT Std 10/13 pt by Toppan Best-set Premedia Limited. Printed and bound in the United States of America.

Library of Congress Cataloging-in-Publication Data

Jinnah, Sikina, 1977–
Post-treaty politics : secretariat influence in global environmental governance / Sikina Jinnah.
    pages cm.—(Earth system governance)
Includes bibliographical references and index.
ISBN 978-0-262-02804-2 (hardcover : alk. paper)—ISBN 978-0-262-52655-5 (pbk. : alk. paper)
1. Environmental policy—International cooperation—Case studies. 2. Environmental management—International cooperation—Case studies. 3. Secretariats—Case studies. 4. Convention on Biological Diversity (Organization) 5. World Trade Organization. 6. Convention on International Trade in Endangered Species of Wild Fauna and Flora (1973). I. Title.
GE170.J56 2014
363.7'056—dc23
                                        2014007219

10 9 8 7 6 5 4 3 2 1

For Lyosha

Contents

Series Foreword

Humans now influence all biological and physical systems of the planet. Almost no species, land area, or part of the oceans has remained unaffected by the expansion of the human species. Recent scientific findings suggest that the entire earth system now operates outside the normal state exhibited over at least the past 500,000 years. Yet at the same time, it is apparent that the institutions, organizations, and mechanisms by which humans govern their relationship with the natural environment and global biogeochemical systems are utterly insufficient—and poorly understood. More fundamental and applied research is needed.

Such research is no easy undertaking. It must span the entire globe because only integrated global solutions can ensure a sustainable coevolution of biophysical and socioeconomic systems. But it must also draw on local experiences and insights. Research on earth system governance must be about places in all their diversity, yet seek to integrate place-based research within a global understanding of the myriad human interactions with the earth system. Eventually, the task is to develop integrated systems of governance, from the local to the global level, that ensure the sustainable development of the coupled socioecological system that the Earth has become.

The series Earth System Governance is designed to address this research challenge. Books in this series will pursue this challenge from a variety of disciplinary perspectives, at different levels of governance, and with a range of methods. Yet all will further one common aim: analyzing current systems of earth system governance with a view to increased understanding and possible improvements and reform. Books in this series will be of interest to the academic community but will also inform practitioners and at times contribute to policy debates.

This series is related to the long-term international research program "Earth System Governance Project."

Frank Biermann, *VU University Amsterdam* and *Lund University*
Oran R. Young, *Bren School, University of California, Santa Barbara*
Earth System Governance Series Editors

Foreword

Students of domestic politics have lavished attention on matters of public administration since the nineteenth century. Research on the role of administrative agencies emerged as a coherent field of study even before the advent of modern political science. During the last forty to fifty years, those interested in such matters have added a concern for bureaucratic politics or the political interactions that take place within and between public agencies. By contrast, studies of public administration at the international level are few and far between. There are a few studies of the secretariats of the League of Nations and the United Nations, but there is no coherent body of literature on the roles of civil servants associated with the rapidly growing collection of international organizations.

The explanation for this contrast is straightforward. Most students of international relations treat international society as a society of states; nonstate actors, including international organizations, are marginal players at best. Both (neo)realists and (neo)liberals think of states as unitary actors, motivated by the pursuit of power in the case of the realists or the effort to maximize interests in the case of the liberals. With its emphasis on the role of ideas, constructivism offers a better prospect for thinking about the roles that international civil servants can and do play. Yet even constructivists show a marked tendency to direct their attention to matters of security and, as a result, to focus on interactions between and among states.

It is easy for those whose thinking is informed by such perspectives to dismiss international civil servants as little more than "administrative lackeys," or, to use more neutral terms, as administrators who confine themselves to the provision of purely technical services. But is this dismissal of the role of international civil servants persuasive? With this book Sikina Jinnah joins a small band of scholars (others include Stefan Bauer, Frank Biermann, and Bernd Siebenhüner) who are questioning this conventional wisdom regarding the insignificance of international secretariats. Basing her analysis on environmental regimes and devoting particular attention to the management of overlaps between distinct regimes, Jinnah builds a compelling case for the proposition that secretariats make an important contribution to the development of international governance systems.

The critical step in this line of thinking centers on an analysis of what has come to be known as soft power, in contrast to the more traditional focus on power in the material sense. Small states and non-state actors are able to exercise influence in international society even though they are poorly endowed with the material resources (e.g., armed forces, natural resources) traditionally associated with the capacity to influence the course of relations among states. They achieve influence through a variety of mechanisms, including identifying emerging issues, framing these issues for consideration at the international level, playing entrepreneurial roles in negotiation processes, promoting the attractions of preferred options, interpreting the provisions of international agreements once they are in place, and providing the administrative resources needed to operate international regimes on a day-to-day basis. Needless to say, it would be a mistake to exaggerate the significance of these roles in what remains fundamentally a society of states. However, as Jinnah shows through a set of substantial case studies, secretariats can and do make a difference in moving international agreements from paper to practice.

How can we document the actual influence of secretariats under real-world conditions? Dealing with such questions is a challenge for all those who must make do with small universes of cases and with little or no opportunity for experimentation. Jinnah employs two intersecting procedures to tackle this challenge. She uses process tracing and the analysis of counterfactuals to interrogate the evidence from her case studies. At the same time, she identifies a set of causal mechanisms that help us to understand the strategies secretariats use to exercise influence. When efforts to deploy distinct strategies show up in the records of specific cases, we can be reasonably confident that the activities of secretariats are making a difference. Of course, this type of reasoning will not convince those who are unwilling to entertain the thought that the efforts of nonstate actors can be effective at the international level. But Jinnah's evidence adds to a growing body of evidence regarding the influence of nonstate actors, including international secretariats, that most students of international relations find convincing.

An appealing feature of Jinnah's analysis is its focus on conditions under which international secretariats are able to exert influence. She does not frame her argument in terms of necessary or sufficient conditions for secretariats to play influential roles in the development and operation of international governance systems. Nevertheless, she makes a strong case for the importance of what she calls preference solidity and substitutability. When member states have preferences that are firm and difficult to adjust, international secretariats will find it hard to influence the course of events. The presence of substitutes for the services secretariats are able to supply will also limit their ability to exercise influence. But when the preferences of states are malleable and when secretariats have few competitors, they can play roles that are highly influential. Jinnah demonstrates the force of these arguments with detailed examinations of the records of her cases.

An interesting feature of this line of analysis is that it points largely to attributes of the setting rather than characteristics of the secretariats themselves as the primary determinants of secretariat influence. But, surely, some secretariats are more capable of exercising influence than others quite apart from the nature of the settings in which they operate. Although Jinnah does not systematically analyze it, she notes that the leadership qualities of executive heads constitute a factor of some importance. Beyond this, we might consider matters such as the strategies secretariats employ, the adequacy of staff resources, and the skill sets of staff members as factors likely to affect the ability of secretariats to play influential roles in the operation of governance systems. Such an analysis would require a loosening of Jinnah's assumption that we can treat secretariats as unitary actors represented by the efforts of their executive heads. Naturally, this would make things more complicated in analytic terms, but it would have the benefit of pointing to things that secretariats (and their supporters) can do to strengthen their capacity to influence the operation of international governance systems.

Interestingly and appropriately, Jinnah concludes by asking whether the growing influence of international secretariats is a good thing. Secretariats can help to make international regimes more effective. However, their actions sometimes favor the interests of some members of international society over others, and there are obvious issues of transparency, accountability, and legitimacy that become increasingly important as the influence of international secretariats grows. It is worth noting that this brings us back to an important concern of long-time students of public administration at the domestic level. Bureaucracies are essential; we cannot do without them. Yet the more influential they become, the more important it is to minimize problems of bureaucratic rigidity and corruption and to maximize the contributions that civil servants make to the pursuit of social welfare.

Oran R. Young
January 2014

Acknowledgments

It's been a long road. I owe a great debt to many friends, family members, mentors, and colleagues for their varied forms of support for this project over the years. I am especially grateful to my dissertation advisor and friend Kate O'Neill. Her scholarship, commitment to graduate advising, and strength of character in the face of immense challenges continue to be a source of great inspiration. Thank you, Kate.

My colleagues at American University have also been particularly important in this journey. Since taking on the leadership of the Global Environmental Politics Program at the university, Ken Conca has spent countless hours reading and commenting on various drafts of this manuscript, often at the expense of his own work. Paul Wapner's guidance has also been invaluable in helping me to see the forest for the trees. I am deeply grateful to both of them for their incredible mentorship. I will never be able to pay back the time, insight, and encouragement you have provided me. I hope you will accept, instead, my deep gratitude and my promise to pay it forward.

My writing group at the School of International Service (SIS) has also been enormously helpful; thanks to David Bosco, Jeff Colgan, Jordan Tama, and Sharon Weiner for our lively and *always* constructive discussions. Thank you for leaving your egos at the door, and for reminding me that I do this work not merely as a means to a professional end, but because with the right intellectual community, this work is loads of fun.

Special thanks are due to SIS Dean Jim Goldgeier for treating my success as an indicator of his own. His support for my book workshop allowed me to benefit from a full-day discussion and critique of my manuscript with Steven Bernstein, Ken Conca, Beth DeSombre, Tammi Gutner, Virginia Haufler, and Sharon Weiner. Those discussions were instrumental in pulling this project across the finish line. I am so grateful to those who participated for their time and candor about the remaining shortcomings of the manuscript and their suggestions for how to address them. I very much hope you will be pleased with the final product.

Thanks are also due to several other mentors and colleagues who have offered varied forms of guidance and insight. These include Mark Axelrod, Sammy Barkin, Pam Chasek, Sally Fairfax, Garrett Graddy, Patrick Jackson, Simon Nicholson, Coleman O'Criodain, Mike Schroeder, Judy Shapiro, Matt Taylor, Steve Weber, David Winickoff, and Mana Zarinejad (and her staff at SIS's International Affairs Research Institute). Thank you all for your generosity.

This research would not have been possible without the access and connections afforded me through my work with the *Earth Negotiations Bulletin* and the United Nations Environment Program's Economics and Trade Branch (UNEP-ETB). Indeed, the endless hours I spent transcribing negotiation proceedings were what led me to the original idea for this project, and the ENB badge and UNEP-ETB letterhead won me the trust of many interviewees otherwise working behind their "veils of legitimacy." Many thanks to Pam Chasek, Kimo Goree, Ben Simmons, and Chris Spence for these opportunities, and to my many ENB colleagues, especially Soledad Aguilar, Karen Alvarenga, Alexandra Conliffe, Stefan Jungcurt, Kati Kulovesi, Kelly Levin, and Miquel Muñoz for sharing their deep empirical expertise and friendship with me over the years. A huge thanks is also due also to the many secretariat staff, state delegates, and NGO representatives who were so generous with their time in speaking with me about what they do both in public view and, in many cases, behind the scenes. I hope you will find that I fairly and accurately represented your work in the pages that follow.

I have also been blessed with an incredible cadre of intelligent and enthusiastic research assistants. Special thanks to Layla Farhat, Sara Lacey, Abby Lindsay, and Michaela Samodelov for their countless hours of work in helping me get this project off my desk. You've saved my sanity … really.

Many thanks to Clay Morgan at the MIT Press for his patience with me through this revision process, and to the three anonymous reviewers for their thorough and incredibly helpful critiques of earlier versions of the manuscript. It should be acknowledged here as well that earlier analyses of two of the case studies included in this book were previously published in the journal *Global Environmental Politics* (MIT Press). The full citations to these articles are included in the reference list at the end of the book (Jinnah 2010, 2011b). Thanks are also due to the Earth System

Governance series editors, Frank Biermann and Oran Young, for their intellectual leadership that has long guided this project from afar. This work attempts to fill out much of the scaffolding you both constructed. It is an honor to be included in your series.

I am also, of course, very grateful for the various organizations and institutes that have financially supported this project, including the National Science Foundation, University of California Institute for Global Conflict and Cooperation, UC Berkeley John L. Simpson Memorial Research Fellowship in International and Comparative Studies, Brown University's Watson Institute for International Studies, Soroptimist International, American University's School of International Service, and UC Berkeley's Department of Environmental Science, Policy, and Management.

Most importantly, I owe a great debt to my family. Thanks especially to my Nanima for setting the bar high, and to my parents for your support in getting me to a place where I had the choice to pursue a PhD at all. To my Nanima, Uncle Akber, and Uncle Kam, thank you for your continued support in ensuring that recent surprises in my personal life didn't derail my professional ambitions. Finally, my gratitude to my husband, Douglas, is overwhelming. Thank you for the many late nights discussing the exciting world of bureaucratic politics, your unyielding confidence in my abilities to complete this project, and most of all, for following me across the country in pursuit of my career, never once mentioning any corresponding sacrifice on your part. One day we'll find our way back home.

List of Abbreviations

AHTEG	Ad Hoc Technical Experts Group (of the Convention on Biological Diversity)
CBD	Convention on Biological Diversity
CITES	Convention on International Trade in Endangered Species
CMS	Convention on Migratory Species
COFI	Committee on Fisheries (of the Food and Agriculture Organization)
COFI/FT	Sub-committee on Fish Trade (of the Committee on Fisheries)
CoP	Conference of the Parties
CTE	Committee on Trade and Environment (of the World Trade Organization)
CTESS	Special Session of the Committee on Trade and Environment
DSB	Dispute Settlement Body (of the World Trade Organization)
DTE	Division on Trade and Environment (of the World Trade Organization Secretariat)
EMIT	Group on Environmental Measures and International Trade (of the General Agreement on Tariffs and Trade)
FAO	United Nations Food and Agriculture Organization
GATT	General Agreement on Tariffs and Trade
GBO	Global Biodiversity Outlook
GEF	Global Environment Facility
GEP	Global environmental politics
IGO	Intergovernmental organization
IISD	International Institute for Sustainable Development
IMF	International Monetary Fund
IO	International organization
IPCC	Intergovernmental Panel on Climate Change
IR	International relations
IUCN	International Union for the Conservation of Nature

MEA	Multilateral environmental agreement
MoU	Memorandum of understanding
NAPA	National Adaptation Programmes of Action (of the United Nations Framework Convention on Climate Change)
NGO	Nongovernmental organization
REDD	Reducing emissions from deforestation and forest degradation
RFMOs	Regional fisheries management organizations
SAICM	Strategic Approach to International Chemicals Management
SBSTTA	Standing Body on Scientific, Technical, and Technological Advice
SC	Standing Committee (of the Convention on International Trade in Endangered Species)
ToRs	Terms of reference
TRIPs	Trade-Related Aspects of Intellectual Property Rights (of the World Trade Organization)
UN	United Nations
UNCED	United Nations Conference on Environment and Development (aka the Earth Summit or Rio Summit)
UNCTAD	United Nations Conference on Trade and Development
UNEP	United Nations Environment Programme
UNFCCC	United Nations Framework Convention on Climate Change
UNHCR	United Nations High Commission for Refugees
WGRI	Ad Hoc Open-ended Working Group on Review of Implementation (of the Convention on Biological Diversity)
WHC	World Heritage Convention
WTO	World Trade Organization
WWF	World Wide Fund for Nature

1

Introduction: Secretariats as Overlap Managers

There are lots of smart people here—and some not so smart—we are not using our brain power enough as it is. ... The Secretariat is a neutral party; it represents the WTO, not governments. Why can't I have ideas? What a loss of capacity!
—WTO Secretariat staff member (interview with author, 2006)

From the outside of an organization, office secretaries are nearly invisible. Simply doing the bidding of their bosses, they take instructions, write up memos, and make appointments for a controlling principal. They have no obvious source of power and are on the receiving end of authority. They appear to play, in other words, a derivative or secondary role. To understand how decision making unfolds within a professional office, many would simply bypass the secretary and go straight to the source of command. Viewed from the inside, however, this is nonsense. Anyone who has ever worked in a professional office knows that a good secretary does much more than is captured within the four corners of his job description. More than anyone else in the office, a good secretary often has the ear and trust of his boss. He likely filters information, controls who talks with whom, and acts as a repository for institutional memory. These things impact office outcomes and have a substantive effect on the success of the organization. A good secretary is a far cry from the coffee-making, nail-filing stereotype of the 1950s.

Secretariats—the administrative arms of international treaties—suffer from similar analytical neglect. On paper, secretariats, like office secretaries, simply do the bidding of states. Their leaders are appointed by the member states to international treaties; they take instruction from these member states and depend on them for financing. This derivative status of secretariats is the reason international relations (IR) scholarship gives them such short shrift.[1] Indeed, most treatment of secretariats in the IR literature has been from the outside and merely reflects what secretariats do on paper, as articulated in their mandates. When secretariats are noticed at all, this scholarship credits them with collecting information, communicating with state actors, tracking scientific information, and coordinating ongoing diplomatic activity. However, most IR scholarship discounts the meaning of these activities and therefore misses the important role secretariats play in political decision making. This book helps to remedy this oversight by showing, from the inside, how secretariats impact international affairs. It does so through the lens of secretariats' participation in the management of overlapping treaty regimes.

Secretariats can have significant governance influence by changing power relations between states, which in turn impacts politics. For example, when secretariats influence how states understand problems, they can affect the way states allocate resources to solve those problems. As this book demonstrates, this influence can have substantial impact on the cooperation between states and the linkages between regimes. Secretariats can also affect interstate relationships and equity issues in international politics. These factors can shape decision making about, for example, what is included in regime goals and who benefits from regime outcomes. Secretariat influence, even when modest, can have important impacts on structural or issue-framing decisions that shape the operation of regimes for long periods of time.

Scholarly neglect of what could be called "secretariat diplomacy" has been endemic in a field that has for so long taken the primacy of states as its bedrock assumption. Realists see states as the main units of analysis and look upon all other actors as politically irrelevant. These scholars generally explain international organization (IO) creation as an attempt to further state interests. For realists, IOs are epiphenomenal. They are created and maintained by the most powerful states, and thus they are not autonomous, nor do they have any impact on political outcomes (Mearsheimer 1994; Strange 1983; Waltz 1979).

Neoliberalism provides a more sympathetic reading. Although neoliberals tend to analytically conflate secretariats with the IOs they are part of, they acknowledge secretariats as part of the bureaucratic apparatus of international regimes and appreciate their roles in gathering information, monitoring compliance, and organizing meetings. The neoliberal ontology similarly adopts a state-centered view of international politics. Neoliberals assert that states create IOs to alleviate problems associated with incomplete information, transaction costs, and efficiency barriers (Abbott and Snidal 1998; Axelrod and Keohane 1985; Martin and Simmons 1998).

Notwithstanding such acknowledgment, neoliberalism still offers a limited view of secretariats as appendages to states. Neoliberals proffer a representative model, in that they understand secretariats merely as delegates of states—representatives who are on a short chain, and who can be recalled or undermined if they go too far out on their own (Hawkins et al. 2006). Secretariats have some autonomy but ultimately serve states—that is their mission and raison d'être. Although IOs have varying degrees of autonomy in the neoliberal institutionalist canon, they have largely been treated as functionaries of state actors, rather than as political actors in their own right (Abbott and Snidal 1998).[2]

The most helpful school of thought within IR for understanding secretariats is constructivism. Constructivism acknowledges that power is not linear. Levels and hierarchies of authority exist. States are certainly central nodes of power within the international system, but power doesn't simply flow from the most powerful to the least. Moreover, power is not simply about regulation, instruction, and giving orders; it is also constitutive. It shapes identities, molds interests, and redistributes capabilities between actors (Barnett and Duvall 2005).

When it comes to secretariats, constructivism offers a framework for appreciating the influence a seeming "functionary" can have. However, few constructivists have offered systematic studies of secretariats. So, while constructivist modes of analysis could in principle help us to make sense of secretariats, in the broad literature of IR, secretariats still play a minor role in the analysis of world politics. Aside from some empirical studies of specific secretariats and some general conceptual works, secretariats as bona fide actors are still deeply in the IR analytical dark.

This is certainly the case within the study of global environmental politics (GEP). No matter which school of thought one turns to for understanding international environmental affairs, states garner the most attention—an ironic situation in a subfield that would naturally lend itself to secretariat studies. The largest literature within GEP focuses on multilateral environmental agreements (MEAs), and studies the challenges and achievements of securing treaties and other institutions to address international environmental problems.[3] GEP also boasts a robust literature on the role of nonstate actors in international affairs.[4] Given that secretariats are at the center of MEAs, it would seem natural that GEP scholars would study secretariats as actors, and try to understand their power and influence in international environmental affairs.

Sadly, there are too few studies of secretariats within the GEP literature. To be sure, there is the pathbreaking work of Frank Biermann and

Bernd Siebenhüner (2009) on environmental secretariats. This work is extremely important for its conceptual and empirical contributions, and it has laid the foundation for "secretariat diplomacy." However, for all its insight, it leaves important questions unanswered and has not fully demonstrated the importance of secretariats such that scholars of GEP, to say nothing of IR in general, will take sufficient notice.

This book attempts to fill in the theoretical gaps surrounding the role of secretariats in global environmental politics. It explains how and when secretariats influence politics and, importantly, how such influence shifts power relations between states. Furthermore, the book demonstrates how an understanding of secretariats advances knowledge of global environmental politics and, indeed, global governance more broadly. As demonstrated by the case studies, secretariat influence matters to the extent that it can shape the way states understand issues, impact equity dynamics in international affairs, and result in a path-dependent dynamic. This book argues that, without an appreciation for the way secretariats develop and capitalize on their unique networks and knowledge, one cannot explain important elements of global environmental governance, especially as related to the ongoing coherence-building efforts that are central to contemporary United Nations (UN) politics.

Regime Overlap and Secretariat Influence

This study explores secretariat influence through the lens of overlap between international regimes. International regimes are collections of formal and informal rules, norms, principles, and practices that guide interstate cooperation in a specific area of IR.[5] International regimes are the centerpiece of international cooperation. They create institutional structures—for example, rules, norms, and practices—that shape cooperation between states on everything from telecommunications, trade, and nuclear weapons, to human rights, traditional knowledge, and organized crime. Within global environmental affairs, regimes address a panoply of issues including disposal of chemicals, protection of biodiversity, transboundary air pollution, stratospheric ozone depletion, and climate change. Indeed, there are currently over 1,000 environmental treaties in operation, and although growth has slowed in recent years, the number continues to climb (data from Mitchell 2013).

As many scholars have noted, the sheer number and scope of international regimes have led to "treaty congestion" (Weiss 1993, 697, 679; Young et al. 2008). One symptom of treaty congestion is the amount of overlap between treaties. Although most treaties aim to address discrete issues, such as trade in endangered species, ozone depletion, or desertification, they are invariably linked to other issues. As John Muir famously reminds us, no issue stands alone: "When we try to pick out anything by itself, we find it hitched to everything else in the universe" (Muir 1911, 110). In some sense, this is what happens within international environmental regimes. We cannot mitigate climate change without attending to deforestation, ozone-depleting substances, and the provision of energy. Furthermore, we cannot address any of these issues without getting into the complicated worlds of international trade, investment, and development.

In the midst of such dense interdependence, treaty overlap is bound to appear. Although treaty overlap indicates an engaged global community, it also creates problems of inefficiency, contradiction, lost opportunities, and sometimes even "sclerosis" (Wapner 2011, 144). When treaties overlap, principles pull at each other, rules conflict, and authority is scrambled. Yet most states lack adequate institutions for cross-issue coordination at the domestic level (UNEP 2000). This capacity deficit has created a space for secretariats to draw on their unique networks and expertise to engage in political decision making. Indeed, five years of observing secretariats in action for this book suggests that secretariat influence is most visible when regimes overlap and require management.

Overlap management has three goals: (1) decreasing duplication of effort across international regimes; (2) increasing synergies and cooperation between regimes; and/or (3) easing tensions resulting from conflicting rules or norms between regimes.[6] It addresses questions such as: How can the Convention on International Trade in Endangered Species (CITES) and the Convention on Migratory Species collaboratively improve the conservation of saiga antelope (a traded *and* migratory species) in ways that neither regime could accomplish alone?[7] How can states reconcile the World Trade Organization's (WTO) prohibition on nontariff trade barriers with CITES's restrictions on trade in endangered species? And how should the competing objectives of dolphin conservation and tuna market liberalization be reconciled within the WTO?

Early scholarship on regime overlap focused on typology development (e.g., Rosendal 2001a, 2001b; Selin and VanDeveer 2003; Young 2002), the impacts of overlap on regime effectiveness (Young et al. 2008), and importantly, the structural determinants of overlap outcomes (Gehring and Oberthür 2009). More recent scholarship has explored how overlapping regimes interact through the lenses of regime complexes (Colgan,

Keohane, and Van de Graaf 2012; Keohane and Victor 2011; Raustiala and Victor 2004), and there is an extensive literature on institutional interplay.[8] Scholars have also begun to explore the consequences of regime overlap (Alter and Meunier 2009). They illuminate the forces that drive the emergence and change of the regime complexes that deal with overlapping issues (Oberthür and Stokke 2011), and like this study, explore the role of agency in managing overlapping regimes (Selin 2010; Selin and VanDeveer 2011). Importantly, recent research points to the key role played by secretariats specifically in managing overlap between regimes (Selin 2010, 168). Yet systematic examination of secretariat work in overlap management is lacking. This study turns its attention to precisely this point.

Secretariat participation in overlap management is not surprising. When issues are new or complex, as overlap management is, states are likely to seek input from nonstate actors (Adler and Haas 1992; Haas 1997; Litfin 1994; Sebenius 1992). States may seek nonstate actor support because they lack either the time to form preferences on new issues or sufficient technical expertise to independently build preferences for complex issues. We know this to be true for nongovernmental organizations (NGOs), scientists, and private-sector actors—this study extends this theory to include secretariats as well.

Overlap management is nowhere more visible than in the environmental realm, where treaty congestion is high and institutional processes are relatively transparent. Because overlap management requires cooperation across otherwise unconnected international regimes, it demands cross-regime knowledge and requires networks to work effectively. Yet overlap management is a relatively new issue, and this type of knowledge and network building is just beginning to take shape institutionally for many actors. This book shows that in the messy world of overlapping regimes, secretariats are well positioned, skilled, and willing to work through the challenges of overlap management. Centrally, this book argues that in drawing from their unique networks and knowledge, secretariats emerge not simply as state functionaries or appendages, but as actors in their own right.

Explaining Secretariat Influence

Secretariats do not always have influence. Their influence varies across organizations (Biermann and Siebenhüner 2009) and within them (Jinnah 2010). This book seeks to explain the factors that condition secretariat influence. As explained above, the book focuses on secretariat participation in overlap management because it is an area where secretariats are well positioned to overcome existing governance challenges, due to a combination of limited state capacity to work across regimes and secretariats' relative strength in this regard. Secretariats are, however, just one part of the "division of labor" that characterizes much of contemporary overlap management politics (Gehring 2011). This study does not attempt to comprehensively evaluate overlap management politics. Rather, because overlap management is creating a new political space for secretariat participation, and because it is on the agenda of most international organizations,[9] it provides rich fodder for an in-depth empirical examination into secretariat behavior across international treaties.

The book, therefore, illuminates how secretariats participate in overlap management. It builds directly on recent studies that have challenged the dominant assumption in IR theory that secretariats are mere functionaries of state actors,[10] and responds to recent calls in the literature for increased attention to secretariats as political actors (Bauer, Andreson, and Biermann 2012, 37) and their role in overlap management politics specifically (Oberthür and Stokke 2011, 335).

This book provides an in-depth look at secretariat behavior. It is interested in how secretariats participate in international affairs and whether such participation impacts political outcomes. The book explains how to identify secretariat influence and asks: *Under what conditions are secretariats likely to influence political outcomes?* In order to answer this question, the book first presents a theory of influence in chapter 3 that explains what secretariat influence is, and how we can recognize it. It builds on previous scholarship by Biermann and Siebenhüner (2009) that focuses on types and mechanisms of secretariat influence, to outline a theoretical framework that allows us to trace the causal links between mechanisms of influence and impacts on political outcomes. The book further explains what types of impacts constitute influence and demonstrates how to measure such impacts empirically.

Building on this theory of secretariat influence, the book posits that secretariat influence is most likely to occur under two conditions. First, secretariat functions must be highly specialized to fit with secretariats' unique knowledge and networks, such that other actors could not easily carry out these tasks on their own. In other words, when the substitutability of secretariat functions is low, secretariats are more likely to influence politics. Second, secretariat influence is likely when state preferences are malleable or unsolidified, as can be the case with new and emerging issues as well as those that are highly technical. Although these two variables condition the likelihood of secretariat influence, they are not all-inclusive. Other factors are also important, such as the structural variables (e.g., problem structure and polity) identified by Biermann and Siebenhüner (2009).

Importantly, this book moves beyond previous scholarship in illuminating *why* secretariat influence matters in international politics. Drawing from constructivist analyses of power in global governance (Barnett and Duvall 2005), this study presents a framework to help us understand how secretariat influence can shape power relations between states and other actors. Specifically, I argue that secretariats change power relations by defining governance architectures/institutions, redistributing capabilities, and shaping shared norms and ideas. Although the book focuses on secretariat activities in the realm of overlap management, the theoretical framework developed in chapter 3 is not specific to overlap management. It could be tested in other areas of international affairs and adapted to evaluate how other types of actors exert influence.

The book's central argument is that when secretariat functions enjoy low substitutability and state preferences are weakly solidified, secretariats can influence politics by changing power relations between states. Secretariats change these power relations by shaping institutions, relationships, and shared norms/ideas.

Empirical Overview

Ecosystems ignore state boundaries. Air, water, shifting soils, migratory animals, and even plants refuse to be cordoned within sovereign, territorial units. And yet the state system remains the main architectonic form of political response to environmental problems (Conca 1994). The mismatch between transboundary environmental dilemmas and the state system is arguably the most important challenge facing humanity's ability to address global environmental challenges such as climate change, ozone depletion, desertification, and ocean pollution. The GEP literature cut its teeth on this mismatch, and the dilemma has inspired some of the most penetrating analyses of both the tragic character of global environmental governance and the international system's most important environmental achievements (e.g., Caldwell 1984; Hardin 1968; Speth 2005).

MEAs are an attempt to overcome the tragedy of the commons in global environmental affairs. As such, they focus on some of the most pressing transboundary environmental challenges. To date, states have negotiated MEAs on everything from sustainable development, genetic resources, and food safety to cetacean conservation, renewable energy, and acid rain elimination. Although these MEAs are created and officially run by states, they all have secretariats that play varying governance roles. To understand how secretariats function in global environmental affairs, particularly in the context of overlap management, I focus on two very different areas of global governance: biodiversity and international trade.

Constituting approximately 30 percent of all MEAs currently in force, biodiversity governance is one of the most well-developed areas of global environmental governance and thus presents rich empirical fodder for a study of overlap management (McGraw 2002a). Although experts struggle to agree on an exact definition, "biodiversity" broadly refers to the diversity of life at the genetic, species, and ecosystem levels (Takacs 1996). Biodiversity is important because species interact with one another and their environments in a complex web of interdependency. Biodiversity has inherent value and ultimately supports human well-being by providing ecosystem services, including food, clean water, and resilience to environmental stressors such as floods and drought.

It makes sense, then, that in the face of these challenges, the international community has negotiated several hundred biodiversity-related MEAs (data from Mitchell 2013). This study focuses on two of the most important of these MEAs, which approach biodiversity governance and, in turn, overlap management in very different ways: the Convention on Biological Diversity (CBD) and CITES. Whereas the CBD is a broad normative convention with a central overlap management agenda, CITES has clear implementation mandates, and overlap management is a peripheral issue for it.

The CBD is the fulcrum of overlap management within the global biodiversity regime complex. It was negotiated in response to demands from the UN Environment Programme (UNEP) Governing Council for a convention that would coordinate among the existing biodiversity treaties (McConnell 1996). Agreed in 1992 at the first UN Conference on Environment and Development (UNCED, or "Earth Summit"), the CBD aims to protect biodiversity, ensure sustainable use of its components, and provide for the equitable sharing of its benefits. At its core, it encourages member states to develop national-level strategies and programs to conserve biodiversity. In essence, the CBD's broad objectives distill the common rules and norms that are reflected in many of the biodiversity treaties preceding it.

As reflected in its near-universal membership, regular meetings, and relatively robust domestic-level institutional commitments, CITES is also a core treaty in global biodiversity governance. Unlike the CBD's overarching conservation objectives, CITES addresses one discrete slice of the conservation pie: it aims to ensure that international trade does not threaten species survival. Since entering into force in 1975, CITES has placed trade restrictions on certain species, such as elephants, orchids, and sharks, in accordance with their level of threat. CITES does not have an expansive coordination mandate, and limits its coordination efforts to functional rather than normative activities. As one interviewee from the CITES Secretariat noted, CITES cooperates with other treaties only when there is a clearly identified common conservation goal in mind. Even though it is more than twice as old as the CBD, CITES has less than half the number of formal cooperative agreements with other organizations (CBD Secretariat 2013c; UNEP Governing Council 1989).

Despite varied levels of engagement with overlap management, CITES and the CBD cannot achieve their conservation objectives alone. Species transgress political boundaries and are threatened by multiple forces. For example, the saiga antelope is both migratory and threatened due to hunting for international trade. Thus, all states within the species' geographic range must implement conservation measures in order to effectively protect it. Yet CITES's mandate is limited to imposing trade restrictions; it has no mandate to establish protected areas. CITES must therefore work with other MEAs, such as the Convention on Migratory Species and the CBD to protect the saiga antelope.

Similarly, because climate change is emerging as one of the largest threats to biodiversity, the CBD must concern itself with work undertaken within the UN Framework Convention on Climate Change (UNFCCC). Biodiversity treaties ignore climate change at their own peril. These secretariats are, therefore, not lone officers able to focus "simply" on conserving biodiversity; they must also design substantive relationships both within and beyond the biodiversity regime. In the midst of such interstitial work, the secretariat must become not simply an implementer or functionary, but also a manager. As this book shows, the biodiversity secretariats work to identify and magnify complementary efforts, negotiate principles of conflict, navigate intersecting lines of practice, and so forth.

Overlap management is not limited to intraregime coordination where normative overlap tends to be synergistic across organizations or treaties. Environmental issues, especially climate change, are now addressed in trade, security, and humanitarian organizations as well (Jinnah 2011a). This study therefore also looks at how secretariats outside the environmental realm interface with environmental issues. The most obvious place to look at this relationship is the WTO. Environmental groups have been trying to get the WTO's attention since it was created in 1994, and it has become the symbolic face of the environmental perils of over-consumption. Indeed, many NGOs address this intersection as part of their regular work program (e.g., International Institute for Sustainable Development, Institute for Trade and Sustainable Development), and a distinct body of scholarship has emerged surrounding trade-environment politics.[11]

Although not a treaty secretariat per se, the WTO secretariat plays a similar role to environmental treaty secretariats. Like treaty secretariats, the WTO Secretariat supports member implementation of the WTO's many trade agreements. Further, its relationship to the WTO membership parallels that of environmental treaty secretariats. Just as parties to the CBD and CITES interact regularly with their members at conferences of the parties (CoPs), the WTO Secretariat interacts regularly with its members at ministerial conferences and regular committee meetings, where policy objectives are defined and implementation details are negotiated.

The WTO's core mandate is to enhance global welfare through trade liberalization. It seeks to do this by reducing trade barriers such as tariffs and quotas, making borders more permeable to foreign service providers, and encouraging foreign investment by streamlining intellectual property rights. However, the WTO also has a mandate, albeit narrow, to cooperate with MEAs, and many of its agreements contain clauses that allow for exemptions to trade rules for environmental purposes.[12]

These environmental mandates are challenging for the WTO. As a trade organization, the WTO primarily focuses on economic issues, and, as reflected in relevant committee reports, members often disagree about the WTO's appropriate role in environmental affairs. Meanwhile, environmental groups continue to protest the WTO's environmental practices at ministerial meetings, as they did in Seattle and Cancun, and actively lobby WTO delegates to take up their environmental preferences. Still, it is difficult for WTO delegates to manage environmental issues because they typically come from trade ministries, and coordination between trade ministries and environmental ministries is weak in most countries (UNEP 2000). In the midst of this tension between core mission and public demand, this book will show, the WTO Secretariat has become a gatekeeper and trainer. It helps WTO members to negotiate the unfamiliar terrain of environmental issues that they, sometimes grudgingly, are required to address.

Methodological Approach

Most scholars who employ process tracing to investigate the workings of international organizations collect data using the same method across cases. This consistency makes sense, as it results in observations that are easy to compare and makes replication of studies more feasible. However, the social world often presents research conditions that do not fit comfortably with this methodological approach. Rather than shying away from this research, this study adopts an innovative methodological approach that allowed me to systematically investigate a question despite significant challenges in collecting data.

Specifically, this book is interested in variation in influence both between and within secretariats. It therefore departs from the literature's more commonly used approach to case definition. Rather than examining secretariats themselves as the unit of analysis, this study looks at instances of overlap management as the unit of analysis.[13] By making instances of overlap management the unit of analysis, it is possible to examine the specific functions that secretariats performed to manage overlap in each case and to identify any causal connections between such functions and impacts on political outcomes. This set-up also enables the researcher to examine the variation of secretariat activities related to a single issue—an approach that complements Biermann and Siebenhüner's (2009) examination of variation across organizations.

However, this approach presents significant data collection challenges due to the wide variety of ways in which organizations operate and secretariats manage overlap. Consequently, the form of overlap management will also vary across cases. As the cases that follow illuminate, overlap management can involve everything from drafting rules that facilitate interregime coordination, to building state capacity to engage in interregime issues, to delivering public speeches aimed at changing the way overlapping issues are understood by state actors. Further, overlap management can range from punctuated unilateral approaches undertaken by a single treaty regime to iterative cross-institutional interactions between two or more organizations over several years.

These challenges are compounded by variation in organizational culture and transparency. Whereas CITES documents and makes much

of its work product publicly available, such as secretariat recommendations, the WTO tends to make available only outputs such as unattrib-
uted meeting reports—the process is hard to trace through public records
alone. Similarly, organizational cultures vary in how readily they allow
outsiders to speak to researchers. Whereas the WTO and CBD Secretariat
staff members were widely willing to grant interviews individually, the
much smaller and capacity-constrained CITES Secretariat preferred to
channel information through fewer points of contact.[14] Finally, my ability
to directly observe secretariats in action varied across cases. Whereas
access to CITES and CBD decision-making forums was easy to secure,
the WTO's decision-making forums are notoriously difficult to penetrate
(Lacarte 2004).

Therefore, although the methodological approach across cases was
identical—process tracing—these challenges demanded variation in data
collection methods. Some cases relied more heavily on interviews, whereas
others relied more heavily on document analysis techniques, such as
coding. For example, whereas the CITES Secretariat's role in decision
making is unusually transparent through sections containing "Comments
from the Secretariat" in all draft decisions, the WTO Secretariat's role in
supporting environment-related dispute settlement and negotiations is
unusually opaque. In the former case, data collection and analysis were
possible through triangulation of interview, participant observation, and
document analysis. In the latter case, where documentation of secretariat
activities is effectively absent, I used interviews with key informants, secondary sources, and participant observation (as possible) of WTO dispute
settlement proceedings.

All cases ultimately sought to understand, however, how the secretariat participated in overlap management, whether such participation
constituted influence, and what conditions enabled or constrained secretariat influence. Therefore, although the data type varies across cases,
the analytical framework that was applied to this data does not. Table
1.1 summarizes the methods utilized in each case, along with a description of each case and an indication of which data sources were most
important in conducting the analysis. More detailed accounts of the
case-specific methods and case selection are included in Appendixes
A and B.

These cases examine different parts of secretariats. Some focus on the
executive head, others on specific divisions within the secretariat, and
others on the whole body. However, the secretariat is treated as a unitary
entity throughout the book. By mandate, all work undertaken by

Table 1.1
Methods

Case #	Management Type	Case	Methods	Case Description
1	Unilateral	CBD biodiversity	*Primary:* document analysis (process tracing) *Secondary:* interviews *Tertiary:* participant observation	CBD Secretariat participation in development of overlap management architecture for all biodiversity treaties
2		CBD climate	*Primary:* document analysis (coding) *Secondary:* interviews *Tertiary:* participant observation	CBD Secretariat participation in framing the relationship between conservation and climate change
3a		WTO negotiations	*Primary:* interviews *Secondary:* secondary sources *Tertiary:* participant observation	Division on Trade and Environment (DTE) participation in environment-related negotiations within the WTO Committee on Trade and Environment in regular and special sessions
3b		WTO dispute settlement	*Primary:* interviews *Secondary:* secondary sources *Tertiary:* participant observation	DTE participation in GATT Article XX dispute settlement
4	Cross-institutional	CITES	*Primary:* document analysis (process tracing) *Primary:* participant observation *Secondary:* interviews	CITES Secretariat participation in shaping the legal relationship between CITES and the UN FAO regarding fish species

secretariats is conducted on the executive head's behalf. She is given a mandate, must delegate to her staff, and is ultimately responsible to the member states for the work undertaken. The CBD biodiversity case, for example, largely relies on documents that the Secretariat as a whole produced for CoPs. Because these documents are produced on the executive head's behalf, they are treated in the same way as the public speeches made by the executive secretary himself that are the primary data source for the CBD climate case. In short, because the structural relationship between the executive head and the rest of the secretariat demands that all secretariat activities are performed on the executive head's behalf, the secretariat is treated as a unitary actor.

Finally, it should be noted that the book focuses on secretariats that support international treaties (or agreements), rather than those that support larger IOs, such as the World Bank and International Monetary Fund (IMF). Treaty secretariats and larger IOs share a common ancestry, which explains their similar norms and structures, such as the nearly verbatim codes of conduct that guide professional behavior across organizations.[15] However, there are also important differences in their mandates and procedures that render direct comparison less useful.

For example, treaty-secretariat mandates, such as those of the CBD and CITES, are typically discrete, aimed at carrying out a specific task, such as monitoring implementation or building a database for collecting and disseminating information. In contrast, larger IO secretariats, such as those of the IMF,[16] often have more far-reaching and ongoing responsibilities, such as advising countries on social spending and environmental policies. The relationship with member states is also different between these two types of international organizations. Treaty secretariats have regular interaction with their member states through annual CoPs, wherein secretariats report on their work and states create, renew, and/ or alter secretariat mandates. The administrative bodies of large IOs tend to have more formal autonomy and "delegated discretion" (Hawkins and Jacoby 2006). The IMF, for example, is mandated to "carry out the business of the Fund" (Article of Agreement of the IMF, Article XII, Section 3). This relationship to member states helps to explain why large IOs can be authoritative actors (Barnett and Finnemore 2004). With their discrete tasks and shorter chain to member states, we might expect that treaty secretariats would be less likely to influence the politics of their organizations. Although the WTO Secretariat shares common features with IOs, in the realm of overlap management it operates in very similar ways to environmental secretariats. As this book will show, however, under certain conditions treaty secretariats can also play important roles in the affairs of their organizations.

The Power of Secretariats

When we study how the secretariats of the CBD, WTO, and CITES manage overlap, the mechanisms of secretariat influence come into sharp relief. The cases reveal how secretariats broker cross-institutional knowledge, strategically market ideas, facilitate negotiations, and guide dispute settlement in ways that influence the tenor and texture of political outcomes.

Frank Biermann and others have laid the foundation for secretariat studies, demonstrating that secretariats influence politics. These authors parcel out the scope, duties, and mechanisms of secretariat behavior, but they don't always explain the causal pathways by which secretariats actually impact political outcomes. This scholarship could go further in explaining *why* these impacts, albeit modest, matter to international affairs and, importantly, how they interact with and shape power relations. This existing literature *suggests* secretariat power—it does not delineate, demonstrate, or give tonality to it.

This book provides this insight and thus uncovers not only how and when secretariats exert influence, but also *why* such influence is important. I argue that, although secretariats may not have the coercive power to dictate their will against state preferences, they influence political outcomes in ways that reflect constitutive forms of power. I illustrate how secretariats can shape power relations between states by designing governance architectures and institutions (institutional power), restructuring relationships between states by redistributing capabilities between them (structural power), and shaping state preferences by constructing shared norms and ideas (productive power) (Barnett and Duvall 2005). By shaping power relations between states in these ways, secretariats themselves become powerful actors.

While the book is based on case studies of overlap management and thus provides a detailed depiction of how secretariats exert influence at the interstices of international environmental regimes, it also provides a general theory of secretariat influence. The theory rests on an analytical framework that parses out and explains the relationships between power, authority, and influence. It shows how observing secretariat behavior can help us to identify mechanisms of influence. However, it is only when such mechanisms can be traced to changes in the institutional, structural, and/or productive power relations between states that we can affirmatively say a secretariat *influenced* a specific political outcome. The book goes on to explain the conditions that enable secretariat influence (i.e., substitutability and state preference solidification), and fleshes out the sources of authority and mechanisms of influence in ways that extend recent work on this topic.

Roadmap of the Book

This book argues that secretariats matter in world politics. This is not to say that we should be on the lookout for a bureaucratic coup d'état. Rather, this book is about *how* and *when* secretariats influence politics and, centrally, *why* such influence matters in international affairs. It illuminates how secretariats impact outcomes as much as, if not more than, other nonstate actors who have garnered scholarly attention in recent years. The book also illuminates the terrain of overlap management within international treaty secretariats. Because this latter topic is still in its infancy, this book, like other recent contributions (e.g., Oberthür and Stokke 2011), takes an inductive approach to help us better understand how overlap is managed and, importantly, who is playing a role—sometimes a leading one—in this governance process.

Chapter 2 details what secretariats are through the lens of IR theory and international law. It draws from the domestic bureaucratic politics literature to explain why secretariats are essentially international bureaucracies. It then explains how scholars of IR have treated secretariats in the IO literature, and why this treatment is in tension with how secretariats are constructed in international law.

Chapter 3 builds a theory of secretariat influence and presents the analytical framework used to evaluate secretariat influence in this study. In constructing this framework, I disentangle the relationship between power, authority, and influence and identify new sources of authority and mechanisms of influence that secretariats employ to participate in overlap management.

Chapters 4 through 7 present four case studies of secretariat participation in overlap management. Chapter 4 traces the evolution of overlap management within the CBD. It argues that the CBD Secretariat designed the original architecture of overlap management in the mid 1990s. Yet the Secretariat's influence declined over time as state preferences solidified and the Secretariat's substitutability increased.

Chapter 5 remains focused on the CBD but illuminates a different mechanism of secretariat influence. This chapter explores the secretariat's role in shaping CBD member states' preferences surrounding overlap management. The case illuminates how the CBD's former executive secretary strategically marketed the relationship between biodiversity and climate change in a way that increased the political saliency of biodiversity issues. He did so by reframing biodiversity from a passive victim of climate impact to an active player in climate solutions. This case also reveals temporal variation in secretariat influence, with secretariat influence decreasing over time as CBD member state preferences become more solid and the Secretariat more easily substitutable.

Chapter 6 shifts focus to the WTO. It presents two subcases of overlap management in which the Secretariat shaped shared understandings of overlap management needs and redistributed capabilities among states to participate in overlap management politics. I argue that in filtering information on trade and environment issues to its membership through legitimated channels, the WTO Secretariat, perhaps inadvertently, reinforces existing developed country norms and understandings of this relationship. Importantly, these cases highlight how the substitutability of secretariat functions and the solidification of state preference vary between developed and developing countries and the problems that arise from this disparity.

Chapter 7 illuminates the conditions under which an otherwise influential secretariat fails to influence political outcomes. It explores the CITES Secretariat's efforts to manage overlap with the UN Food and Agriculture Organization on issues surrounding commercially exploited aquatic species. I argue that, coupled with underlying political issues, the CITES Secretariat was unable to influence overlap management decisions because states' preferences were moderately solidified and the Secretariat's overlap management functions were easily substitutable.

Finally, in addition to summarizing findings and reflecting on the theoretical implications of this study, chapter 8 asserts that path dependence can help to explain why secretariat influence matters, even when such influence is modest or wanes over time. When secretariat influence produces entrenched institutions that yield benefits for key decision makers, the results of its influence can establish a path-dependent dynamic that shapes decision making long after secretariat influence has waned. Chapter 8 further discusses the broader implications of secretariat influence for global governance, arguing that secretariats can strengthen global governance regimes, enhancing them through building developing country capacity, streamlining complex governance tasks, and helping states to capitalize on opportunities for interregime coordination. Chapter 8 also problematizes secretariat influence, exploring the appropriate role of secretariats in global governance broadly. Moreover, it discusses the empirical implications of secretariats as actors in the coherence-building project that dominates much of contemporary UN politics.

2

Secretariats in Theory and Practice

A League Committee, I once heard a delegate say, is composed of a president and a secretary. And his interlocutor asked: Do you think the president is necessary?

—Sir Salvador de Madariaga, former Director of the Disarmament Section of the League of Nations[1]

A secretariat is most simply an international bureaucracy. It is the administrative structure that enables an organization, such as the United Nations (UN), the World Trade Organization (WTO), or the UN Framework Convention on Climate Change (UNFCCC), to operate. Yet secretariats are typically discounted as political actors in their own right.[2] Due to their administrative role, secretariats are assumed to be functionaries of their member states, with little (if any) decision-making authority. Indeed, they often perform mundane tasks such as organizing meetings, distributing documents, and maintaining websites—tasks that have little substantive impact on governance outcomes. Although these administrative tasks are certainly part of a secretariat's repertoire, they by no means complete it. Rather, secretariats are much more than administrative lackeys; they are actors in their own right.

We know very little about secretariat politics, however. State expectations of neutrality make secretariat behavior difficult to study; secretariats go to great lengths to conceal any activities that reflect their own political preferences. The administrative elements of secretariat behavior are generally transparent, and represent the public face of secretariat politics. However, there is also a veiled aspect of secretariat politics. Behind this veil, secretariats perform key regime functions. For example, they draft decisions, filter information, and frame policy ideas. These activities can be critical to regime operation, yet are often informal, unacknowledged, undocumented, and/or obscured.

Secretariat activities that move beyond mere administration are often veiled because their potential for policy influence challenges a fundamental component of secretariat legitimacy: political neutrality (Abbott and Snidal 1998; Bauer, Andresen, and Biermann 2012; Weiss 1982; Mathiason 2007). Secretariats are not expected to have opinions of their own; they are expected to do as they are told by state actors. As one delegate bellowed in a plenary session at the 14th Conference of the Parties (CoP) to the Convention on International Trade in Endangered Species (CITES) in 2007, "the Secretariat is our servant!"[3]

This statement is emblematic of state expectations of secretariats in general.[4] Secretariats, therefore, employ various strategies to maintain an image of impartiality despite their behind-the-scenes maneuvering. Several secretariat staff interviewees noted that they regularly avoid taking credit for their own ideas. For example, several biodiversity secretariat staff highlighted their past efforts in channeling their ideas through state actors sympathetic to their views, and WTO Secretariat staff noted their work in counseling state actors informally rather than making suggestions in formal meetings. One secretariat interviewee reported avoiding the creation of publicly available records of secretariat activities so as to ensure that the secretariat's impartiality would not be questioned. This book illuminates how secretariats influence politics from behind these "veils of legitimacy" (Depledge 2007).[5]

Although secretariats are among the most common of contemporary governance arrangements, scholarly examination of these bodies is thin. They are overlooked because they are assumed to be merely functional, or they are conflated with the much more complex intergovernmental organizations (IGOs) of which they are often part. Their domestic counterparts, however, are well studied. Indeed, the rich literature on domestic bureaucracies lends insight into secretariat structure and function.[6] This chapter draws from this literature to better understand secretariats as a construct in international affairs. It examines how scholars and practitioners alike have treated secretariats in theory and practice. This analysis demonstrates how legal mandates position secretariats to participate substantively in international politics, and why existing theoretical treatments of these bodies fall short of explaining this behavior.

The chapter unfolds in three parts. The first part briefly explains what a bureaucracy is and how well secretariats fit the mold of their domestic counterparts. This is followed by a discussion of how international relations (IR) scholars have treated secretariats theoretically, why such treatment falls short of explaining secretariat behavior, and how this book fills an important gap in this literature. The third part of the chapter focuses on empirical treatment of secretariats in international law and policy. It begins with an analysis of state expectations of secretariats as articulated in the mandates and operational rules of model secretariats, such as the League of Nations and the UN. The League and UN Secretariats are different from the treaty secretariats examined in this study in important ways. For example, treaty secretariats are much smaller and narrower in scope. Nevertheless, as two of the oldest and most important secretariats, those of the League and UN help us understand how states broadly conceive secretariat structure and function. Indeed, the analysis that follows illuminates how the original mandates of these bodies provided a foundation and model upon which most subsequent secretariats are based. The analysis further illustrates how state expectations have changed over time and, importantly, how rules and mandates liberate rather than constrain a secretariat's ability to influence international politics.

Bureaucratic Form and Function

The word "bureaucracy" literally means "power from a desk." The French word *bureau*, which means "office" or "desk," combines with the Greek suffix *-kratia*, meaning "power" or "strength" (*American Heritage Dictionary* 2000). Although the concept can be traced back much further, the contemporary conception of a bureaucracy is largely attributed to Max Weber, who popularized the term in his writings in *Economy and Society* (Weber 1978; originally 1922).[7] Weber asserted that a bureaucracy was not a type of government, as is democracy or monarchy, but rather a means by which a government governs, and a hallmark of the modern Western trend toward rationalization and the capitalist mode of production.

Weber's "ideal type" bureaucracy is characterized by several key features: it has a hierarchical structure and is staffed by salaried, full-time professional experts, who are separated from the means of administration, and who operate by a defined set of impersonal rules (Weber 1978). Weber's bureaucratic form is marked by "precision, speed, unambiguity, knowledge of the files, continuity, discretion, unity, strict subordination, reduction of friction and of material and personal costs" (Weber 2009, 214). For Weber, bureaucratization, a slice of broader societal rationalization, was a superior organizational form because of its ability to efficiently coordinate increasingly complex societies on the basis of rational-legal principles, rather than custom or tradition.[8]

Secretariats are international bureaucracies. They are a diverse set of organizations with substantial variation in terms of size, staff constitution, budget, and, importantly, the types of institutions that they service. Some secretariats support states in negotiating and implementing narrow-issue specific treaties, such as those examined in this book. Others support stand-alone IGOs with substantially larger budgets and staff sizes, such as the World Health Organization (WHO), the Organization of the American States (OAS), and International Monetary Fund (IMF).[9] Further, some "umbrella" secretariats, such as the UN Environment Program (UNEP), provide "subsidiary" secretariats for treaties negotiated under their auspices. This characterizes the relationship, for example, between UNEP and the Convention on Biological Diversity (CBD), the Convention on Migratory Species (CMS) and its series of memoranda of understanding (MoUs), as well as that between the UN and UNFCCC. Non-UN treaties also utilize secretariats, such as CITES or the Ramsar Convention on Wetlands, as do some nongovernmental organizations (NGOs), such as the World Wide Fund for Nature (WWF) International and the Third World Network International. Table 2.1 highlights some of this variation among secretariats.

Despite this variation, secretariats also have core similarities with respect to structure, function, and state expectations. One of the few existing studies on secretariat politics defines international bureaucracies as

agencies that have been set up by governments or other public actors with some degree of permanence and coherence and beyond the formal direct control of single national governments ... that act in the international arena to pursue a policy. ... International bureaucracies are a hierarchically organized group of international civil servants with a given mandate, resources, identifiable boundaries, and a set of formal rules of procedures within the context of a policy area. (Biermann et al. 2009, 37)

Biermann et al. capture the core characteristics of secretariats well. They highlight many of the traits that secretariats share with their domestic counterparts, as well as those that are unique to the former. For example, like their domestic counterparts, secretariats are organized in a hierarchical structure, and are staffed by salaried, full-time professional experts who operate by a defined set of rules. Unlike domestic bureaucracies, Biermann et al. note, secretariats have an international character, coherence, and permanence. Not mentioned in Biermann et al.'s definition, but a defining feature of secretariat politics, is the previously mentioned "veil

Table 2.1

Variation among Secretariats[a]

	Number of Parties	Number of Employees	Annual Budget (Core and Supplementary)	Parent Organization
CBD	193	78	$12,355,100[b]	UNEP
CMS	113	34	$3,257,720[c]	UNEP
CITES	175	27	$10,358,775[d]	NA
Ramsar[e]	160	21	$3,300,000[f]	IUCN
UNFCCC	194	>350	$48,873,303[g]	UN
Water Convention[h]	36	8	$817,667[i]	UN Economic Commission for Europe
WTO	153	629	$182,266,000[j]	NA
IMF	187	~2360	$333,000,000,000[k]	NA
World Bank	187	>10,000	$47,218,800,000[l]	NA

a. For more on variation between international bureaucracies more generally, see Biermann et al. 2009, 37–39.
b. Budget of the 2010 CBD Trust Fund.
c. Budget of the 2008 CMS Trust Fund.
d. CITES Trust Fund annual contributions for 2009–2011 and external funds for 2009.
e. Ramsar Convention on Wetlands.
f. Represents the 2006 core budget only.
g. Average annual budget for 2010–2011.
h. Convention on the Protection and Use of Transboundary Water Courses and International Lakes.
i. Average annual budget for 2010–2012.
j. Annual budget for 2010.
k. Annual budget for 2010.
l. Sum of International Development Association (IDA) Resources, International Bank for Reconstruction and Development Resources, and the total administrative budget for 2009.

of legitimacy" behind which secretariats operate (Depledge 2007). This section considers these commonalities and unique features in the context of how they shape secretariat behavior.

As is the case with domestic bureaucracies, hierarchy is also a defining feature of secretariat structure. Although individual secretariat cultures impact how formally and/or strictly this hierarchy is observed, all secretariats are led by an executive head who then staffs the secretariat with salaried full-time professionals.[10] Secretariat authority is officially seated with the executive head. All activities and output from the secretariat are delivered to member states in the executive head's name, and she or he is ultimately accountable to the member governments.

Also, like their domestic counterparts, secretariats operate on the basis of rules. They are guided by two sets of rules: fixed mandates and evolving mandates. The fixed mandates are those contained in the legal texts, such as treaties and charters, that establish secretariats. All secretariats within the UN system are also guided by the relevant sections of the UN Staff Regulations (United Nations 2009). As detailed in the next section, these fixed rules articulate the general parameters for secretariats' work, such as the *type* of activities in which a secretariat should engage. However, fixed mandates are often not well defined, leaving room for interpretation and allowing secretariats flexibility in determining how to carry out their work.[11]

Precisely because fixed mandates tend to be vague and malleable, a second set of constantly evolving mandates also functions to guide secretariat behavior. These evolving mandates take the form of periodic instructions given by decision-making bodies, such as a CoP, a ministerial conference, or the General Assembly. These instructions dictate specific goals and tasks to guide a secretariat's work on a clearly defined issue in between meetings of the relevant decision-making body. Secretariats, in turn, report back to their decision-making bodies on their progress in completion of these tasks. Although evolving mandates tend to be more specific than fixed mandates, as is discussed in the empirical chapters that follow, they still leave quite a bit of latitude for secretariat interpretation.

Secretariats are also explicitly international in character. Despite national quota systems for staff representation, secretariat staff members are not meant to represent states' positions. Rather, they are expected to act in an impartial capacity with a view to supporting the rules and norms of the institutions they service. This international character is meant to engender cohesive organizations wherein treaties and charters, rather than national loyalties and interests, guide behavior. Although we take this assumption for granted in contemporary global governance, this was a point of much contention during the negotiations surrounding the world's first secretariat, that of the League of Nations (Ranshofen-Wertheimer 1945, 28).[12]

Also important to secretariat politics is that most secretariats are the only permanent bodies (in the physical sense) of the institutions they support. They have brick-and-mortar headquarters where career international civil servants are responsible for making a range of day-to-day operational decisions. In contrast, member states/parties typically send capital-based delegates to attend periodic meetings. Further, whereas secretariats' single-pointed focus is on the issues relevant to a specific treaty regime or organization, several national delegates interviewed for this study noted that they typically juggle regime-specific issues alongside a host of other obligations. As noted by Ranshofen-Wertheimer (1945) in reference to the League of Nations: "Between sessions of the policy-making organs and its numerous committees, the Secretariat was the only concrete evidence of the League's existence" (394). While this may be an overstatement with respect to many contemporary secretariats, it highlights the special permanent position of the secretariat in international politics relative to their member states/parties. This permanent seat positions secretariats at the center of treaty politics—often making them a locus of treaty-relevant information and accountability.

Secretariats in Theory

Scholars of international organizations (IOs) and regimes have tended to discount or ignore secretariats as actors in IR. With some notable exceptions, scholars of IR have typically conflated secretariats with the IOs of which they are often part. As discussed in chapter 1, this can largely be explained by the way dominant theories of IR have conceptualized IOs—as mere functionaries of member states. As such, these scholars have seen little need to study international secretariats per se.

There are, of course, exceptions to this trend. These include a series of commentaries on international bureaucracies following the establishment of the League of Nations (Calderwood 1937; Moats 1939; Wambaugh 1921), and again preceding the establishment of the United Nations (Purves 1945; Ranshofen-Wertheimer 1945; Royal Institute for International Affairs 1944). A more theoretical and analytical lens was adopted later in the twentieth century as scholars turned their attention to matters such as decision making and bureaucratic influence within IOs (Cox and Jacobson 1973), secretariat autonomy and performance (Weiss 1975, 1982), and organizational learning and change (Haas 1990).[13] However, these contributions are few. As IR scholars turned their attention to regime analysis in the late 1970s, IOs and, accordingly, secretariats were "demoted" and largely abandoned in IR scholarship for over a decade (Simmons and Martin 2002, 193).

Recently, however, this otherwise dormant strand of scholarship has begun to awaken. A small but growing body of literature in which secretariats (or international bureaucracies) are examined as political actors in their own right has recently emerged. The first contribution is a collection of studies that adopt a principal-agent framework to analyze the role of secretariats as agents of state principals. These scholars argue that states design IOs with a certain degree of autonomy so that IOs can carry out the functions delegated to them by states. They consider why states delegate to IOs (Green and Colgan 2012; Hawkins et al. 2006; Majone 2001; Nielson and Tierney 2003; Pollack 1997), how states subsequently control IOs after delegation takes place (Hawkins et al. 2006), gaps between state mandate and IO performance (Gutner 2005; Nielson and Tierney 2003), and variation in IO performance more broadly (Gutner and Thompson 2010). For this group of theorists, IOs are actors because they generate autonomy from states to pursue their own strategic interests, sometimes exhibiting slack and/or opportunistic behavior (Hawkins and Jacoby 2006, 5). Nevertheless, these scholars largely see IOs as functionaries; states delegate to IOs because these actors help states to achieve their specified goals.

These rationalist explanations of state delegation hold true much of the time. This book argues, however, that secretariat politics are more complex than a simple principal-agent model would predict. Because the starting points for most of these analyses are instances of delegation, they exclude any examination of how secretariats may operate in the absence of delegation. For example, they do not adequately account for secretariats' behavior when states lack capacity or sufficient time to consider an issue. In fact, the rationalist paradigm makes it difficult to analyze secretariat activities that occur in the absence of delegation, because, despite possessing some autonomy, secretariats are still understood as mere functionaries of states. In contrast, this study's starting point is secretariat behavior, rather than state delegation. It maintains that some of this behavior can be traced directly to delegation, but other elements cannot.

This allows for a more comprehensive understanding of secretariat politics because it does not ipso facto presume that *all* secretariat activities are state defined.[14] Rather, this analysis uncovers how secretariats themselves can play a role in shaping the very state preferences and practices that drive delegation to begin with. In short, this study argues that rationalist explanations of secretariat behavior as rooted in delegation are useful but incomplete. It understands secretariats as agents, but also as constitutive actors who shape the state preferences that determine what gets delegated and what does not.

There are other important limitations to focusing mainly on delegation as an organizing concept for understanding secretariat behavior. State mandates are often vague and open-ended, leaving much room for interpretation.[15] As such, it can be difficult to trace specific secretariat activities back to an explicit mandate or instance of delegation. Paradoxically, if challenged, most secretariat activities can be legally justified in some way. As one CBD Secretariat staff member put it, "I can find a decision to justify anything I want to do."[16] Similarly, secretariats can hide autonomous behavior or make it appear that autonomous behavior was in fact delegated. For example, some of the secretariats explored in this study draft decisions and negotiating texts that, while originating within the bureaucracy, are formally attributed to states. The secretariat never takes the credit. The way secretariats operate within their zones of discretion is the meat of secretariat politics; that these activities can be justified by implicit delegation (i.e., states don't object) that mirrors overarching institutional rules or norms does not preclude a constitutive role for these actors. As such, secretariat politics are not of interest here because they necessarily thwart state interests, but because, under certain conditions, they *shape* them.

The concept of "agent strategies" is helpful in understanding secretariat politics (Hawkins and Jacoby 2006, 205). Agent strategies are the ways that agents attempt to reinterpret their mandates in order to increase their autonomy (202). This study is similarly interested in how secretariats interpret their broad mandates, but it does not see increasing autonomy as a goal of secretariat politics per se. Rather, the cases examined here suggest that secretariat politics are motivated by a desire to enhance regime goals as defined in treaty texts, irrespective of how state preferences fracture and drift over time with respect to these goals. This sentiment is reflected in the way some WTO delegates interviewed for this study characterized the WTO Secretariat as the "guardian of the agreements."[17] This book illustrates how secretariats employ something akin to "agent strategies" in order to further regime objectives and, under certain conditions, influence political outcomes.

This argument finds support in a second strand of scholarship focused on bureaucratic influence in international affairs. This book provides strong support for arguments that secretariats (and IOs more generally) are authoritative actors (Barnett and Finnemore 2004) who influence political decision making in important ways (Bauer 2006; Bauer, Andresen, and Biermann 2012; Biermann and Siebenhüner 2009; Busch 2006; Shaffer 2005; Stanford 1994). Like these contributions, this study also finds that secretariats play an important role in shaping knowledge and belief systems, pointing to "cognitive" influence as a particularly important dimension of secretariat politics (Biermann and Siebenhüner 2009).

This book builds directly on Biermann and Siebenhüner's (2009) foundational study that outlined a typology of secretariat influence. It highlights new sources of authority (i.e., social networks and institutional memory) and mechanisms of influence (i.e., marketing and litigation facilitation), and presents variables that begin to explain variation in influence across organizations. It also moves beyond a mechanistic view of secretariat influence by building a new theory of influence that helps us to better understand the relationship between secretariat influence and power relations between states. It draws from constructivist-oriented discussions of power in global governance (Barnett and Duvall 2005) to shed light on how secretariat influence can change state power relations by shaping institutions, relationships, and shared norms/ideas.

The remainder of this chapter turns to an empirical examination of secretariat form and function through the lens of state expectations for these secretariats. It does this through an examination of secretariat legal mandates, which provide the foundation for secretariat influence in international politics—including in overlap management.

Secretariats in Practice

The most obvious place to look to understand state expectations of secretariats is the mandates that states give to them. As discussed above, secretariat mandates are both fixed in treaty texts (fixed mandates), and evolve over time through official decision-making processes (evolving mandates). The fixed mandates that govern secretariat behavior are generally fairly consistent across organizations; similar rules and norms tend to be reproduced and reinforced in fixed mandates. However, there is substantial variation among secretariats in terms of their evolving mandates, which reflect institution-specific norms and cultures. Although the rules and norms governing secretariat behavior have evolved to some extent over time, the basic contours of state expectations have remained fairly consistent.

This section traces state expectations of secretariats over time by examining expectations as articulated in the documents creating the world's first and most important secretariats. This analysis begins therefore with the 1919 Covenant of the League of Nations. The Covenant created the world's first secretariat, which provided a model for all such bodies that came after it. This section then traces the evolution of the secretariat form through the UN and the UNEP before turning to an examination of the central rules that govern UN secretariats (i.e., UN Staff Rules and Regulations), and state proposals to reform them (i.e., the 2005 World Summit Outcome on Secretariat Management and Reform).

Although the League and UN Secretariats are quite different in important ways from the treaty secretariats examined here, as two of the oldest and most important secretariats, they help us understand how states broadly conceive secretariat structure and function. As we shall see, the structure and mandates of the League and the UN provided a model for subsequent international bureaucracies. Indeed, the mandates of the treaty secretariats examined in this study are clearly derivative of those that governed the League and the UN. As such, these larger predecessor organizations help us to understand what states expect of secretariats writ large.

Covenant of the League of Nations

Created by the Treaty of Versailles in 1919, the League of Nations Secretariat has been characterized as "a great experiment in international administration" (Ranshofen-Wertheimer 1945). The League Secretariat, therefore, is the blueprint from which our contemporary notion of the secretariat form is derived. As a "great experiment," it was unclear in 1919 exactly what role international bureaucracies would play in global governance. Would they be mere functionaries of their member states, as contemporary IR theory tells us, or would they be more active participants in political decision making?

Reflecting this uncertainty, League members created a secretariat with vague and malleable rules that could be interpreted broadly and adapted over time to emerging needs. The League of Nations Secretariat's mandate was limited to basic structure (Covenant Article 6). The Covenant also enumerated a few specific tasks for the Secretariat, including serving as a depository for declarations of accession to the League, and registering and publishing a list of all treaties that League members are party to. The sole line of substantive direction to the Secretariat articulates that: "Subject to the consent of the Council and if desired by the parties, [the Secretariat shall] collect and distribute all relevant information and shall render any other assistance which may be necessary or desirable" (Article 24).

The Secretariat's mandate reflects several core elements of state expectations for secretariat structure and function. First, Article 6 clearly reflects expectations for a secretariat. It delineates a hierarchical structure, a permanent nature, and international character. Further, it reflects states' desire for strict bureaucratic control in the explicit consent the Secretariat must seek for simple tasks, such as to "collect and distribute information." Although secretariat discretion in this regard has increased over time, this original articulation indicates that secretariats were clearly not originally conceived of as political actors but as functionaries of state actors. Finally, Article 6 mandates that the Secretariat "render any other assistance which may be necessary or desirable," thereby providing great latitude for secretariat functions to evolve in response to changing needs.

The Secretariat's functions did indeed evolve. As reflected in contemporary discussions of Secretariat reform, the League Secretariat took on a much more political role over time. For example, although this role was not reflected in the majority report, the minority report of the 1930 Committee of Thirteen Inquiry on the Organization of the [League] Secretariat noted:

In practice, the work of the Secretariat to-day is quite different from what was anticipated in 1921. The division of work between the different capitals and Geneva has developed in such a way that the political character of the Secretariat's work has become much more accentuated than thought likely. Not only does the execution of decisions taken by the various organs of the League constantly require interpretations and judgments of a political nature, but the preliminary work entrusted to it makes it an adviser in the various spheres of the League. (Committee of Thirteen 1930)

As is argued in the empirical chapters that follow, this characterization remains true today.

UN Charter

Following World War II, the League was replaced by the United Nations in 1945. Similar to the League Secretariat, the UN Charter (Chapter XV,

Articles 97–101) established a Secretariat with a broad mandate with respect to size, structure, and function. It provided broad dictates and overarching principles to guide Secretariat behavior.

Parroting the League Covenant, the UN Charter calls for a hierarchical secretariat with an international character. The Charter also goes beyond the Covenant in three key ways. First, and most important, Article 99 removes the central mechanism for bureaucratic control. No longer does the Secretariat need state approval to bring information and issues to the attention of the membership; it can now do so based on its own "opinion" of what is necessary (Chapter XV, Article 99). Second, in expanding upon the notion of the Secretariat's "international character," Article 100 provides the foundation for secretariat influence. It divorces secretariat accountability from individual member states, stressing that the Secretariat is "only responsible to the Organization," and underscoring that members should not "seek to influence" the Secretariat. This creates a way for secretariats to advocate for positions that may or may not be in line with those of powerful states. Finally, reflecting Weberian notions of the bureaucratic form, the Charter calls for "the highest standards of efficiency, competence and integrity" (Article 101). This statement defined the overarching norms and principles that should govern secretariat behavior and, in doing so, shaped secretariat identity as an impartial actor in world politics.

General Assembly Resolution Establishing UNEP

The next relevant branch in the secretariat family tree is the United Nations Environment Program (UNEP). The UN General Assembly established UNEP and its Secretariat in 1972, following a recommendation in the Stockholm Declaration (UN General Assembly 1972). Although the UNEP Secretariat's mandate was far more detailed than that establishing the UN Secretariat in 1945, it still left much room for interpretation and thus further wedged open the window for secretariat influence in international affairs, more specifically in overlap management.

The functions outlined in the General Assembly Resolution establishing UNEP mirror, and far extend, those in the UN Charter. Not only does the resolution mandate the Secretariat to bring to member states any matter "[she or] he deems appropriate," it also explicitly articulates the Secretariat's advisory role, its ability to provide "substantive" (rather than merely administrative) support, and, importantly, its ability to act on its own initiative. The resolution also gives the Secretariat disguised but important agenda-setting capabilities. Perhaps even more far-reaching is the responsibility to oversee implementation of programs "and assess their effectiveness" (UN General Assembly 1972). In entrusting the Secretariat with assessing regime effectiveness, the resolution gives it the power to shape rules and practice by highlighting and framing issues of critical importance to regime operation. Finally, the resolution sets the stage for secretariat influence on overlap management specifically by entrusting the Secretariat to serve as a focal point and to coordinate among the UN's various environmental programs.

UN Staff Regulations

The UN has rules and regulations that apply to all UN staff, including all secretariat staff. Although these rules are primarily procedural in nature, outlining guidelines for such things as accepting gifts and taking sick leave, they also further enshrine some of the core principles by which the Secretariat is expected to operate. Of particular importance are Regulations 1.2(b) and (d). Regulation 1.2(b) recalls the UN Charter, stating, "staff members shall uphold the highest standards of efficiency, competence, and integrity." It further defines integrity as including, but not being limited to, "probity, impartiality, fairness, honesty, and truthfulness." Also recalling the UN Charter, Regulation 1.2(d) further entrenches the Secretariat's international character. It underscores that "in the performance of their duties staff members shall neither seek nor accept instructions from any Government or from any other source external to the Organization." These regulations reinforce norms that guide secretariat behavior writ large, including national impartiality, expertise, and hierarchy, and aim to protect the UN secretariats from capture by powerful interests.

Also incorporated into the UN Staff Rules are the recommendations of the 2001 International Civil Service Commission, an expert panel established by the UN General Assembly (2001). These recommendations reiterate and expand upon many of the guiding principles contained in the UN Charter, including an emphasis on international character, hierarchy, and integrity.

Following 82 years of state experience with secretariats, the recommendations further elaborated key elements of what secretariats are and should be. They expanded an advising role for executive heads, articulating for the first time that they can hold and advocate for their own positions and, importantly, draft important documents such as resolutions. The latter will emerge as a key mechanism of influence for some of the secretariats examined in the empirical chapters that follow. Finally, the most striking aspect of the recommendations is the credit they give to secretariats for the success of global governance writ large. They state: "ultimately, it is the international civil service that will enable the United Nations system to bring about a just and peaceful world." Taken together, secretariat functions as articulated in the recommendations reflect state recognition of secretariats as more than mere administrators. Rather, the 2001 recommendations reflect an evolving (albeit tacit) state understanding of secretariats as actors with the capacity to shape political decision making in ways not previously conceived.

Reform Proposals

Finally, state demands regarding UN Secretariat reform are a useful guide to understand what states expect from secretariats. Reform proposals have waxed and waned in the UN system since its creation. They have been launched by various actors, with the most high-profile proposals covering Security Council and General Assembly reform. Former Secretary-General Kofi Annan launched a comprehensive reform agenda for the Secretariat itself. Although Annan's proposals for institutional and management reforms were largely aimed at providing additional authority and flexibility, including that related to discretionary funding, member states saw reform as a way to make the Secretariat more efficient, effective, accountable, and transparent (Martinetti 2008). Nevertheless, many of Annan's proposals were taken up in the 2005 UN World Summit on Sustainable Development Outcome, which was subsequently adopted by the UN General Assembly (2005).

The UN Resolution clearly reflects state demands for increased bureaucratic control through increased transparency and accountability in UN Secretariats. This suggests that secretariats have, to some extent, escaped state control, stoking in states a desire to rein them in. It also highlights the political importance of secretariat evolution from an actor that once needed state consent to merely provide information (the League) to one that can advocate for positions and advise (UNEP) and "enable the United Nations system to bring about a just and peaceful world" (International Civil Service Commission 2013).

Case Study Secretariat Mandates

The structure and function of the secretariats examined in this study are derivative of the larger organizations discussed above. In some cases, this makes good sense because the treaty secretariat is formally administered by a larger organization. This is true for the CBD and CITES, which are both administered by UNEP. In other cases, such as the WTO, the secretariat is an entirely independent organization. In either instance, however, secretariat structures and fixed mandates are very similar to those of the League, UN, and UNEP. These similarities across vastly different organizations highlight the commonalities of secretariats as an organizational form and, importantly, the expected relationship between a secretariat and its member states.

The remainder of this section briefly summarizes the mandates of the secretariats examined in this study. It highlights the commonalities with their predecessors and focuses attention on how their mandates position them to participate in overlap management specifically.

Convention on Biological Diversity   The CBD Secretariat's mandate is surprisingly short. Unlike its predecessors, it is silent on structure and norms of behavior. However, because the CBD Secretariat sits within the UN system and is hosted by UNEP, these details of its structure and norms are implicit in those of its predecessors. That is, UN rules apply to all UN secretariats and UNEP rules apply to all secretariats hosted by the central organization. State expectations regarding elements such as hierarchy, international character, and competence were established elsewhere, such as the Declaration establishing UNEP, and did not need to be articulated again in the Convention text. Rather, the Secretariat's mandate articulates a simple relationship to the CoP: the Secretariat is to do what the CoP asks of it and report back to the CoP on its progress. States' desire for bureaucratic control is clearly embedded in this mandate.

The CBD Secretariat's mandate regarding managing overlap, however, is new, explicit, and far-reaching. The mandate not only allows but instructs the Secretariat to "coordinate with other relevant international bodies and, in particular to enter into such administrative and contractual arrangements as may be required for the effective discharge of its functions" (CBD 1992, Article 24(d)). Although the latter clause has resulted in the negotiation of many paper tigers, this mandate also opened the door for the Secretariat to develop and drive overlap management.

The Secretariat's leadership role in overlap management is further developed through Article 23 paragraph 4(h) of the Convention and Goal 1 of CBD's Strategic Plan, adopted by CoP6 in 2002. Article 23 instructs the parties to "contact, through the Secretariat, the executive bodies of the conventions dealing with matters covered by the

Convention, with a view to establishing appropriate forms of coopera- tion with them." Goal 1 calls for the CBD to fulfill its "leadership role in international biodiversity issues" by "promoting cooperation between all relevant international instruments and processes to enhance policy coherence." Although the Secretariat is not explicitly mentioned in the latter goal, its fixed mandate (embodied in Article 24) and Article 23 clearly identified the Secretariat as the leadership figure in carrying out overlap management functions. The Secretariat's evolving mandates on overlap management are detailed in chapters 4 and 5.

World Trade Organization   The WTO Secretariat also has fixed and evolving mandates. Its fixed mandate, as contained in Article VI of the Marrakesh Agreement Establishing the WTO (1994), draws nearly entirely from the UN Secretariat mandates described above. As with the UN secretariats, states expect the WTO Secretariat to be structured hier- archically, international in character, and responsible for meeting the evolving needs of member states.

The WTO's mandate remains silent, however, on Secretariat functions, leaving those to be determined by the Ministerial Conference at a later date. The mandate is also silent on any Secretariat functions relevant to overlap management. Instead, the WTO Secretariat's capacity to influ- ence overlap management between the WTO and various environmental regimes is built into the Secretariat's organizational structure. The WTO Secretariat has a division specifically dedicated to supporting work on issues of overlap between trade and the environment (i.e., the Division on Trade and Environment [DTE]). The DTE does not have an individu- alized fixed mandate. As discussed in chapter 6, its work on overlap management is largely determined by its evolving informal mandates from member states.

Convention on International Trade in Endangered Species   Established in 1973, the CITES Secretariat has the most far-reaching mandate of all the secretariats examined thus far in this chapter. Like the CBD Secre- tariat, the CITES Secretariat is administered by UNEP and its fixed mandate is short on structure. Further, like all mandates examined thus far, the CITES Secretariat mandate contains language leaving room for interpretation and change as states' needs evolve over time. The CITES mandate is unique, however, in that it enumerates various specific activi- ties that the Secretariat can engage in, many of which are central to regime operation.

For example, expanding on the UNEP Secretariat's mandate to advise and advocate, the CITES Secretariat is mandated to "undertake scientific and technical studies" relevant to regime operation (CITES 1973, Article XII 2(c)). Whereas its predecessors were permitted to gather and distribute information to states, the CITES Secretariat is explicitly mandated to produce such information on its own. Further, in being mandated to review party reports and request additional information as needed, the CITES Secretariat is also given a role in enforcement. Finally, the Secretariat is mandated to make recommendations to parties regarding implementation of the Convention. This might include, but is not limited to, suggestions for which species should be protected under the Convention or how well a particular country is doing in meeting its obligations. Unlike the CBD, the CITES Secretariat does not have an overlap management mandate. However, the CITES Secretariat's mandate provides a strong platform for its participation in making a broad range of political decisions.

Conclusions

The legal mandates and theoretical treatments of secretariats analyzed above illuminate commonalities that engender a similar politics across secretariats, despite their diversity. Three aspects of secretariat structure are central to understanding secretariat politics more generally. First, secretariats' international character is critical to understanding how secretariat interests are formed. Secretariats are generally responsible first and foremost to their organizations, not to individual member states. This allows secretariats to circumvent power politics and advocate for positions that reflect organizational rules and norms rather than the interests of powerful states. To be sure, states originally defined these rules and norms in, for example, treaty texts. For this reason, many scholars have ignored secretariats as actors in their own right. However, these treatments obscure secretariats' role in maintaining treaty integrity as state interests creep over time.

Second, the "delegated discretion" (Hawkins et al. 2006) endowed to secretariats through state mandates lays the foundation for secretariat influence in political decision making. Delegated discretion articulates areas where secretariats can act autonomously, substantively, and/or constitutively. For example, the UN Secretariat can advocate for positions, the UNEP Secretariat can bring anything to parties' attention that it deems appropriate, and the CITES Secretariat can review state implementation reports and request additional information. These functions all move beyond simple administrative duties, extending into the substantive work of these organizations. They are broad enough to rationalize a host of potentially influential activities.

Finally, these mandates merely generate the legal capacity for influence. They articulate what is possible but are often vague on details. Mandates leave much room for entrepreneurial secretariats to expand their zones of discretion. Further complicating secretariat politics, what is delegated and what is not can be unclear. If states fail to object to secretariat activities, does their silence constitute implicit delegation? In addition, vague mandates can be used to justify many types of secretariat activities, whether or not these activities were intended by member states. Recent discussions of secretariat reform within the UN system reflect the disconnect between theory and practice in this regard.

The empirical chapters that follow detail how secretariat practice emerges through evolving (as opposed to fixed) mandates and in the absence of mandates entirely. Although the very different secretariats described above have very similar fixed mandates, the empirical chapters illuminate variation between secretariats in terms of their ability to influence decision making. This variation is a result of differences in secretariat expertise and networks, as well as the nature of state preferences on a given issue. The next chapter unpacks these ideas and their relationship to secretariat influence in more detail. It demonstrates how secretariats exert influence, when such influence is possible, and when it persists over time.

3

The Analytics of Influence

It's about changing attitudes among individuals. The role of the Secretariat is being there and talking to Parties, trying to get them to buy in—not pushing too hard or they tend to back off. Demonstrating the value of collaboration [across treaties]. It is a progressive, trust-building process. The Secretariat's role is large in building this norm among Parties.

—Biodiversity Secretariat staff member (June 2006)

This chapter lays out the theoretical underpinnings and analytical framework deployed in this study to understand secretariat influence. The first half of the chapter explains how the core theoretical concepts of power, authority, and influence are understood and deployed in this book. It presents a new theory of secretariat influence that builds on emerging understandings of power in global governance. The second half of the chapter presents a theoretically derived analytical framework for understanding when secretariats are most likely to influence overlap management politics. That analytical framework is applied to the empirical cases that follow in chapters 4 to 7.

Specifically, the framework presented in this chapter argues that secretariats influence politics by shaping the institutional, structural, and productive power relations between states. Secretariats have this ability because they have authority, rooted in delegation and network position. Their influence operates through various mechanisms, including knowledge brokering, marketing, and facilitating negotiations and dispute settlement. Finally, this chapter argues that secretariats are likely to influence politics when certain conditions are met—namely, when other actors cannot reasonably carry out secretariat functions (i.e., substitutability is low), and when state preferences surrounding a particular issue are weak and/or underdeveloped (i.e., when preferences are weakly solidified).

As noted above, the chapter is divided into two major sections. The first section discusses the conceptual relationship between power, authority, and influence. It disentangles the theoretical relationship between these three core concepts—often conflated in the scholarly literature—which underlie the analysis undertaken in this book. This section is written for readers who are keenly interested in the thick theoretical relationship between these three concepts. This first section is purely conceptual in nature; it does not seek to answer any specific empirical questions. The second half of this chapter presents an analytical framework that deploys the concept of bureaucratic influence and power that was detailed in the first half of the chapter. The analytical framework is central to this study. It is deployed in all empirical chapters that follow to explain (1) how we know secretariat influence when we see it, and (2) the conditions that enable/constrain secretariat influence.

Theoretical Foundations: Disentangling Power, Authority, and Influence

Influence is often understood in line with Cox and Jacobson's classic definition as "the modification of one actor's behavior by another" (1973, 3). This definition is useful because it focuses attention on behavioral impacts. It is also imprecise and has led to much analytical confusion, contributing to the frequent conflation of influence, authority, and power throughout the scholarly literature. For example, Barnett and Finnemore's (2004) definition of authority is very similar to Cox and Jacobson's definition of influence. Barnett and Finnemore define authority as "the ability of one actor to use institutional and discursive resources to induce deference from others" (5, 20). Similarly, Dahl's (1957) classic definition of power (the ability of actor A to get actor B to do something it otherwise would not) deviates only slightly from Cox and Jacobson's definition of influence. Polsby (1980) explicitly considers "power" and "influence" to be "serviceable synonyms" (3). Although this section does not claim to settle decades of debate on the topic, it disentangles the relationship between power, authority, and influence for the purposes of better understanding *secretariat* politics in the cases that follow.

In short, power and authority are capacities to impact outcomes, whereas influence is the mobilization of power or authority to realize those outcomes. Although these three concepts are closely linked, scholarly discussions surrounding them have evolved in an uncoordinated fashion—mobilizing these concepts to ask different types of questions. As such, the analytical tools that can be extracted and applied to the case of secretariat politics are different. The influence literature helps us to understand *how* secretariats influence; the power literature helps us to understand *when* such influence matters; and the authority literature helps us to understand *why* secretariats are able to influence. Although this study is fundamentally interested in explaining secretariat influence, such influence cannot be understood without first clarifying how power and authority are conceptualized in this book.

Secretariat Power

Power is the capacity to impact outcomes (Giddens 1984, 257). While power may include obvious instances of coercion, it also involves A's ability to persuade B, or even to shape the options that B believes are available through, for example, agenda setting (Bachrach and Baratz Morton 1962), discursive practices (Hajer 1995), and/or the mobilization of bias (Lukes 1974). When these more subtle modes of power are exercised, "some issues are organized into politics while others are organized out" (Schattschneider 1975, 69). Put another way, power is not only the ability to prevail in a political discussion but also the ability to predetermine the content of the discussion itself (Perenti 1970). As such, power is not simply a coercive mechanism but a constitutive one as well.

Barnett and Duvall's (2005, 3) constructivist-oriented model of power defines power as "the production, in and through social relations, of effects [or impacts] that shape the capacities of actors to determine their own fates." This definition is particularly appropriate for an analysis of secretariat behavior because secretariats are not typically decision makers themselves. That is, they are not explicitly entrusted with the ability to make binding decisions, nor do they enjoy coercive strength. Rather, secretariats' capacity to impact outcomes is more often reflected indirectly in their ability to shape preferences and (re)distribute capacities among decision makers. They can, for example, participate in framing key governance concepts that privilege some states' interests over others, and/or regulate the flow of information that shapes these decisions to begin with. In this way, secretariats are able to shape power relations between states.

Power is difficult to observe empirically because it is, by definition, a capacity—not a tangible resource. As such, it is typically observed by proxy. When understood through the coercive lens adopted by scholars such as Dahl and Polsby, power can be measured through tangible proxies such as guns, bombs, and dollars. However, when understood as the capacity to shape preferences and (re)distribute capabilities, such tangible proxies remain elusive. In this situation, an actor can be understood as powerful if certain types of impacts can be attributed to that actor post facto.

This study also employs power as a concept to understand how secretariats can shape power relations between states. Barnett and Duvall's (2005) typology of power helps us to envision the suite of potential ways that secretariats can shape such power relations. They outline four forms of power: compulsory, institutional, structural, and productive. Changes in power relations between states can be observed empirically by overlaying these forms of power onto specific types of impacts. That is, institutional, structural, and/or productive changes in the power relations between states can be observed through changes in rules/institutions, relative capacities/relationships, and/or norms/ideas, respectively. Although my interpretation deviates slightly from Barnett and Duvall's original articulation (and indeed simplifies it), the concepts of institutional, structural, and productive power are very useful to our understanding of how secretariats matter most in world politics. I explain below how each of these forms of power applies to the case of secretariat behavior.

Compulsory power reflects the realist and institutionalist understandings of how power operates in international politics. It refers to the "ability of one actor to exert direct control over another" (Barnett and Duvall 2005, 3) and is clearly most in line with Dahl's definition cited above. However, compulsory power is rarely, if ever, exerted by secretariats; it is more reflective of the power states have over secretariats on issues such as the budget, which might detail, for example, what projects the secretariat can engage in or how many staff positions it can add or must eliminate. Compulsory power is necessarily coercive. It is not particularly relevant to the analysis undertaken in this book, except to the extent that it highlights the softer nature of secretariat power when compared to more state-centered understandings of the concept.

Institutional power is far more relevant to secretariat activities than is compulsory power. Institutional power is an actor's capacity to shape the formal and informal institutions (e.g., rules, procedures, norms) that mediate relationships between state actors (Barnett and Duvall 2005, 15–16). Correspondingly, changes in these formal and informal institutions indicate a change in institutional power relations between states. For example, rule changes can redistribute capabilities by (re)allocating responsibilities in ways that privilege certain actors' participation and/ or expertise over that of others. These impacts are particularly important because, once institutionalized, they can persist for long periods of time. In this way, institutional power is necessarily indirect; it does not involve explicit instruction or overt pressure that changes actor behavior. Yet institutional power is important because it can shape power relations by changing the institutional structures that mediate state interactions in world politics.

Although closely related, institutional and structural power differ in how they impact relational identity and capacities. Whereas institutional power produces rules, norms, and procedures (i.e., formal and informal institutions) that enable and constrain actors' capacities for political decision making, structural power is the ability to shape how actors understand and operationalize their relationships to one another. Structural power can produce subject positions (e.g., master-slave, laborer-capitalist, member state–secretariat, developed-developing) that determine how actors will interact, or it can further entrench existing structures. As explained by Barnett and Duvall (2005, 18), "structural power shapes the fates and conditions of existence of actors [by] ... allocat[ing] differential capacities, and typically differential advantages, to different positions." More simply, structural power shapes relationships between states and their relative capacities to engage in world politics.

Correspondingly, changes in the way states understand and operationalize their relationships to one another indicate a change in structural power relations between them. For example, structural changes can shape power relations between developed and developing states by filtering information flow that reinforces existing power dynamics. Secretariats can do this by organizing workshops and distributing studies and reports to state actors. In regulating outside organizations' access to member states, secretariats enable some ideas, information, and actors while excluding others. Although this filtering role may be less relevant for well-resourced states that have plenty of options for acquiring information, it can be quite important for underresourced actors who rely more heavily on secretariats for such capacity-building work. In filtering which information reaches underresourced states, secretariats can shape structural power relations between them by distributing information that confers differential advantages to different groups of actors.

Finally, productive power is the capacity to "constitute ... social subjects ... through systems of knowledge and discursive practices" (Barnett and Duvall 2005, 20). As Barnett and Duvall explain, whereas structural power shapes relationships in a hierarchical or binary way, productive power shapes relationships more broadly. Productive power constitutes actors through classification systems such as "civilized," "democratic," or "rogue." Productive power as discussed in this study also reflects an actor's capacity to change significance and meaning in ways that redefine how actors understand what is actual, possible, and/or should be possible. In other words, productive power is the ability to shape norms and ideas that are important to regime operation.

Correspondingly, changes in key regime norms and ideas indicate a change in productive power relations between states. For example, secretariats can shape how member states understand the significance or strategic role of linkages between international regimes. They can reframe previously peripheral elements of regime operation or problem structure in ways that attract additional attention and resources. The rise of climate change, for example, has catalyzed the forging of new and creative linkages across a wide variety of forums, with secretariats at the helm in some cases (Jinnah 2011a). Such changes in systems of knowledge and discursive practices shape power relations between states by creating systems of meaning and networks that shape interstate relations (Barnett and Duvall 2005, 20).

In summary, secretariats can shape the institutional, structural, and/ or productive power relations between states by driving changes to institutions, relationships, and/or norms/ideas.

Secretariat Authority

Authority is the exercise of legitimate power (Cronin and Hurd 2008, 6; Cutler, Haufler, and Porter 1999, 5; Hall and Biersteker 2002, 4; Ruggie 1982, 198). Broadly speaking, power is legitimate when the object thinks such power ought to be obeyed (Hurd 1999, 381), or when it results in the institutionalization of formal and/or informal rules or practices that objects understand as obligatory (Bernstein 2005, 156). However, states rarely "obey" secretariats or understand their rules and practices as "obligatory." Rather, secretariat authority is more commonly indirect in that it can shape state preferences, which in turn can institutionalize formal and informal rules, practices, and norms that direct state behavior and interaction. How then do we know when secretariat behavior is legitimate?

Most discussions of legitimacy requirements in global governance identify principles of democracy (e.g., participation and transparency) as the necessary ingredients (e.g., Bodansky 1999; Held 1995). Democratically derived legitimacy has limited applicability for international bureaucracies, however, as bureaucratic activities generally lack these ingredients. Yet, as measured through impacts, bureaucracies enjoy authority. Bernstein's discussions of political legitimacy help us to better understand why this is so (2005, 2011). Bernstein defines political legitimacy as "the acceptance and justification of shared rule by a community" (2005, 142; 2011, 20). Although the concept of bureaucratic "rule" is an uneasy one in global governance, Bernstein's definition of legitimacy is important in that it focuses attention on acceptance, rather than obligation, as the necessary ingredient for bureaucratic legitimacy.

Drawing from Weberian understandings of domestic bureaucracies (Weber 1978), a burgeoning literature on international bureaucracies further helps us to understand when secretariat activities are legitimate. Specifically, this literature provides three key concepts for understanding the conditions under which bureaucratic activities are accepted by states as legitimate (e.g., Barnett and Finnemore 2004; Bauer 2006). In addition to rational-legal authority, the literature identifies delegation, morality, and expertise as the primary sources of legitimate bureaucratic behavior.[1] In the context of secretariats, shared norms can be a better way to describe the dynamic of moral authority described by Weber and others. When bureaucracies draw from these legitimate resources to change power relations between states, such changes can (generally) be understood as legitimate themselves, and therefore, authoritative.

Rational-legal, delegated, moral/normative, and expert resources are legitimate because they frame bureaucratic behavior in relation to a chain of command that begins with state actors (directly and indirectly). Authority derived from law and/or delegation is the clearest example. Morality/norms and expertise also reflect this dynamic because state actors play an important role in defining these regime-specific ideas as well. For example, shared norms or morals (e.g., neoliberal understandings of development or conservation-based understandings of environmentalism) are often defined in the preamble of treaty texts, which are negotiated and endorsed by member states. These ideas define the boundaries of regime operation and secretariat activities, which also evolve over time (Bushey and Jinnah 2010). Similarly, most treaties contain articles that outline secretariat functions, such as identifying issues of concern to member states, analyzing implementation, or evaluating proposals. These functions articulate states' treaty-specific expectations for secretariat expertise in, for example, conservation biology, law, and/or economics. Therefore, authority that draws from delegation, shared morals/norms, and expertise is generally legitimate to the extent that it is rooted in state expectations and/or delegation. As we will see in the World Trade Organization (WTO) cases, however, when state expectations are unclear or diverge, this legitimacy can erode.

Drawn primarily from Weber's studies of domestic bureaucracies, delegation, morality/norms, and expertise capture the rough contours of legitimate *secretariat* behavior as well. However, these concepts of bureaucratic authority obscure some important differences between secretariats and their domestic counterparts. Importantly, secretariats derive legitimacy—and thus authority—not only from their relationship to states but also from their position in global governance networks. This source of authority is largely a function of the changing nature of global governance, which is becoming increasingly interconnected and complex, with problem-solving needs crossing institutional boundaries (Young et al. 2006). A governance void has opened, wherein "accepted rules and norms according to which policy making and politics is to be conducted" are lacking (Hajer 2003, 175). As demonstrated in the empirical chapters that follow, states increasingly rely on secretariats to fill this void.

It is secretariats' unique position in governance networks that allows them to operate in this political space. Secretariats are the only permanent seat of most intergovernmental organizations (IGOs), and they are made up of career civil servants who often work across different organizations on similar issues.[2] These characteristics position secretariats to derive additional authority from institutional memory and social networks, both of which are sources of secretariat authority related to expertise. Indeed, institutional memory is akin to Weber's "knowledge of the files" (2009, 214), and social networks enable power because they facilitate the rapid transfer of knowledge between relevant actors. However, these two sources of secretariat authority warrant further explication because they derive legitimacy not necessarily from delegation alone, but also from positioning that legitimizes deference.

The remainder of this subsection, therefore, details the three relatively well-understood forms of bureaucratic authority that are rooted in state delegation (delegated, moral/norms, expertise), as well as two previously undiscussed forms of secretariat authority that are rooted in subject position (institutional memory and social networks).

Authority Rooted in State Delegation   Delegated authority results from direct instruction from states to secretariats to carry out specific tasks. Elsewhere described as "delegated discretion,"[3] delegated authority is built into a secretariat's fixed or evolving mandate.[4] This delegation articulates where and when a secretariat can act in the absence of direct instruction from member states. While delegated authority creates a zone of discretion for secretariat action, secretariats can also play an important role in (re)constructing and expanding their zones of discretion. As we will see in chapter 4, the Convention on Biological Diversity (CBD) Secretariat shaped the architecture of overlap management in a way that cements its own position as the most qualified actor to lead the process, leaving states little choice but to delegate discretion to it on this issue. Together with rational-legal authority, delegated authority lays the foundation for secretariat influence by providing secretariats with the legitimacy for discretionary action.

While delegated authority in global governance can be traced to specific state mandates and instructions, moral authority is more implicit. Moral authority is the ability to draw from shared normative belief systems to advocate for or defend particular activities or ideas. As Hall (1997, 594) explains, moral claims can be authoritative when they become "socially embedded in a system of actors whose social identities and interests impel them to recognize [such claims] as a power resource." Bureaucracies draw on moral authority when they "claim to be the representative of a community's interest or the defender of the values of the international community" (Barnett and Finnemore 2004, 23). Such shared moral justification is often found in treaty texts or in the norms underlying regime operation. For example, the WTO Secretariat's economic expertise embodies a morality that is bound up in a widely held worldview associated with market liberals.[5] Similarly, the CBD Secretariat's expertise in conservation issues reflects a morality derived from a "bioenvironmental" worldview (Clapp and Dauvergne 2005, 9–11). Because powerful states create IGOs, these worldviews tend to align normatively with powerful states' interests within these organizations, and as such can be drawn upon to motivate state behavior. In this way, claims based in moral authority are legitimate and persuasive to the extent that they are seen as endogenous to the regime itself.

Expertise-based authority is derived from technical knowledge and training. Such expertise is often required of secretariat staff in order to carry out their functions as articulated in fixed and evolving mandates. For example, most secretariats are mandated to support the legal life of treaties by drafting decisions or supporting dispute resolution. Similarly, environmental treaties tend to be science-based, requiring their secretariats to do such things as evaluate ecological impacts and suggest modes of addressing those impacts. In these cases, legal and scientific expertise are requirements for secretariat operation. Secretariat expertise is reflected in academic literature, technical reports, papers, and analyses that demonstrate their in-depth knowledge of convention rules, processes, and related contemporary issues.[6] As such, secretariats have expert authority to the extent that they have highly trained and experienced staff that create and manage knowledge and channel information and data flow, thereby shaping regime operation.

Authority Rooted in Position   Institutional memory is a specific type of expertise. It is derived from years of collective experience with institutional rules, norms, and practices. Institutional memory moves beyond general expertise in that it incorporates not only technical know-how and formal training but also authority derived from informal knowledge about the history and evolution of institutional processes. For example, secretariat staff interviewed for this study who deal with biodiversity issues noted that state delegate turnover is not uncommon. In contrast, when they were asked about their career paths, it became clear that many secretariat staff members are highly specialized career professionals, experts on a particular aspect of international law, and often stay within the secretariats (or closely related ones) for many years. Secretariats' institutional memory is reflected in their comprehensive understanding of the complex dynamics of national circumstances that drive member positions and, importantly, how and why those positions have changed over time. It is not uncommon, for example, for secretariats to utilize past state decisions to justify future actions (see chapters 4 and 7). Institutional memory can therefore provide secretariats with a legitimizing basis for decision making when they draw on such things as legal precedent and political intent.

Similarly, social networks are a source of secretariat authority, which is derived from the web of professional relationships that develop among actors working on interrelated issues over extended periods of time. The increased density, overlap, and connectedness of international treaties suggest that networks between organizations are increasingly important for effective governance (Young et al. 2006). Indeed, many secretariat staff interviewed for this study highlighted their regular interactions (e.g., meetings, informal consultations on issues of common interest) with staff at other IGOs, nongovernmental organizations (NGOs), and state actors who work in their issue area. These interactions reflect relatively well-developed extraorganizational networks that can contribute to governance effectiveness. As highlighted in the empirical chapters that follow, secretariats often selectively broker connections between their extra- and intraorganizational networks. For example, the WTO Secretariat uses these networks to set up workshops and/or information sessions for its member states on issues under negotiation. Through activities like these, secretariats can play an important role in filtering information between outside organizations and delegates to their respective IGOs. These networks can function to facilitate learning across organizations through information flow and, when well managed, can even increase the stability of a network (Young et al. 2006). As such, secretariat authority sourced from social networks derives its legitimacy from its connection to enhanced regime effectiveness through organizational learning.[7]

In summary, authority is legitimate power. Secretariats derive legitimacy from at least five sources: delegation, morality, expertise, institutional memory, and social networks. The first three of these authoritative sources garner their legitimacy in large part from their connection (albeit sometimes indirect) to chains of state delegation or mandate. The latter two capitalize on secretariats' subject position in international politics, deriving their legitimacy from secretariat claims to legal intent/precedent (institutional memory) and their ability to enhance regime effectiveness (social networks). When changes to institutional, structural, and/or productive power relations between states can be traced to secretariat activities that rely on these legitimacy resources, a secretariat has authority.

Secretariat Influence

Whereas power and authority are capacities to impact outcomes, influence is the mobilization of power or authority to realize those outcomes.[8] Because secretariats do not enjoy the coercive power exerted by states, secretariat influence *most often* relies on the mobilization of legitimate power resources, or authority. Secretariat influence, therefore, is the mobilization of authority, rooted in delegation or network position, to impact political outcomes. Moreover, those impacts matter most when they reflect institutional, structural, and/or productive changes in the power relations between states.

For example, Barnett and Finnemore (2004) describe how the International Monetary Fund (IMF) developed policies that ultimately reconstituted member state economies, and how the UN High Commission for Refugees (UNHCR) shaped the way the international community understood who was a "refugee," and therefore who fell under the UNHCR's mandate. In both instances, the secretariats drew from their authoritative resources (i.e., morality, expertise, social networks, delegation, institutional memory) to participate in political decision making. In the first example, the IMF Secretariat deployed its expert authority to yield an impact that reflected institutional changes in member state economies. In the latter example, the UNHCR Secretariat deployed its moral authority to yield an impact that reflected productive changes in the way member states understood a key concept. In both cases, the secretariat influenced political decision making by shaping the institutional and productive power relations between states.

The literature illuminates some ways that secretariats mobilize their bureaucratic authority to exert influence. In other words, it describes their mechanisms of influence. Biermann and Siebenhüner (2009) identify three such mechanisms: knowledge brokering, negotiation facilitation, and capacity building. The empirical cases examined in this study put forward two additional mechanisms of secretariat influence: litigation facilitation and marketing. These new mechanisms overlap with, but are not fully captured by, existing categories, and thus lend some additional nuance and texture to our understanding of how secretariats operate in international politics.

Knowledge brokering operates by changing knowledge and belief systems (Biermann et al. 2009, 47). Secretariat knowledge brokering includes such activities as gathering, synthesizing, processing, and disseminating information to states or other objects of influence. Negotiation facilitation is a mechanism of normative influence in its ability to shape procedures and law making, frame issues, and define participation (Biermann and Siebenhüner 2009, 48). It includes such activities as creating, supporting, and shaping norm-building processes for issue-specific international negotiations through, for example, agenda setting or facilitating access to organizational forums for outside organizations. Finally, capacity building is aimed at direct assistance to member states (Biermann and Siebenhüner 2009, 48). It includes such activities as assisting countries to comply with international rules or shape domestic policies through, for example, workshops or providing formal or informal technical advice.

Litigation facilitation overlaps with knowledge brokering, such as through the provision of technical information to support dispute settlement (e.g., negotiation history of a specific topic or adjudicative histories). It also includes functions that move well beyond provision of technical information. These functions include drafting key legal documents for justices, providing direct legal support, overseeing panel composition, and even helping underresourced countries to more effectively participate in litigation processes.

A subset of knowledge brokering, marketing moves well beyond provision of technical information to the strategic use of information to shape shared opinions and understandings about political processes, norms, and/ or institutions. Whereas knowledge brokering can be as simple as providing states with a list of studies published on a particular topic, marketing involves an inherent element of strategic framing and dissemination.

Marketing is the strategic filtering, framing, and iteration of a concept or idea that is important to a particular political discourse. It involves the conscious selection and uptake of specific pieces of information (filtering); the digestion and transformation of that information to meet specific political ends ((re)framing); and the repeated presentation of that information across multiple political forums (reiteration). Finally, marketing is a combination of cognitive and normative influence due to its ability to "frame international and transnational processes of bargaining and arguing ... [in order to advance] ... the codification and development of international law." (Biermann and Siebenhüner 2009, 47–48)

In summary, secretariat influence is the mobilization of authority to shape power relations between states. Secretariats do this by engaging in activities (knowledge brokering, marketing, etc.) that result in institutional, structural, or productive changes to institutions, relationships, and/or norms/ideas.

Analytical Framework: How and When Do Secretariats Influence Politics?

The first half of this chapter fleshed out what influence is, how it functions in secretariat politics, and its relationship to power and authority. That discussion illuminated the analytical potential of all three concepts for understanding secretariat influence specifically. Using that conceptual foundation, this section builds a two-pronged analytical framework for studying how and when secretariats influence politics. First, it explains how to evaluate whether a secretariat has influenced political outcomes in global governance. Second, it proposes a framework for understanding the conditions under which such influence is likely to occur.

Prong #1: Did the Secretariat Influence Political Outcomes?

There are three steps involved in evaluating whether a secretariat has in fact influenced political outcomes. First, we must empirically evaluate *if* the secretariat deployed any mechanisms of influence (i.e., knowledge brokering, negotiation facilitation, marketing, etc.). If the secretariat engaged in politics through one of these mechanisms, then influence is possible and further inquiry is warranted. We must be able to trace those mechanisms of influence to specific impacts, however, in order to confirm that a secretariat did in fact influence political outcomes. Moreover, those impacts must be substantive, rather than merely functional. Whereas functional impacts are those that enable or facilitate collective action among actors without necessarily changing political preferences (e.g., logistical support) (Betsill and Correll 2008), substantive impacts, as understood here, are those that shape power relations between political actors. For example, substantive impacts include those that alter how funds are distributed, how issues are framed, which policy tools are favored, how legal issues are interpreted, and which scientific studies are considered most relevant.

The second step, therefore, is to determine *if* observed mechanisms of influence yielded impacts that reflect institutional, structural, or productive changes to power relations between states. We can do this by identifying changes in institutions, relationships, and/or norms/ideas and using process tracing to determine whether such changes can be plausibly attributed to the secretariat's observed mechanisms of influence (or vice versa). Finally, the third step involves a counterfactual analysis to rule out alternative explanations for the observed changes.

Once we have determined whether a secretariat influenced a particular outcome, we can generally evaluate the strength of that influence by examining the characteristics of the relevant impact. This study considers influence to be strong if the relevant impacts reflect a change in core institutional rules and/or norms that dictate state behavior. Influence is considered moderate if it reflects a change in at least some state practices

Table 3.1
Influence

None	Weak	Moderate	Strong
No change in power relations	Change in flow/ availability of information	Change in some state practice not required by rules	Change in core rules/norms

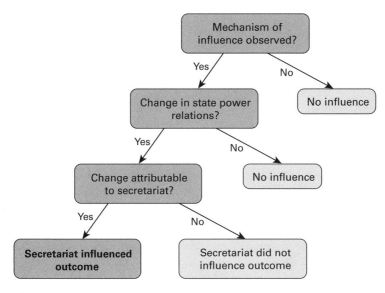

Figure 3.1
Did the secretariat influence political outcomes?

that are not required by changes in official rules or widely adopted normative changes. Finally, influence is considered weak in this study if it reflects changes in the flow and/or availability of information that states use for decision making (table 3.1). Again, influence is absent if no change in power relations between states can be attributed to any secretariat mechanisms of influence. Figure 3.1 summarizes the overarching approach to answering Prong #1's core question: Did the secretariat influence political outcomes?

Prong #2: Under What Conditions Can Secretariats Influence Outcomes?

A host of variables condition a secretariat's ability to influence political outcomes. Biermann and Siebenhüner (2009) convincingly argue that problem structure, polity, people, and procedures are critical to understanding when secretariats influence outcomes and when they do not. This study adds two relational variables (i.e., those that account for differentials in experience and positioning between secretariats and other actors in the political system) that are also important in conditioning secretariat influence. Specifically, this study posits that secretariat influence is likely when (1) secretariat services have low substitutability and (2) state preferences are weakly solidified.

This hypothesis draws strongly from the literatures on NGOs and epistemic communities. Like NGOs and many epistemic communities, secretariats are nonstate actors—by definition, they do not have national affiliations. However, state relationships with secretariats and their relationships with other nonstate actors are different in important ways. Although secretariats are not perfect agents, the secretariat-state dynamic in most circumstances closely resembles a principal-agent relationship; states control secretariat budgets and give orders that secretariats are obligated to follow. In contrast, NGOs and epistemic communities are largely independent from states; they are not necessarily reliant on states for finances or mandate. Nevertheless, secretariat functions and mechanisms of influence in international affairs overlap substantially with those of NGOs and epistemic communities. Centrally, like many NGOs and epistemic communities, secretariats can shape state preferences through provision of expertise in ways that allow them to strategically frame issues. As such, insights from these literatures help to illuminate the conditions under which secretariats too can influence international politics. This section unpacks the two variables considered in this study, which are distilled from these literatures: preference solidification and substitutability.

Preference Solidification This study presents a new variable—preference solidification—that helps to explain the likelihood of secretariat influence. Preference solidification is related to the more commonly used metric of preference heterogeneity. Heterogeneity measures similarity across state preferences and predicts that greater heterogeneity yields lower levels of delegation (Hawkins et al. 2006, 21). Solidification, in contrast, is interested in how the qualities of delegated tasks themselves (i.e., administrative vs. analytical) help us to understand how well-developed state preferences are—that is, whether they are weakly, moderately, or strongly solidified. This, in turn, helps us to understand how much room secretariats have to maneuver and, accordingly, the likelihood of secretariat influence.

This study posits that secretariats are most likely to influence outcomes when state preferences are less well developed—that is, when preferences are weakly solidified. As detailed below, the types of things that states might delegate when their positions are strongly solidified are likely quite different from the types of things they would delegate when those preferences are weakly solidified. When preferences are weak, states may care little about the outcome, and are thus more likely to delegate more substantive tasks and/or to tolerate a more proactive, autonomous secretariat than they might when their preferences are strong and they care deeply about the specifics of a particular political outcome. The level of state preference solidification can be measured by looking at how new the issue is and how states cost the possibility of unfavorable outcomes and/or preference development itself. The next section explains each of these concepts in more detail.

New issues indicate weakly solidified preferences. When issues are new, states simply may not have had the time to form strong preferences on a particular topic, creating space for nonstate actors to influence politics (Betsill and Corell 2001; Joachim and Locher 2008). In comparison to most core regime objectives, overlap management is a relatively new issue across all cases examined in this book. However, because this study examines overlap management over time whenever possible (i.e., as issues in this area move from infancy to maturity), we can also observe changes in newness over time within a single case. Accordingly, we can measure variation in preference solidification, and thus the likelihood of secretariat influence over time. This points to the importance of relational variables (i.e., substitutability and preference solidification) in understanding secretariat influence, alongside the structural ones (e.g., problem structure and rules/procedures) that have been the focus of previous investigations.

Newness alone, however, cannot explain variation in preference solidification. States often introduce new issues to the policy-making forum precisely because they have specific preferences (often developed domestically) that they wish to see institutionalized in international agreements (DeSombre 2000).[9] As such, weakly solidified preferences do not always correlate with an early stage in the policy cycle. A second variable that helps us to understand preference solidification is related to how states cost preference development.

Rational choice theory suggests that when the costs of developing preferences are high and/or when the costs of an unfavorable outcome are perceived to be low, it is more likely that preferences will be weak. The costs of preference development may be high when there is a substantial amount of research, coordination, or institutional capacity needed to fully understand an issue. In these situations, states may deem it too costly to develop their own expertise, and are instead interested in pooling resources and having the secretariat work on a specific problem or issue to lower the transaction costs of decision making (Koremenos 2008). On the other hand, states may perceive that the costs of an unfavorable outcome are low when they view an issue as unimportant. In these situations, preferences are weak simply because states care little about the outcome.

The distribution of costs can also impact the degree of solidification. For example, when the costs of an unfavorable outcome are high but evenly distributed, states will likely disagree on the value of a particular issue depending on, for example, how the issue is prioritized domestically or depending on their share of perceived or actual benefits. In these situations, preference solidification is considered moderate in this study. In contrast, if costs of an unfavorable outcome are high and distributed *un*evenly (i.e., concentrated with one or a small group of actors or bifurcated), preferences are more likely to be stronger. Preference solidification is considered strong in these situations because those states bearing the high costs are likely to demand greater control over the issue, leaving less room for a secretariat to maneuver.

Similar dynamics are at play when costs of an unfavorable outcome are low. In these situations, if costs are also evenly distributed, preference development is considered weak because there is little reason to form a preference at all. Similarly, when unfavorable outcome costs are low and either concentrated or bifurcated, preferences are likely to be moderate to weak, depending on the specific context. Again, how the issue is prioritized domestically or whether the uneven distribution is seen as equitable or fair may be important in evaluating solidification in these instances (table 3.2).

In summary, newness and the costs of unfavorable outcomes (and/or preference development) allow us to evaluate the degree of preference solidification on a particular issue. This theoretically derived approach to preference solidification helps us to predict when secretariat influence is likely, and/or to explain post facto why it was possible. How, then, do we measure perceived costs of unfavorable outcomes?

Table 3.2
Preference Solidification, Direct Measurement

Cost of Unfavorable Outcome	Distribution of Costs		
	Even	Bifurcated	Concentrated
High	Moderate	Strong	Strong
Low	Weak	Weak/moderate	Weak/moderate

Empirically measuring how states evaluate these costs is tricky. Thick description and economic analysis can be used to understand how states cost unfavorable outcomes (and/or preference formation). However, direct evaluation of costs is quite difficult, and the resources available for this study prevented a quantitative measurement for each case. Instead, this study proposes a new framework for indirectly measuring perceived costs by examining state mandates. In order to do this, we must assume that high costs of unfavorable outcomes are correlated with states' desire to keep secretariats on a short chain. Although there are likely situations where this is not the case, rational choice theory and recent studies, which identify policy externalities as rationales for delegation, suggest that this relationship is true most of the time (Hawkins et al. 2006).

We can get a sense of how states perceive costs, and thus the degree of preference solidification, by examining state mandates and instructions for action on a specific topic, including the specific mandates (i.e., instructions) they give to secretariats on this issue. We would expect that instructions based on strongly solidified preferences would be restrictive and administrative in nature, articulating specific strategies for meeting identified outcomes. These mandates might request, for example, that the secretariat organize meetings, collect and disseminate specified information, maintain a database, etc. Such mandates would leave little room for interpretation or discretion—they are designed to support prearticulated goals or, perhaps, to avoid pursuing a goal at all. In contrast, instructions based on weakly solidified preferences would likely be analytical and open-ended in nature, possibly asking the secretariat to conduct analyses or make policy proposals, or leaving room for them to make policy recommendations. These types of mandates may be aimed at helping states understand complex issues or fill low-risk policy gaps.

Analytical mandates that restrict a secretariat's analytical autonomy indicate moderately solidified preferences. These might include mandates that ask a secretariat to conduct technical analyses but restrict its ability to make analytical recommendations, and/or identify specific sources of data that should be included in the analysis. These mandates may be aimed at mediating disagreements between states with strong but divided preferences. Finally, mandates that are administrative and open-ended are not covered by this framework; in these cases, states could be strongly divided and therefore are reining in secretariat autonomy, or don't care about the issue enough to request that the secretariat carry out substantive work on it. In these situations the broader political context must be

Table 3.3
Preference Solidification, Indirect Measurement

Characteristics of Mandate	Open-Ended	Restrictive
Administrative	—	Strong
Analytical	Weak	Moderate

more carefully evaluated to understand the nature of state preferences (table 3.3).

Open-ended secretariat mandates are particularly important to secretariat politics, because such mandates provide opportunities for creative interpretation and open the door for influence. This is not to say that secretariats are always able to convert the potential energy of an open-ended mandate into the kinetic energy of influence. Rather, other variables, including substitutability and problem structure, condition a secretariat's ability to do so. For example, an open-ended mandate could be the result of disagreement between states on policy issues (i.e., due to a particularly difficult problem structure). States may provide open-ended mandates based on lowest common denominator areas of agreement. Under these conditions, however, it is unlikely that states will afford secretariats much latitude in creatively interpreting these mandates. They may also reject secretariat proposals responding to such mandates. In these situations, preferences are likely strongly solidified and secretariat influence is unlikely. As such, understanding preference solidification requires an iterative process tracing analysis in which state mandates are compared first to secretariat activities and subsequently, when possible, to state responses to those activities.

Substitutability   Whereas preference solidification helps us to understand whether secretariat influence is possible, substitutability helps us to understand why a secretariat is more likely to exert influence in comparison to another actor in the political system. Substitutability is the degree to which secretariat functions could be carried out by another actor. Secretariat functions that could easily be carried out by another actor have high substitutability, and secretariat functions that are less easily farmed out to other actors have low substitutability. This study is, of course, focused on secretariat functions related to overlap management. There are a set of functions that are central to effectively managing overlapping regimes, including wielding cross-institutional knowledge and straddling institutional networks (Alter and Meunier 2009; Jinnah 2010; Oberthür and Stokke 2011). This study posits, therefore, that the lower the substitutability of these central functions in a particular political context, the more likely a secretariat will be able to influence outcomes.

How, then, can we evaluate the substitutability of these functions in a particular case? The NGO and epistemic community literatures suggest conditions under which knowledge providers are likely to play central roles in decision making. Given the nature of the secretariat-state relationship, some of these variables are less relevant to secretariat politics. For example, Sebenius (1992) suggests that epistemic communities are more likely to play central roles when their beliefs are more cohesive and consistent. Since secretariats are essentially unitary actors, acting on behalf of an executive head, this variable is less transferable to the secretariat context. However, two other variables are transferable and worth exploring in the secretariat context: the degree of access as well as competition. Secretariats are more likely than other actors to play central roles in decision making when they have deeper access in key decision-making forums than do other actors and little competition from other actors to carry out central functions (Betsill and Correll 2008; Sebenius 1992). Each is considered in turn below.

Access   "Access" refers to both physical access and participation rights. Physical access is measured through rules and/or norms that regulate nonstate actor presence in decision-making forums. For example, Geneva is filled with organizations working on trade-environment issues just outside the WTO's front gates. However, WTO access restrictions often prohibit outside organizations from participating in critical negotiations on this topic, while the Secretariat is a standard presence at these meetings. In contrast, most environmental treaty regimes grant substantial access rights to many NGOs through participation in meetings and requests for technical support and advice.

"Participation access" refers to the *quality* of access enjoyed by nonstate actors. Participation access includes things such as the right to speak and/or make submissions within decision-making forums, as well as the establishment of any unusual venues through which nonstate actors can shape state preferences. For example, secretariats are often invited to formally address state actors on issues of common interest both within and beyond their own organizations. Although such platforms are not unheard of for other nonstate actors, these actors are more commonly given the side stage, such as through expansive side event programs at United Nations (UN) climate negotiations (Schroeder and Lovell 2012).

The deeper a secretariat's physical and/or participation access to decision-making forums relative to that of other actors, the less substitutable are the functions secretariats perform. By nature of their position in treaty regimes, secretariats always have some access rights not enjoyed by outside organizations. For example, secretariats sit at the dais alongside state actors during Conferences of the Parties (CoPs), sometimes providing counsel to key states (Depledge 2007). However, these access rights vary in terms of how they impact a secretariat's ability to carry out central overlap management functions. Access, therefore, cannot be determined by participation rules alone, but must be evaluated using in-depth analysis of both fixed and evolving mandates, as well as patterns of practice and informal requests from state actors.

This study categorizes secretariat access as deep when a secretariat has participation rights/privileges that differ substantially from those granted to other nonstate actors. This may be the case when organizational rules or norms facilitate a secretariat's physical access to key decision-making forums but restrict other actors' physical access, and/or when a secretariat is formally granted broader participation rights in these forums than other actors are permitted. For example, secretariat access is deep when other nonstate actors are not physically allowed into decision-making forums, or when their participation is restricted to listening to the proceedings without intervention rights.

Access rights are considered equal in this study when rules and norms do not substantially differentiate between secretariats and other actors. This might be the case when the secretariat has been reined in on a specific issue, or when states explicitly ask a secretariat to incorporate analysis from an outside organization when developing its own proposals or analyses. Although more rare, secretariats may also have less access than other actors in certain circumstances. This may be the case, for example, when states explicitly allocate a central function to an alternative actor.

Competition   Competition from other actors increases the substitutability of secretariat functions. This is intuitive. There are a host of reasons why states may prefer that an NGO or scientific organization perform a task rather than a secretariat. For example, the secretariat may not have the right expertise or its budget may be limited. However, the mere presence of alternative actors does not on its own increase substitutability.

In addition to having the technical and financial resources to complete a particular task, alternative actors must also be politically available to complete that task. As an example, if member states do not trust an NGO to provide a negotiation history for fear of bias, they might disable that NGO from being politically available to provide that service through a resolution or by blocking consensus on adoption of such information. In this type of case, the secretariat might well be the only politically available actor, and thus lack competition.

The cost of creating an alternative actor to carry out central functions is also important in evaluating competition. Rational choice theory suggests that competition from other actors will be low when the cost of creating a suitable alternative actor to perform these functions is high. Conversely, when the cost of creating a new actor to carry out that function is low, competition is high. In the context of global environmental governance, costs may be low because a particular function requires little specialized or technical competence.

This study, therefore, evaluates competition by looking at nonstate (including secretariats) proposals to states and state responses to those proposals. Specifically, it looks at formal proposals to state decision-making bodies (i.e., CoPs) from nonstate actors, state requests that such actors carry out central functions or be consulted when a secretariat carries out those functions, and proposals by one or more states that suggest actors other than the secretariat carry out central functions. These data can be used to evaluate the level of competition because they provide a paper trail of which actors are competing to influence decision making in specific activities and, importantly, state preferences for which actors should participate in these activities. This too is intuitive. When states formally request that outside actors carry out critical overlap management functions (i.e., through CoP decisions or evolving mandates), competition is strongest. Competition is also strong when states formally request that a secretariat consult with an outside actor in carrying out overlap management functions. When one or more states propose that outside actors carry out overlap management functions but the decision-making body does not adopt that proposal, competition is low. When no such proposals/requests exist, no competition is present (table 3.4).

To be clear, it is the secretariat *function*, not the secretariat itself, that has high, low, or moderate substitutability. Within a single secretariat, some functions may be highly substitutable while others have low substitutability. For instance, under the Convention on International Trade

Table 3.4
Substitutability of Secretariat Functions

Access	Competition		
	None	**Low**	**Strong**
Deeper	Very low	Low	Moderate
Equal	Low	Moderate	High
Less	Moderate	High	Very high

in Endangered Species (CITES), rapporteuring is an essential function that can just as easily be carried out by an NGO. Indeed, the International Institute for Sustainable Development (IISD) provides a very similar function through its *Earth Negotiations Bulletin*. However, one CITES Secretariat interviewee noted that due to concerns about bias, CITES parties require the Secretariat to produce parallel reports and at times has restricted IISD access to key decision-making forums. Therefore, competition for rapporteuring under CITES is moderate. In contrast, participant observation of several CITES meetings during the study period demonstrates that despite strong efforts to wield knowledge surrounding budgetary decisions, the CITES Secretariat is often reined in by parties who prefer to rely on domestic institutions to allocate funding. This occurred at CoP14, for example (personal observation 2007). In this case, competition is high because there is another actor readily available to carry out budgetary analyses.

The substitutability of a function can change over time as the availability of alternative actors or the costs of creating such alternatives changes. The CBD Secretariat's work in drafting decisions on overlap management had low substitutability in the early 1990s, as the issue was new and other actors lacked the cross-institutional knowledge and networks to compete with the Secretariat in designing governance structures. However, substitutability increased over time as other actors developed the necessary knowledge and networks to compete with the Secretariat in developing these rules. This variation helps to explain why secretariats can influence politics surrounding some issues but not others, and why influence can vary over time.

In summary, this study hypothesizes that secretariat influence is most likely when state preferences are weakly solidified and when secretariat functions have low substitutability. State preferences are weakly solidified when secretariat mandates are substantive and open-ended in nature,

Table 3.5
Likelihood of Influence

Substitutability	Preference Solidification		
	Strong	Moderate	Weak
High	Very unlikely	Unlikely	Likely
Moderate	Unlikely	Possible	Likely
Low	Unlikely	Likely	Very likely

and substitutability is low when secretariats have deep access to decision-making forums and low competition from alternative actors to carry out central functions (table 3.5).

Finally, when secretariat influence is indicated as "possible" in table 3.5, the likelihood of influence cannot be determined by this framework alone. In these cases, structural variables, such as costs of regulation and problem saliency, become critical to the analysis (Biermann and Siebenhüner 2009). If secretariat functions are highly substitutable and preferences are moderate, Biermann and Siebenhüner suggest that the costs of regulation will determine the likelihood of secretariat influence. If another acceptable actor can perform the task at a lower cost, a secretariat is unlikely to exert influence.

Conclusions

In building a theory of bureaucratic influence that is rooted in broader concepts of authority and power, this chapter lays a foundation for understanding the dynamics of secretariat politics. It helps us to understand how and when secretariats are likely to influence politics, and why such influence matters in global governance. Further, the framework helps us to understand how secretariat influence varies not only between organizations but also over time and across issue areas as state preferences change and issues mature.

This chapter presented a two-pronged analytical framework that allows us to (1) determine whether a secretariat influenced political outcomes; and (2) understand the conditions under which such influence is likely to occur. Specifically, the first prong asserts that secretariats influence politics when their activities shape the power relations between states, as measured by institutional, structural, and productive changes to political outcomes. These institutional, structural, and productive changes include such things as changes to institutions, relationships, and/or key norms/ideas that mediate how states interact and understand core regime issues. These changes can be attributed to secretariat activities through a combination of process tracing and counterfactual analysis. The second prong argues that substitutability and preference solidification are particularly important variables to consider in evaluating the potential for secretariat influence. The study posits that secretariats are most likely to influence political outcomes when substitutability is low and state preferences are weakly solidified. The four empirical chapters that follow apply this two-pronged analytical framework to several case studies of secretariat participation in overlap management governance in an effort to better map the topography of secretariat politics.

4

Origins of Overlap Management in the Biodiversity Regime Complex

We can always find a [CoP] decision to justify what we want to do.
—CBD Secretariat staff member, June 2006

Biodiversity loss is an intractable global environmental problem. Despite some of the oldest international regimes, widespread nongovernmental organization (NGO) activity, and a plethora of national-level institutions to address species and habitat loss, biodiversity loss continues to accelerate at an alarming rate. Current extinction rates are estimated to be 1,000 to 10,000 times faster than the background extinction rate derived from the fossil record (Singh 2002, 646), with 27,000 species lost per year in tropical forests alone (Myers 1993, 74). Scientists estimate that if current extinction rates continue, we will lose 50 percent or more of all species by the end of the twenty-first century (Myers 1993, 75). Sadly, the most recent scientific studies indicate that the rate of loss does not appear to be slowing, despite a wide array of policy initiatives aimed at abating this problem (Butchart et al. 2010). In short, we are losing biodiversity quickly, and our current political strategies are doing little to solve the problem.

The reason curbing biodiversity loss is difficult is not a lack of knowledge about drivers or available solutions. Although scientific uncertainty exists surrounding precise figures and many species disappear before scientists have even named them (Singh 2002), broad consensus exists that biodiversity loss is happening quickly and that it is largely driven by habitat loss and, increasingly, by climate change. The reason biodiversity loss is so difficult to address is because conservation is a value-laden enterprise with varied understandings of not only *why* biodiversity is important, but also what it *is* to begin with. Indeed, leading scientists diverge in opinion about what "biodiversity" actually means (Takacs 1996). More importantly, even when a definition can be agreed on for the purposes of political action, biodiversity conservation often pits the privileged conservation-oriented "green" concerns of the industrialized world against the development-oriented "brown" concerns of the developing world—a division that characterizes much of global environmental politics (Allen and You 2002). This problem is enflamed by the mismatch between the geographic reality of where biodiversity and those most concerned about its loss are physically located: most of the world's biodiversity is located in developing countries (Myers et al. 2000), while most of those with the financial capacity to prioritize it are located in developed countries. Further, those most concerned with biodiversity loss cannot seem to find a justification for conservation that sticks. Justifications include everything from aesthetic and inherent value to economic (e.g., ecosystem services) and medicinal values. Unfortunately, none of these framings have yet gained enough traction to actually solve the problem.

As a result of this complexity, global biodiversity governance has evolved in a stepwise and fragmented manner. Countries have found common ground on which to cooperate only by focusing on narrow slices of the broader biodiversity loss problem. Accordingly, there are well over 150 international treaties chipping away at the problem, with biodiversity-related treaties making up the vast majority of multilateral environmental agreements (MEAs) currently in force (data from Mitchell 2013).[1] Together, these agreements attempt to govern global biodiversity loss via a "collective of partially overlapping and nonhierarchical regimes"—what we might call the biodiversity "regime complex" (Raustiala and Victor 2004, 277). Table 4.1 lists some of the treaties that make up the biodiversity regime complex, highlighting the diversity of topics addressed and the long time span along which they have emerged.

Although fragmentation of governance is a symptom of broader ailments in global environmental politics (Biermann et al. 2009), the trend is especially problematic for global biodiversity regimes. Ecosystems are complex webs of life, with species dependent on one another and their biophysical environment for survival and propagation in ways that we are just beginning to understand. In contrast, the fragmented political context of conservation largely assumes that species and small areas of land can be protected in isolation, when in fact biologists have long asserted that a holistic ecosystem approach to conservation is necessary to success. Although some MEAs, such as the Convention on Biological Diversity (CBD), do adopt an ecosystem approach, their ability to employ it on a large scale is heavily impeded by the political complexities

Table 4.1

Sample of Biodiversity Treaties (1935–2013)

MEA	Entry into Force (year)	Biodiversity Objective
Convention for the Regulation of Whaling	1935	Evolved over time from ensuring sustainability of whaling industry to the protection of whales for conservation
Convention on International Trade in Endangered Species (CITES)	1975	Prevention of species extinction resulting from international trade
Ramsar Convention	1975	Protection of wetlands, especially for water fowl habitat
Convention Concerning the Protection of the World Cultural and Natural Heritage	1975	Protection of biological formations which are of outstanding universal value from their aesthetic or scientific point of view
Convention on Migratory Species (CMS)	1983	Conservation of migratory species and their habitat
Convention on Biological Diversity (CBD)	1993	Conservation and sustainable use of biodiversity and equitable sharing of benefits arising from such use
Cartagena Protocol on Biosafety	2003	Ensure the safe transfer, handling, and use of living modified organisms that may have adverse effects on the conservation and sustainable use of biological diversity
International Treaty on Protection of Genetic Resources for Food and Agriculture (ITPGRFA)	2004	Ensure the conservation and sustainable use of plant genetic resources for food and agriculture and the fair and equitable sharing of the benefits arising out of their use
Nagoya Protocol on Access and Benefit Sharing	2010*	Ensure the fair and equitable sharing of the benefits arising from the utilization of genetic resources, including by appropriate access to genetic resources and by appropriate transfer of relevant technologies

* Adopted

described above. In short, our fragmented political architecture does not overlay well with the holistic demands of conservation science.

In efforts to bridge this divide, actors within the biodiversity regime complex have taken on the task of fusing fragmentation between these various treaties. They have done this by identifying legal and scientific points of overlap between regimes and defining and driving the rules and practices for managing that overlap. Their work not only avoids duplication of effort in an environment of scarce resources (although this provides a popular justification for member states), but also identifies ways to use one another's tools and strategies to enhance effectiveness of their own conventions and of the biodiversity regime complex as a whole. This chapter will examine the CBD Secretariat's important role in this process.

Specifically, this chapter will show how the CBD Secretariat's efforts are critical in adapting the political architecture for global biodiversity conservation to fit with the scientific realities of what is necessary to solve the problem. Different biodiversity conventions protect different species, in different locations, for different uses. Never does one regime comprehensively protect a species (or ecosystem for that matter) through all aspects of its life history. For example, whereas the Convention on International Trade in Endangered Species (CITES) protects the saiga antelope from threat due to international trade by requiring confirmation that "take" of an individual specimen does not threaten species survival, the Convention on Migratory Species (CMS) ensures that habitat destruction does not threaten saiga survival by creating protected areas, for example.

This elegant overlap of convention norms does not always fit neatly with empirical political practice, however. More often than not, potential synergies between international regimes go unharnessed, wasting valuable time and resources as actors continually reinvent the wheel under separate treaty regimes. For example, reporting requirements tend to require states to replicate information in different formats in order to demonstrate compliance under different treaties (UNEP World Conservation Monitoring Centre 2004). Indeed, developing harmonized reporting requirements among the biodiversity MEAs has been a long-standing agenda item at the CBD (CBD Secretariat 2013b).

This chapter argues that the CBD Secretariat influenced overlap management within the biodiversity regime complex in important ways. It brokered knowledge and facilitated negotiations in ways that shaped state preferences about how overlap *should* be managed and, subsequently, *was* managed. The chapter sheds light on the Secretariat's key role in designing and building the overlap management governance architecture that was widely adopted by states within the CBD and beyond. More broadly, this chapter shows how secretariats can influence international cooperation by changing the institutional power relations between states. In this case, the Secretariat did so by shaping the rules that guided state behavior surrounding overlap management for many years with the CBD.

The chapter is organized as follows. The next section introduces the CBD. It briefly details the CBD's organizational structure, including a description of the Secretariat and how its mandate makes overlap management possible. The two subsequent sections introduce the political context of overlap management in the CBD and chronicle the emergence of overlap management under the CBD, focusing on the Secretariat's role in this process. The analysis that follows applies the two-pronged analytical framework presented in chapter 3 to explain how the Secretariat influenced overlap management in this case.

CBD: A Brief Overview

The CBD has three official objectives: biodiversity conservation; sustainable use of its components; and equitable sharing of its benefits (Convention on Biological Diversity 1992, Article 1). The Convention entered into force on December 29, 1993, and as of June 15, 2011, the CBD has near universal membership with 193 parties. The CBD's organizational structure is quite similar to that of other MEAs. It has three operational bodies: the Conference of the Parties (CoP); the Standing Body on Scientific, Technical, and Technological Advice (SBSTTA); and the Secretariat. The CoP is the governing body of the Convention, and meets regularly to direct the course of the Convention through decisions on specific issues and programs of work. It has the power to adopt protocols and budgets, establish subsidiary bodies (at the time I am writing, there are five),[2] and further define both its own functions as well as those of the SBSTTA, Secretariat, and subsidiary bodies as it sees fit (CBD 1992, Article 23). It typically meets on an annual or biannual basis for two weeks at a time.

The SBSTTA is the scientific arm of the Convention. The CoP determines the length and frequency of its meetings, which are intended to provide the CoP and its subsidiary bodies with scientific, technical, and technological advice relevant to implementation of the Convention.[3] The

SBSTTA submits recommendations to the CoP, which the CoP can then adopt, revise, or reject.

The CBD Secretariat is, of course, the administrative arm of the Convention. Hosted by the United Nations Environment Program (UNEP), it is located in Montreal and is broadly responsible for coordinating meetings for the CoP, SBSTTA, and working groups as well as for coordinating with other international organizations. As of July 2011, the CBD Secretariat is organized into five major divisions: (1) Social, Economic, and Legal Matters; (2) Scientific, Technical, and Technological Matters; (3) Biosafety; (4) Implementation and Technical Support; and (5) Resource Management and Conference Services. One staff member heads each program area within the Secretariat, and "each programme establishes a vision for, and basic principles to guide future work. They also set out key issues for consideration, identify potential outputs, and suggest a timetable and means for achieving these."[4] The Secretariat also works on 19 issues that cut across its work programs, including biodiversity and climate change, traditional knowledge, alien invasive species, and trade.

As of July 2010, the Secretariat had approximately 102 staff members, consisting of 50 professional staff, 51 administrative staff members, and the executive secretary.[5] In addition, CBD staff interviewed for this study noted that the Secretariat hires a varying number of consultants who typically work on six- to 18-month contracts. Most CBD Secretariat staff members hold advanced degrees and have extensive experience in international politics. Of those interviewed for this study, 14 staff (approximately 25 percent of total professional staff) held postgraduate degrees in fields such as law, biology, plant physiology, biotechnology, and geography. Of this group, four (28 percent) held PhDs, four (28 percent) held a master's degree, and five (36 percent) held law degrees. Many CBD staff members also have practical experience in international politics. Four of the 14 staff (28 percent) had worked on their government delegation to an international environmental agreement or in a domestic environmental agency prior to joining the Secretariat, two of whom indicated that prior to joining the CBD Secretariat, they had served on their home country's delegation for negotiating the CBD or its Cartagena Protocol. Another six (43 percent) had worked for other United Nations (UN) organizations prior to coming to the CBD Secretariat, including one interviewee who had worked in the UN system for at least 13 years.

The CBD Secretariat's mandate is surprisingly short. It is silent on structure and norms of behavior. However, it stands to reason that because the CBD Secretariat sits within the UN system and is hosted by

UNEP, these details of structure and norms were implicit. State expectations regarding elements such as hierarchy, international character, and competence were established elsewhere, such as the UN Declaration establishing UNEP, and did not need to be stated again in the Convention text. Rather, the Secretariat's mandate articulates a simple relationship with the CoP: the Secretariat is to do what the CoP asks of it and report back to the CoP on its progress. States' desire for bureaucratic control is clearly embedded in this mandate.

The CBD Secretariat's mandate on managing overlap, however, is new, explicit, and far-reaching. The mandate not only allows, but instructs, the Secretariat to "coordinate with other relevant international bodies and, in particular to enter into such administrative and contractual arrangements as may be required for the effective discharge of its functions" (CBD 1992, Article 24(d)). Although the latter clause has resulted in the negotiation of some empty agreements, this mandate also opened the door for the Secretariat to develop and drive this new area of global governance.

The Secretariat's leadership role in overlap management is further developed through Article 23 paragraph 4(h) of the Convention and Goal 1 of the CBD's Strategic Plan, adopted by CoP6 in 2002. Article 23 instructs the parties to "contact, through the Secretariat, the executive bodies of the conventions dealing with matters covered by the Convention, with a view to establishing appropriate forms of cooperation with them." Goal 1 calls for the CBD to fulfill its "leadership role in international biodiversity issues" by "promoting cooperation between all relevant international instruments and processes to enhance policy coherence." Although the Secretariat is not explicitly mentioned in the latter, the Secretariat's fixed mandate (CBD 1992, Article 24) and Article 23 above clearly identify it as the leadership figure in carrying out overlap management functions such as these.

Early Political Context of Overlap Management in the CBD

The CBD is essentially, albeit unofficially, a framework convention, in that its norms and goals encompass those of all other international biodiversity agreements. Indeed, the CBD was originally conceived as an overlap management convention. During the negotiations of the CBD in the early 1990s, the United States (a non-party) tried to frame the CBD as a "coherence building" treaty, designed to coordinate preexisting international biodiversity agreements such as CITES, CMS, and the World

Heritage Convention (WHC) (McGraw 2002a, 2002b). As such, overlap management was envisioned to be part of the CBD's raison d'être from the very beginning.

Despite being central to the original US proposal for the CBD, this overlap management role faded into the background as preparatory negotiations for the CBD evolved in the early 1990s. Feeling "colonized" by the demands of developed countries in the parallel climate treaty negotiations, developing countries fought particularly hard to secure their core interests under the CBD (McGraw 2002a, 2002b). Central to these demands was that biotechnology issues be included under the CBD (Chatterjee and Finger 1994; McConnell 1996). Against the backdrop of bioprospecting from the pharmaceutical and biotechnology industries based in the developed world, developing countries fought to secure sovereign rights to genetic resources within their territories, as well as for a system of sharing benefits that derive from the use of those resources (McGraw 2002a, 2002b). Their ability to secure these demands in the face of opposition from developed countries can in part be explained by their possession of the majority of the world's biodiversity. As one senior CBD negotiator described the developing countries' negotiating position at the time, "we've got most of it: you want it; you'll have to pay for it" (McConnell 1996, 76).

This dynamic shifted the inertia of CBD politics from one focused on conservation as envisioned by the Unted States to one focused on the intersection between conservation, sustainable use, and benefit sharing as demanded by the developing world. Indeed, the United States became increasingly marginalized from CBD preparatory negotiations due to its strong resistance, along with Japan, to the inclusion of biotechnology in the CBD (McConnell 1996). However, having lost that battle as a precondition for the engagement of developing countries, early CBD negotiations focused on how (not *if*) biosafety should be operationalized in practice, alongside technical financial issues, such as whether or not contributions should be mandatory (McConnell 1996).

This change in political focus helps to explain why the United States—a strong proponent in early negotiations—ultimately refused to ratify the CBD. Further, it demonstrates why overlap management, which was largely conceived as a way for the CBD to coordinate conservation politics across organizations, fell into the background of political discussions in the CBD's early years. This is evidenced in the exclusion of overlap management from the list of core issues identified by CBD states for priority action in 1992, which focused instead on financial issues and biosafety (McConnell 1996). The fading of overlap management in CBD negotiations is further evidenced in the focus of CBD protocol negotiations. Formal negotiations on the Biosafety Protocol were launched at CoP2 in 1995, and the Nagoya Protocol on Access and Benefit Sharing was more recently adopted in 2010. The CBD still lacks, however, a protocol on its first objective: conservation.

In its early years, overlap management was thus present but not central to CBD negotiations. It was enshrined in the treaty and therefore a subject of ongoing CoP discussions, yet many developing countries—supported by the EU—were pushing the CBD away from a conservation discussion toward one focused on sustainable use and benefit sharing (McConnell 1996). In this way, overlap management too was pushed to the margins of CBD discussions in the early 1990s.

Nevertheless, overlap management was included in the treaty text and is therefore regularly reflected on the agenda at CBD CoPs (CBD 1992, Article 24(d)). Importantly, overlap management objectives are articulated in the CBD's 2002 Strategic Plan, which identifies concrete goals for action under the Convention. The first of these goals is to assure that the CBD is "fulfilling its leadership role in international biodiversity issues" by "setting the global biodiversity agenda" and "promoting cooperation between all relevant international instruments and processes to enhance policy coherence" (CBD CoP6 2002c, Sec. C.1). Therefore, although underlying politics drove the CoP's attention away from overlap management in the early years of CBD negotiations, it remained a constant on the CoP agenda, typically in the form of mandates to the Secretariat to enhance the overlap management process (e.g., CBD CoP1 1994b).

In recent years, overlap management has become more politically charged, with divisive issues such as linkages between biodiversity and climate change, geoengineering, and biofuels entering CBD discussions (IISD 2010b). This chapter focuses its attention on early overlap management, but the subsequent chapter explains and explores overlap management debates within the CBD in this more contemporary politicized context.

The CBD Secretariat: Designing the Architecture of Overlap Governance

The CBD treaty text (1992) provides the original mandate for overlap management, and identifies the Secretariat as a key participant in fulfilling this mandate. Specifically, Article 23 paragraph 4(h) mandates the

CoP to "contact, through the Secretariat, the executive bodies of Conventions dealing with matters covered by this Convention with a view to establishing appropriate forms of cooperation with them." Similarly, Article 24.1(d) mandates the Secretariat to "coordinate with other relevant bodies, and in particular to enter into such administrative and contractual arrangements as may be required for the effective discharge of its functions." While these mandates identify cooperative activities as an important goal of the Convention, they provide little direction as to *how* these cooperative activities, or overlap management, should be pursued.

The analysis that follows argues that this vague delegated discretion from the CoP allowed the CBD Secretariat to take on a highly entrepreneurial role, positioning it to assume key functions in defining the architecture of overlap management. In short, it demonstrates how the Secretariat designed the core rules and norms for overlap management within the CBD. Specifically, the Secretariat produced a key document on overlap management for CoP2 in 1995 that defined, and continues to shape, overlap management architecture within the biodiversity regime complex (CBD Secretariat 1995). Prior to the Secretariat's action in this area, overlap management was all but absent in this realm of international biodiversity politics; thereafter, the CBD Secretariat's thumbprint became visible on overlap management activities not just within the CBD but across the entire biodiversity regime complex.

Evolution of Overlap Management

This section traces the emergence of overlap management within the CBD beginning at CoP1 in 1994 and ending at CoP10 in 2010. Historically, there are two overlap management–related agenda items on the CoP and SBSTTA dockets: cooperation with other international organizations, and scientific and technical cooperation. The scope of this analysis is limited to the former, although the latter is another important area of overlap management (e.g., in the development of the CBD-Ramsar Joint Work Program). In order to trace how overlap management evolved within the CBD, this case examines the cooperation decisions taken under the "cooperation with other international organizations" agenda item at each of the CBD's 10 CoPs to date. It traces these decisions back through pre-session information (referred to as "INF" documents) and official documents, as well as any relevant SBSTTA recommendations on which they are based.[6] All documents analyzed for this study are available on the CBD Secretariat's website.[7]

CoP1: Constructing Secretariat Autonomy

The CBD CoP identified "Cooperation with other Organizations" (i.e., overlap management) as a standing agenda item at its first meeting in November 1994, and has since addressed and adopted decisions on the issue at each subsequent CoP (CBD Secretariat 2013d). As evidenced in their first official decision on the matter, CBD parties did not have a clear vision for the future of cooperation activities in the early 1990s (CBD CoP1 1994b). Aside from inviting other organizations to make cooperation proposals to the Secretariat, this decision merely restates the treaty text (quoted above), giving the Secretariat the broad mandate to enter into contractual arrangements and coordinate with other international bodies. Of note, however, is another decision taken by CoP1, which explicitly states the need for Secretariat autonomy in carrying out these functions (CBD CoP1 1994a). As such, while overlap management did not prove central at this meeting, CoP1 set the stage for the Secretariat to emerge as a leader in overlap management by establishing cooperation with other biodiversity conventions as a standing agenda item (CBD CoP1 1994c, paragraph 2.6), and by giving the Secretariat much autonomous control over this governance process (CBD CoP1 1994a).

CoP2: The Blueprint

In November 1995 at CoP2, the Secretariat very tactfully and strategically defined the architectural framework that continues to support overlap management politics today. Although *not* explicitly requested to do so by the parties, the Secretariat submitted a critical document to CoP2, which outlined the architecture for overlap management that structures governance in this area today (CBD Secretariat 1995). Specifically, this document "considers why cooperation is needed, how the Convention on Biological Diversity could cooperate with related Conventions, what might be appropriate forms that such cooperation could take, and what the CBD might expect to gain from cooperation with related Conventions" (paragraph 2). As this content analysis will show, the CBD CoP has taken very few, if any, cooperation (i.e., overlap management) decisions that were not originally suggested by the Secretariat in this 1995 document. This document effectively served as a *blueprint* for all future overlap management decisions under the CBD.

The two most important contributions from the Secretariat's "blueprint" are its identification of seven[8] areas where cooperation might be pursued and four specific "recommendations for action." On the seven areas of cooperation, the Secretariat suggests:

- coordinated implementation across Conventions (i.e., development of mutually reinforcing policies aimed at conservation);
- coordination between institutional bodies (i.e., CoPs, scientific bodies, etc.);
- coordination of CoP agendas (i.e., making "Cooperation with other Conventions" a regular agenda item);
- harmonization of national reporting between biodiversity conventions (i.e., rather than stretching capacity through multiple overlapping reporting requirements);
- partnerships between secretariats;
- development of joint work programs;
- the supportive role of the UNEP (i.e., as a coordinating entity).

As this section will show, all of these ideas subsequently became fodder for CoP discussion and action on overlap management.

Of the four "recommendations for action," three—advocating for harmonized reporting, a joint working group between the biodiversity conventions, and, critically, Secretariat leadership in these activities—were included in the CoP's final decision (CBD CoP2 1995). Although the fourth recommendation (suggesting that other biodiversity conventions include "cooperation between conventions") was not included in the CoP decision, this recommendation has nonetheless emerged as a point of discussion across the core biodiversity conventions—within and beyond the CBD. This suggests that the Secretariat capitalized on its cooperation mandate (quoted above) to catalyze the CoP's decision to address this fourth recommendation in other biodiversity forums.

Importantly, the blueprint moves well beyond the Secretariat's actual mandate on overlap management from CoP1. Whereas CoP1 merely mandated the Secretariat to make contact with other biodiversity secretariats, the Secretariat was now charged with (1) identifying practical reasons to cooperate and examining how parties might benefit from cooperation, (2) presenting the "salient elements" of other biodiversity conventions, (3) discussing the forms cooperative arrangements might take, and (4) suggesting which cooperation-related options the CoP should adopt. As such, through its creative interpretation of its open-ended CoP1 mandate, the Secretariat positioned itself as the de facto leader in overlap management by defining the initial rules and norms for governance in this area. This is further reflected in the open-ended mandate that CoP2 gave the Secretariat, which instructed it to, inter alia,

report to CoP3 on modalities for future cooperation with relevant biodiversity conventions (CBD CoP2 1995).

CoP3: Institutionalizing Secretariat Authority
In the interim between CoP2 (1995) and CoP3 (1996), the Secretariat
not only finalized memoranda of cooperation (MoCs) with three other
conventions (Ramsar, CITES, and CMS)—a notable achievement in a
one-year period[9]—but also coproduced with the Ramsar Convention
Secretariat a document outlining specific modalities for cooperation
between the two conventions. All of these documents draw substantially
from the Secretariat's recommendations to CoP2 as contained in the
blueprint.

In accordance with its CoP2 mandate to identify future cooperation
modalities, the Secretariat produced two key documents for CoP3 (CBD
Secretariat 1996a, 1996b). The first summarized cooperative activities
undertaken by the Secretariat to date and, importantly, reemphasized the
Secretariat's proposed architecture for overlap management as contained
in the blueprint. The second document further developed the Secretariat's
normative justification for overlap management, reviewed existing
overlap management strategies outside the biodiversity regime complex,
and made specific suggestions for which of those should be pursued
under the CBD (CBD Secretariat 1996b). Importantly, the Secretariat's
proposals marketed the Secretariat as a central actor in these governance
processes through, for example, emphasizing its potential role in harmo-
nizing work programs and attending CoPs of overlapping biodiversity
conventions.

CoP4 and CoP5: Executing the Blueprint
Cooperation between the biodiversity conventions took a technical
turn at CoP4 (1998) and CoP5 (2000). The Secretariat's overlap
management–relevant submissions to these meetings were far less normatively constitutive than their earlier submissions: they aimed at facilitating implementation of cooperative initiatives proposed in the blueprint.
The Secretariat set forth ways to formally institutionalize its suggestion
for coordinated implementation, in particular as it relates to in situ conservation (e.g., protected areas and restoration), and with respect to
developing a joint work program with CMS as suggested in the blueprint's recommendations for action.

Importantly, at CoP4, the Secretariat's efforts to market itself as the
CBD's central overlap manager began to pay off, with CoP4 formally

designating overlap management as a "key" component of the Secretariat's work. Specifically, the CoP asked the Secretariat to "consider matters of liaison, cooperation and collaboration as a *key* responsibility" [emphasis added] (CBD CoP4 1998a).

CoP6 and CoP7: Mainstreaming the Blueprint

Overlap management activities at CoP6 (2002) and CoP7 (2004) reflected pivotal progress in institutionalizing the Secretariat's overlap management agenda. In addition to steady progress on blueprint implementation through, for example, the further development of joint work programs and MoCs,[10] CoP6 and CoP7 institutionalized and expanded (i.e., mainstreamed) the blueprint's reach. CoP6 welcomed the Joint Liaison Group (CBD CoP6 2002a) between the Rio Conventions (CBD, United Nations Framework Convention on Climate Change [UNFCCC], and United Nations Convention to Combat Desertification);[11] and, more importantly, following verbatim the blueprint's second recommendation for action, CoP7 requested that the Secretariat establish the Biodiversity Liaison Group among the biodiversity conventions (CBD CoP7 2004b).

Both the Joint Liaison and Biodiversity Liaison Groups continue to provide an institutionalized mechanism through which the executive heads of the biodiversity Secretariats meet to discuss overlap management activities between them. These groups remain important institutional structures that have provided a mechanism for the CBD Secretariat to diffuse its overlap management agenda both within and beyond its own member states. The establishment of these groups highlights an unexpected dynamic in secretariat activities: secretariats defining mandates to guide their own activities.

Finally, decisions taken at CoP6 and CoP7 reflect another important milestone in expanding the Secretariat's participation in overlap management. Overlap management architectures identified in the blueprint began to percolate beyond decisions on "cooperation with other organizations," and were mainstreamed into the core work of the Convention. For example, CoP6 incorporated blueprint suggestions, such as coordinated implementation across Conventions, in its decisions on forest biological diversity (CBD CoP6 2002b), among others.

CoP8: Beyond the Blueprint

By CoP8 (2006), tools identified in the blueprint had become common practice across the biodiversity regime complex. The use of joint work programs, lead implementation partners, and MoCs provided the core foundation of overlap management governance architecture within the CBD and beyond. Yet little attention had been paid to the effectiveness of these governance approaches. In the lead-up to CoP8, at the first meeting of the Ad Hoc Open-ended Working Group on Review of Implementation (WGRI-1) (CBD Secretariat 2005b), the Secretariat began to evaluate the status of overlap management efforts and make specific suggestions for improvement based on this analysis. For example, the Secretariat strongly advocated for three ideas that would dominate overlap management discourse for the next five-plus years: enhanced national-level cooperation, a global partnership on biodiversity, and enhanced cooperation with the climate change regime (CBD Secretariat 2005a).

At CoP8, following the Ad Hoc Working Group meeting, the Secretariat stressed the need for a more "systematic approach," proposing that, inter alia, it should inventory existing partners,[12] assess the current state of cooperation, and identify and prioritize overlap management activities that should be pursued into the future (CBD Secretariat 2006b). In outlining a prioritization framework, the Secretariat's third proposal marks the Secretariat's reentry into the realm of constitutive overlap management governance (CBD Secretariat 2006b, paragraph 58).

At the heart of the Secretariat's proposal was a strong push for a new institutional framework to guide overlap management called the "global partnership on biodiversity." Although the partnership idea was previously introduced at CoP7 by the EU, very few details were given at that time (IISD 2004). The Secretariat fleshed out this proposal in two documents that it produced for the first meeting of the WGRI (CBD Secretariat 2005a, Add. 1–3; CBD Secretariat 2005b).[13] Many of these ideas made their way to CoP8 via a resulting WGRI1 recommendation reflecting the Secretariat's suggestions. The Secretariat ran with the partnership idea, detailing its possible rationale, tools, and trajectory. The partnership was the centerpiece of the Secretariat's proposal for a renovated overlap management architecture that would build on existing partnerships and tools created by its original blueprint. The primary difference between this second constitutive phase of overlap governance and the one that preceded it in the mid 1990s was that while the first phase was focused on creating institutional structures to facilitate cooperation, the second phase was focused on adjusting those structures to enhance conservation outcomes.

Despite the Secretariat's efforts in developing the partnership idea, member states disagreed on the need for such an institution and were concerned about costs (IISD 2004). As such, the idea did not make it into

CoP8's decision on overlap management. Nonetheless, the Secretariat's suggestion for an evaluation and corresponding enrichment of the overlap management process *was* reflected in the CoP decision. The Secretariat's proposal called for, among other things, the integration of biodiversity concerns across sectors and their coordination among national actors (CBD CoP8 2006a). Although the Secretariat's draft decision on the matter attributes some of these ideas to WGRI1 (CBD CoP8 2006b), tracing these ideas back through input documents to WGRI-1 reveals that the analytical and constitutive nature of these recommendations in fact derive from the Secretariat's recommendations produced for that meeting (CBD Secretariat 2005a, Add. 2). This is notable in that it brings our attention to an important mechanism by which the Secretariat constructed its veil of legitimacy; the Secretariat channeled its ideas through a smaller subsidiary body and subsequently allowed that subsidiary body to take credit for the original ideas when presenting them to the CoP.

CoP9 and CoP10: Beyond Biodiversity

With institutional structures to support overlap management between the biodiversity conventions firmly in place, and concrete recommendations for improving these structures under discussion, CoP9 (2008) and CoP10 (2010) focused on extending overlap management beyond the biodiversity regime complex. For example, parties encouraged further development of existing collaborative relationships such as the Biodiversity Liaison Group (CBD CoP9 2008b), and updating existing joint work plans (CBD CoP10 2010a). However, CBD parties' interest in overlap between biodiversity and other issues began to take center stage at this time.

CBD parties focused their attention on overlap between climate change and biodiversity, and especially on issues such as biofuels, geoengineering, and reducing emissions from deforestation and forest degradation (REDD) (IISD 2010b). The CBD Secretariat played a role in the emergence of these topics of discussion; however, as will be shown in chapter 5, it did so in a way that framed debates rather than initiated them. Indeed, CBD parties had long been interested in this relationship, and CoP10 in particular saw lengthy and heated discussions among parties on these issues, leaving less room for Secretariat participation (IISD 2010b).

Understanding Secretariat Influence

This section evaluates whether the Secretariat's overlap management activities identified above had any impact on power relations between states. It argues that the CBD Secretariat exerted strong influence on overlap management within the CBD in the mid to late 1990s. By defining the institutional architectures that moderated state interactions on this issue, the Secretariat shaped power relations between them. This section further argues that the Secretariat was able to exert this influence at the time because state preferences surrounding the particulars of overlap management were weakly solidified, and because the Secretariat's overlap management functions had low substitutability.

Did the Secretariat Exert Influence?
In order to ascertain whether the Secretariat influenced overlap management, we must undertake a three-step analysis. First, we must evaluate whether Secretariat participation in overlap management reflects any mechanisms of influence (i.e., knowledge brokering, capacity building, marketing, negotiation/litigation facilitation). The presence of these mechanisms is necessary but not sufficient to attribute influence. Second, if any mechanisms of influence are identified, then we must determine through process tracing whether such activities shaped power relations between states. Finally, we must confirm that these changes can be attributed to Secretariat activities through a counterfactual analysis. For a graphic representation of this process, see figure 3.1.

Mechanisms of Influence?   The CBD Secretariat participated in overlap management via knowledge brokering, facilitating negotiations, and to a lesser extent, marketing. That these three mechanisms of influence are present in this case suggests that Secretariat influence on member state interests is possible. This section briefly recounts how the Secretariat brokered knowledge, facilitated negotiations, and marketed its ideas.

On the first two mechanisms, the Secretariat utilized its expertise in conservation science and its networks with other biodiversity organizations to broker knowledge on how the global biodiversity treaties overlap with one another and, accordingly, to facilitate negotiations by developing proposals on how this overlap should be managed. This is evidenced not only in the blueprint, but in several other Secretariat submissions to the CoP. These submissions reflect the Secretariat's deep knowledge of overlapping conventions by delineating specific modalities and strategies for overlap management across the biodiversity regime complex (e.g., CBD Secretariat 1995, 1996a, 2002). Importantly, the Secretariat also facilitated negotiations by regularly making proposals for its own mandate. As explained above, the parties adopted many of these proposals, including proposals that the Secretariat take the lead on overlap management activities by defining ways to move forward (e.g., CBD CoP2 1995).

On the third mechanism, marketing, the CBD Secretariat also went to great lengths to position itself as the central actor on issues related to overlap management. It repeatedly framed overlap management solutions in ways that placed itself as a leader in overseeing the issue. For example, the blueprint proposed joint work programs between the biodiversity conventions, directed collaboration between secretariats, and harmonized national reporting to the CBD Secretariat (CBD Secretariat 1995). The Secretariat's suggestion and the CoP's subsequent creation of the Biodiversity Liaison Group as a forum for intersecretariat discussions on overlap management are a key example of the Secretariat's successful marketing efforts in this regard.

In summary, the Secretariat exhibited several mechanisms of influence in its work on overlap management issues within the CBD, suggesting that influence is possible. The subsequent section evaluates whether the Secretariat did indeed influence overlap management, by tracing these mechanisms of influence to any observable changes in power relations between states.

Change in Power Relations?   This section argues that the CBD Secretariat activities detailed in the preceding section did yield impacts that shaped key rules and norms that guide state behavior surrounding overlap management, and that such impacts reflect changes in productive power relations between states. The CBD Secretariat broadly interpreted its open-ended coordination mandate in a manner that allowed it to develop specific overlap management proposals, many of which were adopted verbatim by the CoP (e.g., CBD CoP7 2004b). More importantly, the Secretariat's blueprint shaped the CoP's subsequent decisions on overlap management in unambiguous ways. Most notably, the majority of the Secretariat's proposed "recommendations for action" in the 1994 blueprint were formally adopted by the CoP, and continue to be standard practice within the CBD today (CBD Secretariat 2013a). As explained in chapter 3, because these Secretariat activities shaped the formal and informal institutions (e.g., rules, procedures, norms) that mediate relationships between state actors, these impacts reflect changes in institutional power relations between states.

One important example of the Secretariat's impact on overlap management was CoP3's decision in 1996 to formally adopt the Secretariat's suggestion that the Ramsar Convention be a legally designated "lead implementation partner" for issues related to wetlands.[14] Lead implementation partners, a new idea at the time, remain a central tool to legalize and legitimize cooperative arrangements between the biodiversity conventions today.[15] Indeed, aside from harmonization of reporting, which has not yet materialized despite significant interest,[16] all of the policy proposals contained in the blueprint have been adopted and institutionalized by CBD parties through decisions on cooperation. Further, following the Secretariat's suggestion, CoP4 formally recognized overlap management as a "key" component of the Secretariat's overall responsibilities (CBD CoP4 1998a).

Another important example of the Secretariat's impact on overlap management was CoP7's nearly verbatim adoption of the Secretariat's proposal for the creation of the Biodiversity Liaison Group (CBD CoP7 2004b). The Group's creation signaled the increased importance of overlap management across the biodiversity regime complex by placing overlap management on the limited docket of the executive leadership of each of the biodiversity conventions. The proposal's smooth adoption by all relevant conventions further reflects the importance of the Secretariat's networks in developing a proposal that was palatable across all involved organizations (e.g., CBD CoP8 2006a; CBD CoP9 2008b; CBD CoP10 2010a; CITES Secretariat 2007f, 2007g; and CMS CoP8 2005; CMS CoP9 2008).

These impacts shaped institutional power relations between states by defining the institutions (i.e., the rules, procedures, and norms) that guide overlap management under the CBD. Indeed, the blueprint outlined the specific institutions that structure how states interact on overlap management issues by creating the rules to govern these interactions. Further, the Secretariat enhanced its own capacity for future influence by proposing overlap management institutions that further entrenched practices that rely on secretariat authority. For example, because the CBD does not have an implementation mandate per se, the creation of "lead implementation partners" (as suggested by the Secretariat) relies heavily on the Secretariat's expertise and its networks with other biodiversity MEAs. In using its open-ended mandates to make suggestions for the future of overlap management, the CBD Secretariat mobilized "agent strategies" (Hawkins and Jacoby 2006) that shaped overlap management options and architectures. Importantly, it did so in ways that expanded its own zone of discretion by asserting its ability to *lead* this political process (e.g., CBD CoP7 2004b).

Alternative Explanations?   In many cases, the language adopted in CoP decisions on overlap management can be traced verbatim back to the Secretariat. As such, it is highly unlikely that these impacts can be attributed to another actor. The chain of causality in this case is crystal clear: CBD Secretariat recommendations were taken up by the CoP and incorporated directly into formal decisions on the matter. Had states wanted (or been able) to direct this process, they would have submitted proposals on the topic themselves, as they do most of the time on other issues. Such proposals on overlap management were absent in the mid to late 1990s. As such, the CBD Secretariat's participation in overlap management yielded changes in institutional power relations between states, which were unlikely to have been the result of another actor's activities on the issue. As explained above and in chapter 3, these changes reflect *strong* Secretariat influence because such Secretariat activities resulted in changes in core institutional rules and norms that guide state behavior.

Why Was the Secretariat Able to Exert Influence?

Chapter 3 presents a framework for predicting when secretariats are most likely to influence overlap management. Specifically, the framework suggests that preference solidification and substitutability help us to understand the factors that enable or constrain a secretariat's ability to influence political outcomes, including those related to overlap management. The framework posits that a secretariat is most likely to exert influence when its functions have low substitutability and when state preferences are weakly solidified.

Preference Solidification   Newness and state mandates (as a proxy for costs) can help us to understand the degree to which state preferences on a given issue are solidified. As detailed in chapter 3, when issues are new, state preferences are likely to be less solidified. Further, state mandates that are administrative and restrictive reflect strongly solidified preferences, whereas those that are open-ended and analytical reflect weakly solidified preferences, and analytical yet restrictive mandates reflect moderately solidified preferences (see table 3.3). The more strongly solidified state preferences are, the less likely a secretariat will be able to influence overlap management (see table 3.5).

The role of newness can be determined by examining political documents from biodiversity treaties that predate the CBD (e.g., CITES and CMS). These reveal a dearth of overlap management—it does not show up anywhere on meeting agendas or reports, thus suggesting that overlap management was largely absent from global biodiversity politics prior to the CBD's entry into force. Further, coordination between domestic ministries dealing with the international conventions was poor in many countries at the time (interview with Secretariat staff, 2005; United States of America 2004). When the CBD was in its infancy, therefore, member states were largely inexperienced in *coordinated* international (conservation) politics. Although they had been working for many years on more discrete slices of the conservation pie, through agreements such as CITES and CMS, the CBD framework called for a more holistic approach to conservation that required coordination between the various biodiversity regimes (McGraw 2002a, 2002b). Overlap management was thus a new issue in the early 1990s, suggesting weakly solidified state preferences.

CBD CoP decisions on overlap management also suggest that state preferences were weakly solidified during the study period because mandates were largely analytical and open-ended. The first CBD CoP decision on overlap management was very clearly analytical and open-ended, asking the Secretariat to identify areas for cooperation with other biodiversity conventions and report back to the CoP at its next meeting (CBD CoP1 1994b). In response to this open-ended analytical mandate, the Secretariat produced a comprehensive analysis of existing overlap between the biodiversity conventions, and policy proposals for managing overlap between them (i.e., the blueprint). CoP mandates continued in this vein—asking the Secretariat to identify modalities and strategies—for over a decade. As explained in chapter 3, this open-ended analytical mandate (and the Secretariat's response to it) suggests that states' perceived costs were low and thus their preferences were weakly solidified during this period (see table 3.3).

CoP mandates suggest that state preferences solidified over time, however. We see this solidification as states began to reassert control of the institutional dimensions of overlap management by limiting the scope of Secretariat mandates. For example, at CoP10, the Secretariat's mandate was limited to "convey[ing] a proposal to develop joint activities" and "hold[ing] a retreat of the biodiversity-related conventions ... to consider the Strategic Plan for Biodiversity 2011–2020" (CoPX/20). These restrictive and largely administrative mandates are a far cry from the open-ended analytical mandates that states gave the Secretariat in the mid to late 1990s. This shift in the tenor of state mandates to the Secretariat suggests that state preferences solidified over time, and helps to explain why the Secretariat has been less able to influence overlap management in more recent years.

Substitutability   Whereas preference solidification helps to explain the conditions under which outside actors are likely to influence policy making, substitutability helps to explain when that outside actor is likely to be a secretariat. If a secretariat's overlap management functions could have been carried out just as easily by another available actor, those functions are highly substitutable, and secretariat influence is less likely. As detailed in chapter 3, the substitutability of secretariat functions can be evaluated through an examination of secretariats' access to key decision-making forums relative to the access of other actors, and the level of competition from such actors to perform that function. These factors can be evaluated through a qualitative examination of relevant CoP mandates and rules of access to decision-making forums. Secretariat substitutability is lowest when access relative to that of other actors is deep and competition is absent. As relative access decreases and competition increases, substitutability increases (see table 3.4), and accordingly, the likelihood of secretariat influence decreases (see table 3.5).

As for competition, the CBD is a relatively open forum. Nonstate actors regularly attend and participate in CBD formal meetings and side events, alongside the Secretariat. Although the CBD Secretariat likely has more direct access to many state actors at and between meetings, this alone does not represent a major substantive difference in access. The Convention text, however, explicitly extends the Secretariat's access rights beyond those enjoyed by other actors and effectively curtails competition from outside actors. Because the Convention mandates the Secretariat to manage overlap with other international organizations (Article 24(d)), states regularly request that the Secretariat engage in CBD politics on this issue. Outside actors are given no such participation rights in the Convention, and accordingly are rarely, if ever, granted the deep access to CBD decision making enjoyed by the Secretariat on these issues.

It is particularly notable that the CBD Secretariat has used these access rights to construct overlap management in a way that further deepens its access to governance processes. In the blueprint, for example, the Secretariat framed overlap management in a way that could realistically be operationalized only by the CBD Secretariat itself. It identified activities, such as joint work between the biodiversity conventions and coordination of agendas, that reflected its own domain of authority as measured through social networks and expertise across biodiversity conventions. Similarly, the Secretariat framed overlap management as a long-term progressive endeavor. This approach has the convenient implication of positioning the CBD Secretariat (i.e., as permanent, full-time, career professional experts) as the only actor who could oversee this task on a day-to-day basis. For example, the proposed approach relies on a steady communicative relationship between organizations over time—a task state actors are much less able to fill due to the diffuse nature of these tasks, states' lack of relevant networks, and staff permanence issues (see chapter 2). In framing overlap management in this way, the Secretariat made it less likely that outside actors could perform overlap management functions, effectively decreasing the substitutability of its functions.

As reflected in participation rules and the highly specialized tasks the Secretariat has outlined for overlap management, the Secretariat enjoys deeper access than outside actors and low competition from outside actors. As explained in chapter 3, under these conditions, the framework categorizes the Secretariat's overlap management functions as having low substitutability.

In summary, the CBD Secretariat's influence can in part be explained by the degree of state preference solidification and the substitutability of its overlap management functions. State preferences were initially weakly solidified, as evidenced in their analytical and open-ended mandates to the Secretariat. Secretariat influence can be further explained by the low substitutability of its overlap management functions. With overlap management enumerated as a Secretariat task in the Convention text itself, outside actors had a difficult time competing with the Secretariat to perform this management function due to the nature of state mandates to the Secretariat on this issue and the participation rules of the Convention.

The central finding in this case (i.e., strong secretariat influence) supports the hypothesis outlined in chapter 3: when state preferences are weakly solidified and secretariat functions enjoy low substitutability, secretariat influence is very likely (table 4.2).

Further, as state preferences solidified over time, the CoP's rejection of Secretariat proposals related to such things as the global partnership

Table 4.2
Summary of Findings—CBD Biodiversity Overlap Management

Cases	Preference Solidification	Substitutability	Predicted Influence	Observed Influence
CBD Secretariat	Weak	Low	Very likely	Strong

on biodiversity suggests that Secretariat influence waned, a finding that is also supported by the framework.

Conclusions: Secretariat Influence on Governance Architectures

The CBD Secretariat shaped institutional power relations in this case by shaping the design and construction of overlap management architecture under the CBD. By interpreting its analytical and open-ended mandates from CBD states to identify strategies for cooperation between the biodiversity conventions, the Secretariat shaped core rules and norms that guide state behavior. As explained in chapter 3, these types of impacts reflect strong secretariat influence.

Central to the Secretariat's efforts was a highly prescriptive document (i.e., the blueprint) that positioned the Secretariat itself at the center of overlap management governance. This document not only identified areas for cooperation as requested, but went well beyond this task in advocating for specific recommendations for action. The recommendations contained in the blueprint were adopted by the CBD CoP and provided the foundation for overlap management within the CBD for over a decade. The CBD Secretariat was able to position itself in this way because state preferences on the issue were weakly solidified (in the early years) and the substitutability of its overlap management functions was low.

This case demonstrates how secretariats can influence the way states understand new issues and shape the institutions for managing those issues, even in the absence of state delegation. Two processes are particularly notable. First, secretariats can play a role in refining their own mandates for action. Second, secretariats can actively expand their "zones of discretion." The process-tracing exercise above illuminates the former process at work, with the Secretariat steadily and strategically marketing itself as a leader in overlap management until CoP4 finally institutionalized this as a "key" Secretariat activity in 1998. The CBD Secretariat expanded its "zone of discretion" by initiating three important MoCs in the mid 1990s, which, while often weak on substance, expanded its discretion with respect to how and when to cooperate directly with other international bodies. A similar dynamic emerged through the designation of "lead implementation partners," which, to some degree, circumvent the need for member state approval to engage in certain activities. This dynamic is reflected in this chapter's epigraph, when a CBD staff member interviewed for this study noted: "We can always find a [CoP] decision to justify what we want to do."

This case also shows how secretariat influence can vary over time. Whereas previous studies have explained variation across secretariats, this case demonstrates how one secretariat's influence has ebbed and flowed as state preferences and substitutability changed over time. The CBD Secretariat's influence was most powerful in the mid to late 1990s when overlap management was new and relatively undefined. During this period, state preferences were weakly solidified, as evidenced in the open-ended analytical mandates that they gave to the Secretariat. The Secretariat's deep access rights as contained in the Convention text effectively eliminated competition, decreasing the substitutability of Secretariat overlap management functions. As state preferences solidified over time, secretariat influence decreased, despite the continued low substitutability of Secretariat functions surrounding overlap management.

Finally, this case demonstrates how secretariats can engage in and sometimes influence politics even in the absence of state delegation. Open-ended analytical mandates were central to the CBD Secretariat's ability to exert this influence. The CBD Secretariat liberally interpreted such mandates to make strategic and substantive policy proposals that effectively shaped the way states managed overlap in that forum for many years. The Secretariat was not operating in contravention with state preferences; rather, by liberally interpreting open-ended mandates at a time when preferences were weakly solidified, the Secretariat was able to shape what those interests were to begin with—with little to no contestation from parties. A far cry from being the mere functionary and apolitical bureaucracies assumed in most IR theory, secretariats can thus deliberately and strategically position themselves to shape not only state preferences but also policy responses and, ultimately, global governance of overlap management writ large.

5

Marketing the Climate-Biodiversity Interface

Biodiversity is an essential asset in the fight against climate change.
—Former CBD Executive Secretary Ahmed Djoghlaf, May 22, 2007

It is my view that the tragic loss of our planet's biodiversity should be as well known to the general public as the issue of climate change. Indeed, they are intrinsically bound together.
—Former CBD Executive Secretary Ahmed Djoghlaf, September 17, 2007

Scientists have long discussed the current and projected impacts of climate change on the decline and loss of species due to increasing stressors on ecological systems (Parry et al. 2007). While this causal relationship between climate change and biodiversity loss is the dominant discursive frame of biodiversity-climate overlap in the scientific literature, political actors seeking to jump on the "climate change bandwagon" have adeptly and creatively diversified the ways overlap between these issues is framed to strategically shape governance of the intersection between these two issues (Jinnah 2011b).

This chapter examines how the Secretariat of the Convention on Biological Diversity (CBD) managed overlap between biodiversity and climate change by engaging in one form of "climate bandwagoning" in the mid-2000s (Jinnah 2011a). The chapter demonstrates how the Secretariat constructed a new, shared understanding of the relationship between biodiversity and climate change by filtering, (re)framing, and reiterating (i.e., marketing) strategic discussions of the overlap between these two issues. It did so in ways that aimed, not necessarily to carry out CBD member state instructions, but rather to shape how member states themselves understood the biodiversity-climate interface and consequently approached solutions to both issues.[1]

The chapter demonstrates how the Secretariat reframed biodiversity from a passive recipient of climate impacts to an active player in addressing the climate change problem. The chapter shows how, in efforts to increase the political saliency of biodiversity conservation, the Secretariat went to great lengths to reframe conservation as a climate adaptation strategy and a means to ameliorate the human security impacts of climate change. It did this through a targeted campaign of written and verbal statements delivered by the CBD's former executive secretary (ES), Ahmed Djoghlaf. Most notably, from 2006 to 2007, the Secretariat launched an aggressive marketing campaign through over 100 public statements aimed at reframing biodiversity-climate overlap in a way that emphasized biodiversity's active role in climate solutions, rather than merely its role as a victim of climate change.

This marketing campaign strategically framed biodiversity conservation—the CBD's first objective and an issue historically (and understandably) of higher political priority for industrialized countries—in a way that aimed to incentivize developing country interest. That is, whereas developing countries, who are both biodiversity rich and most heavily impacted by climate change, have tended to be more active in politics surrounding the CBD's third objective, (equitable sharing of benefits arising from the use of biological resources), the political framing marketed by the CBD Secretariat highlighted why conservation (CBD objective #1) should also be a priority for these countries. In essence, the Secretariat reframed biodiversity conservation as a development issue in the way it strategically linked it to climate change. In doing so, the Secretariat not only makes clear a mechanism by which regime overlap can be actively managed to enhance regime effectiveness (i.e., marketing), but also provides strong empirical support for emerging understandings of secretariats as important political actors in their own right (Biermann and Siebenhüner 2009; Jinnah 2010).

Ultimately, this chapter argues that the CBD Secretariat moderately influenced climate-biodiversity overlap management politics by changing the way some states approached management of the issue in practice, as evidenced in their national reports. It exerted influence, however, in very different ways than we saw in chapter 4. Rather than mobilizing expertise to shape institutional structures, in this case the Secretariat strategically reframed and marketed a core political construct (i.e., the role of biodiversity in climate solutions) that had important implications for problem solving under the Convention. It was able to do this because, as reflected in CBD states' analytical but restrictive mandates to the Secretariat, CBD state preferences surrounding overlap management on this issue were only moderately solidified in this case. Further, because the

Secretariat enjoyed substantially deeper access than other outside actors and had low competition for managing this issue during the time period examined, its overlap management functions had very low substitutability. Together, these factors help to explain why the Secretariat was able to exert moderate influence on overlap management in this case. More broadly, this chapter shows how secretariats can influence international cooperation by impacting productive power relations between states. In this case, the Secretariat shaped norms and ideas that guided how CBD states understood and responded to overlap management needs as related to climate change.

This chapter proceeds as follows. The next section introduces the contemporary political context of overlap management politics in the CBD. The story picks up CBD overlap management politics where the last chapter leaves off, focusing specifically on CBD overlap with climate change. The subsequent section explains how the CBD Secretariat participated in managing overlap with climate change through a content analysis of relevant political documents, before applying the two-pronged analytical framework presented in chapter 3 to show how the Secretariat shaped norms and ideas that guided how CBD states understood and responded to overlap management with respect to climate change.

Contemporary Political Context: Overlap Management Politics in the CBD

Whereas chapter 4 focused on how the CBD Secretariat managed overlap in the mid to late 1990s when overlap management was just emerging on the CBD agenda, this chapter focuses on more recent overlap management efforts under the CBD, specifically in the mid to late 2000s. There are two key differences between these time periods within CBD politics. First, following its coordination mandate, in the 1990s overlap management within the CBD was largely a unilateral policy-making process that sought to enhance its coordination with other biodiversity treaties. In contrast, by the mid 2000s, overlap management had expanded greatly to include not only biodiversity treaties but other issues as well—most notably, climate change through discussion of issues such as biofuels and forest conservation (IISD 2010b). Second, in the 1990s, overlap management was largely internally focused. That is, CBD overlap management goals were largely aimed at creating institutions for CBD parties to manage overlapping issues within the Convention. In contrast, overlap management in the CBD in recent years became more outward-looking.

As this chapter will show, CBD overlap management goals during this period aimed to shape not only CBD policies, but also policies within other organizations such as the UN Framework Convention on Climate Change (UNFCCC).

The focus on climate change here is not incidental. Climate change has likely garnered more political attention than any other environmental issue ever has, in part because the breadth and depth of climate impacts are so extensive. Climate change is expected to affect most economic sectors and geographic regions, with many of these impacts projected to be highly disruptive given the levels of greenhouse gas mitigation currently agreed to under the UNFCCC (IPCC 2007). Indeed, climate change is not merely an environmental issue but an issue of development, economics, and even security (Lee 2009). These impacts have brought unprecedented levels of funding to global environmental governance with, for example, various climate funds established under the World Bank, and pledges of USD 100 billion per year by 2020 to support mitigation and adaptation (IISD 2009). Given this influx of funding, it is no wonder that many actors outside the climate regime have attempted to frame their efforts in terms of climate mitigation and adaptation (Jinnah 2011b).

The CBD states are no different. Overlap management with climate change first emerged on the CBD Conference of the Parties (CoP) agenda at CoP5 in 2000 with a decision asking for scientific assessment of the climate impacts on biodiversity (CoPV/4). It emerged as a regular agenda item four years later at CoP7 (CoPVII/15), and has steadily diffused throughout the CBD work programs since that time. Early discussions focused on the technical elements surrounding how to minimize climate impacts on biodiversity and have become steadily more political in nature over time (IISD 2007b). For example, contemporary CBD discussions focus on deforestation and geoengineering, with hopes that negotiations on safeguards for Reducing Emissions from Deforestation and Forest Degradation (REDD), for example, will feed directly into UNFCCC negotiations on the topic (IISD 2012b).

The analysis undertaken here focuses on how climate change issues made their way onto the CBD agenda. Although a seemingly simple process, given the clear and direct scientific linkages between biodiversity and climate change, it was in fact deeply politicized. Developing countries had felt "deeply colonized" by the developed world through the UNFCCC negotiations (McGraw 2002b, 13). Until the late 2000s when adaptation was firmly ensconced in the UNFCCC negotiations, climate change negotiations had largely focused on mitigation, which was widely regarded as a developed country issue (IISD 2007b). In contrast, because developing countries possess four-fifths of the world's biodiversity, they were able to take a leadership role in CBD negotiations—confidently thwarting powerful US interests (McGraw 2002a). Specifically, developing countries had little interest in the conservation-focused agenda of the United States, and were able to steer CBD negotiations toward their core interests in benefit sharing and sustainable use.[2] Because scientific discussions surrounding biodiversity-climate overlap are inherently conservation-oriented in their focus on climate as a driver of biodiversity loss (see analysis below), linkages between the CBD and UNFCCC needed to be handled with great care in order to secure developing country buy-in. This chapter demonstrates how the CBD Secretariat adeptly negotiated this difficult terrain by reframing biodiversity-climate overlap from a conservation-focused, developed country issue to a development issue that should be of primary interest to the developing world as well.

Shared Understandings of Biodiversity-Climate Overlap

This section compares the ways that CBD states and the Secretariat each understand and seek to manage biodiversity-climate overlap. Measuring how actors understand the relationship between biodiversity and climate change in the aggregate is extremely difficult. This is in part because the meaning of "biodiversity" itself is contested (Takacs 1996). Further complicating this analysis, biodiversity value is constantly being reconstructed from inherent value to ecosystem service value to economic value. It is an extremely malleable term, which can be reframed to meet the shifting needs and values people assign to it. David Takacs (1996) said it best: "Don't know what biodiversity is? You can't. Perhaps bio*diversity* is an appropriate term. The confusion it conveys reveals our pathetic weakness in thinking we can define, know, and control a nature that will always dance just beyond our grasp" (341).

Despite this definitional ambiguity, we can still obtain a crude measure of how states and the Secretariat understand biodiversity-climate overlap. We can do so by analyzing documents that reflect how states understand the relationship between biodiversity and climate, and coding those documents according to various framings of biodiversity-climate overlap. To understand the various ways that CBD states frame and discuss biodiversity-climate overlap, this study systematically codes all official CBD documents, including CoP decisions, public speeches, and state and

Secretariat proposals on the issue. Because CBD states often instruct the Secretariat to make recommendations on the basis of specific scientific reports, all such reports are also included in this analysis. If the CBD Secretariat is merely an agent of its member states (Nielson and Tierney 2003, 243–244), we would expect to see a high degree of similarity between the Secretariat's activities surrounding biodiversity-climate overlap and member state instructions, including instructions to base any Secretariat activities and/or recommendations to the CoP on specific scientific reports. If the Secretariat is more than merely an agent of member states, we would expect to see some divergence between state instructions and Secretariat activities and/or recommendations.

In order to make this comparison, this study identified a universe of eleven frames used to describe biodiversity-climate overlap, and subsequently conducted a systematic content analysis of relevant documents that compared state frames of biodiversity-climate overlap to Secretariat frames of this issue (see table 5.1 for a full list).[3]

State Frames: Scientific, CoP, and Standing Body on Scientific, Technical, and Technological Advice (SBSTTA) Documents

CBD member states discuss biodiversity-climate overlap primarily in three sources: state-sponsored scientific documents, CoP decisions, and recommendations taken by CBD subsidiary bodies. This study looks to these three sources to identify how CBD states frame biodiversity-climate overlap. Specifically, this study examines state-sponsored scientific documents, such as CBD Ad Hoc Technical Expert Group (AHTEG) reports, the Millennium Ecosystem Assessment (MA), and assessment reports produced by the Intergovernmental Panel on Climate Change (IPCC). Although the link between CBD AHTEG's and CBD member states is clear, clarification of this link is needed for documents not produced by CBD states themselves. CBD member states formally endorsed the MA as a mechanism through which to meet their assessment needs in 1999–2000 (Millennium Ecosystem Assessment 2012). In the case of the IPCC, states nominate the scientists to serve on the Panel and provide the funding for the IPCC to carry out its work. Therefore, all of these documents, whether implicitly or explicitly, reflect framings of biodiversity-climate overlap that are endorsed by CBD member states.

The second place where CBD states discuss biodiversity-climate overlap is in CoP decisions on the issue. CoP decisions outline state views, needs, and objectives on all issues within the purview of the Convention, including overlap management. Third, state framings of

Table 5.1

Universe of Frames Used to Describe Biodiversity-Climate Overlap

#	Frame	Explanation/Example
1	Climate change causes biodiversity loss	Climate change is projected to be one of the two most important drivers of biodiversity loss by the end of the century
2	Mitigation/adaptation-response measures impact biodiversity	Biodiversity loss due to conversion of "natural" forests to plantation forests in order to enhance sequestration benefits
3	Adaptive capacity of biological systems to climate change	Resilience; the ability of species to adapt to warmer climates or changes in water availability
4	Conservation contributes to human adaptation	Wetland conservation helps buffer coastal communities from sea level rise and some extreme weather events
5	Conservation contributes to mitigation	Forest conservation creates carbon sequestration opportunities
6	Biodiversity loss impacts the rate of climate change	Albedo effects of land use change; deforestation as a loss of sequestration capacity
7	Conservation contributes to ecosystem adaptation (or unspecified aspects of adaptation)	More-diverse ecosystems are more resilient to changing climatic conditions due to species redundancy and other factors—a relationship that is still a topic of active debate in the scientific community (Folke et al. 2004; Hooper et al. 2005)
8	General cooperation	Institutional or scientific cooperation between conventions; the need for "mutual supportiveness" between conventions
9	Coupling biodiversity and climate change funding	Encourages parties to incorporate biodiversity concerns into climate change adaptation projects through, for example, funding requests to the Global Environment Facility
10	Traditional knowledge as means of climate change adaptations/mitigation	Highlights the role indigenous and traditional knowledge can play in helping ecosystems and humans adapt to climate change through, for example, agricultural practices
11	Climate change and biodiversity loss as security concerns	After clearly establishing a link between climate change and the loss of biodiversity, frames climate change and/or biodiversity as a security issue related to, for example, water access or as a driver of violent conflict

biodiversity-climate overlap are articulated through recommendations made by the CBD's Subsidiary Body on Scientific, Technical, and Technological Advice (SBSTTA), which include a mix of scientific and political content. This study coded all scientific reports, CoP decisions, and SBSTTA recommendations produced between 1994 and 2010 in order to identify state framings of biodiversity-climate overlap and trace how these changed over time.

Examination of scientific documents reveals that the scientific discourse between 2000 and 2007 emerging from the climate change community (e.g., IPCC) clearly, and nearly exclusively, emphasized one distinct frame of biodiversity-climate overlap: the increasingly important role climate change is playing in accelerating biodiversity loss (Frame #1). While scientific reports from biodiversity-focused scientific communities (e.g., MA and AHTEG reports) mirror this emphasis, they also incorporate in-depth discussions of some of the secondary framings identified in IPCC discussions. Namely, these scientific reports also emphasize the potential impacts of climate change mitigation and adaptation measures on biodiversity (Frame #2); the role that conservation can play in mitigation efforts (Frame #5); and in the case of CBD Technical Series 25, the adaptive capacity of biological systems to climate change (Frame #3) (CBD Secretariat 2006a).

In contrast to these scientific reports, CoP decisions on biodiversity-climate overlap tended to focus on general, nonsubstantive statements of cooperation, such as encouraging the continued cooperation between the UNFCCC and CBD political and scientific bodies or establishing an AHTEG to examine a particular issue recommended by the Secretariat (Frame #8). To a lesser degree, the CoP also reiterated the frames identified in the scientific literature, in particular Frames #2 and 7. However, these were typically used as a way to justify establishing broad institutional cooperation rather than for defining a particular overlap management trajectory. That is, the CoP did not offer much substantive guidance on how exactly overlap between the CBD and UNFCCC should be managed. The one exception to this is a dominant frame that emerged in a decision at CoP6 that initiated the discussion of coupling biodiversity and climate change funding through national implementation of the Convention (Frame #9) (CBD CoP6 2002a).

Finally, like the scientific inputs, SBSTTA discussions also focused on the impacts of adaptation/mitigation activities on biodiversity (Frame #2) and the role of climate change impacts on biodiversity (Frame #1). Similarly, paralleling CoP discussions and reflecting the SBSTTA's hybrid nature at the science-policy interface (Koetz et al. 2008), the SBSTTA also emphasized elements of general institutional cooperation (Frame #8).

In the aggregate, state-produced documents tended to frame biodiversity as a victim of climate change and/or focus on the general need to enhance cooperation between biodiversity climate regimes. Specifically, scientific documents focused strongly on climate change as a driver of biodiversity loss (Frame #1), CoP documents focused on general cooperation (Frame #8), and SBSTTA documents focused on the role of mitigation and adaptation response measures relating to biodiversity (Frame #2).

Secretariat Frames

While the Secretariat certainly draws from the same frames identified in the state-produced data, the diversity of frames employed and the order of emphasis of these frames are quite different. In fact, the only frame from the three state sources to emerge as highly emphasized (≥9 percent) in the Secretariat discourse is the foundational frame, "Climate Change Causes Biodiversity Loss" (Frame #1). Rather, the Secretariat emphasizes the frames that highlight biodiversity's anthropocentric attributes, such as the role it can play in human adaptation (Frame #4) and the linkage between climate change, biodiversity loss, and security concerns (Frame #11)—neither of which are highly emphasized in the state data. Table 5.2 below summarizes findings and compares them across each of the data sources discussed above.

Table 5.2
Emphasis of Frames by Actor: Frame # (Percentage of Total Discussion of Issue)

Scientific	CoP	SBSTTA	Secretariat
1 (40%)	8 (50%)	2 (37%)	1 (28%)
5 (18%)	2 (14%)	8 (23%)	4 (14%)
2 (16%)	9 (10%)	1 (15%)	7 (12%)
3 (12%)	1 (9%)	7 (12%)	11 (10%)
7 (6%)	7 (8%)	5 (7.5%)	8 (8%)
4 (3%)	5 (6%)	3 (5%)	5 (8%)
			3 (7%)
			2 (6%)
			10 (3%)
			9 (2%)

In summary, there are at least eleven dimensions of overlap between biodiversity and climate change that are deployed by state actors and the Secretariat. Although the core relationship describing climate change as a driver of biodiversity loss is important in the way all actors discuss this linkage, the Secretariat also discusses the linkage in ways that diverge from state articulations. This suggests that the Secretariat is not merely following the lead of its member states in managing overlap on this issue; rather, it is strategically choosing which frames to deploy and amplify to meet specific political objectives. The next section explores how the Secretariat deployed these frames in an effort to influence overlap management politics.

Understanding Secretariat Influence

This section evaluates whether the Secretariat's overlap management activities identified above influenced power relations between states. It ultimately argues that the CBD Secretariat did impact power relations by marketing a new framing of biodiversity-climate overlap—focused on the human security impacts of climate change—that is beginning to shape the way CBD member states understand this issue and address it through policy and discourse. The Secretariat was able to influence power relations because state preferences on biodiversity-climate overlap management were only moderately solidified during the study period, and, critically, because the Secretariat was able to decrease the substitutability of its overlap management functions by strategically justifying new functions for itself in this area that faced low competition from other actors.

Did the Secretariat Exert Influence?
A three-step analysis (outlined in figure 3.1) is necessary to ascertain whether the Secretariat influenced overlap management. First, we must assess whether the Secretariat deployed any of the five mechanisms of influence described in chapter 3 (i.e., knowledge brokering, capacity building, marketing, negotiation/litigation facilitation). If so, we must trace those mechanisms of influence to observed changes in power relations between states. Finally, we must conduct a counterfactual analysis to rule out alternative explanations for the observed change in state power relations.

Mechanisms of Influence?   The data presented in the preceding section highlights that CBD Secretariat activities did indeed reflect one mechanism of bureaucratic influence: marketing. As explained in chapter 3, marketing involves the conscious selection and uptake of specific pieces of information (filtering), the digestion and transformation of that information to meet specific political ends ((re)framing), and the habitual and repeated presentation of that information across multiple political forums (reiteration). In this case, the Secretariat marketed a particular framing of biodiversity-climate overlap. Drawing on the content analysis conducted above, this section explains how the Secretariat carried out its marketing campaign by secretariat filtering, (re)framing, and reiterating a particular framing of biodiversity-climate overlap.

Filtering   The content analysis above reveals that the Secretariat strategically filtered information related to biodiversity-climate overlap by emphasizing some frames and deemphasizing others. As one might expect from existing treatments of secretariats as functionaries in the scholarly literature, there is a high degree of similarity between the universe of frames used by state actors and those used by the Secretariat. Indeed, nine of the eleven frames identified by this study can be traced back to state-produced sources (i.e., CoP decisions, SBSTTA recommendations, and state-sponsored scientific documents). However, this analysis reveals that the Secretariat also acted autonomously and politically by strategically choosing which state-produced frames to emphasize and which to ignore. Indeed, if we look at the frames utilized by the various actors 9 percent or more of the time, aside from the foundational scientific relationship (Frame #1), the Secretariat emphasizes very different aspects of biodiversity-climate overlap than do any of the state actors from whom their activities should theoretically be derived (table 5.3).

It is not surprising that the CoP, SBSTTA, and external scientific organizations would utilize different frames in discussing biodiversity-climate overlap. However, if secretariats are indeed merely pawns of their member states as international relations theory suggests, then we would expect

Table 5.3

Most Emphasized Frames: Frame # (Percentage of Total Discussion of Issue)

Secretariat	CoP	Scientific	SBSTTA
1 (28%)	8 (50%)	1 (40%)	2 (37%)
4 (14%)	2 (14%)	5 (18%)	8 (23%)
7 (12%)	9 (10%)	2 (16%)	1 (15%)
11 (10%)	1 (9%)	3 (12%)	7 (12%)

to see the Secretariat framing biodiversity-climate overlap in a manner that mirrors the way state actors frame the issue.[4] In fact, as the content analysis above shows, the Secretariat emphasized frames of biodiversity-climate overlap that diverged dramatically from those chosen by states, suggesting that the Secretariat acted autonomously in filtering particular framings of biodiversity-climate overlap.

(Re)Framing   In filtering certain frames into and out of its discourse on biodiversity-climate overlap, the Secretariat reframed the issue in a way that increased the global salience of conservation, in particular for developing countries. It did so by marketing biodiversity conservation as a way to, first, help humans adapt to climate change and, second, enhance human security. Whereas the state actors tended to emphasize the *passive* climate impact–oriented relationship between biodiversity and climate change (Frames #1 and 2) as a justification for general cooperation (Frame #8), the Secretariat emphasized the relationship in a way that gave biodiversity conservation an *active* role in climate response. Critically, in emphasizing the role biodiversity conservation can play in climate change adaptation (Frame #4), the Secretariat reframed biodiversity-climate overlap as an issue with significantly more international political traction than the need to protect the largely nonhuman world of biodiversity (Takacs 1996; Dickson and Lewis 2010). In Djoghlaf's (2007c) oft-repeated words, this reframing provides the "human face of climate change."

The Secretariat also reframed existing state discussions of biodiversity-climate overlap by introducing a new frame (#11) to the CBD discourse. This new frame focuses on the human security impacts of climate change and the role that biodiversity conservation can play in ameliorating those impacts. For example, the Secretariat often references the role that agrobiodiversity can play in enhancing food security by making agricultural systems more resilient to climate impacts. The way the Secretariat utilizes the security frame is peculiar because the Secretariat only implicitly links human security and climate change to biodiversity loss. Moreover, it does so through an adaptation approach, which, as previously mentioned, has greater political traction than does conservation alone.

Rallying countries to engage climate change promises indirect problem-solving benefits for the CBD as well. This is, of course, because climate change is a major driver of biodiversity loss. As such, it is in the CBD's interest to encourage action on climate change—as it did by marketing conservation as an active player in this battle—irrespective of the specific rationale for such action. For reasons discussed above, focusing on human security rationales for climate action, especially in the context of adaptation, is more salient for many countries than are rationales based on curbing biodiversity loss alone. This reframing allowed Djoghlaf to circumvent discussion of the less politically tractable concept of halting biodiversity loss through conservation, yet nevertheless advocate for this same outcome by instead focusing on those climate impacts that are likely to better engage developing countries.

The Secretariat's reframing of biodiversity-climate overlap in these ways was deeply strategic and political. In emphasizing how conservation can aid in climate adaptation, the Secretariat made conservation, which has historically been a "developed nation issue" (National Research Council 1992, vii), more attractive to developing countries, who have significant adaptation needs that are largely unfulfilled (IPCC 1998). Similarly, the human security framing worked to encourage indirect action on biodiversity loss (i.e., through climate action) by focusing on climate impacts of central concern to developing countries. Albeit circuitously, these Secretariat activities generate benefits for CBD member states by reframing biodiversity loss in a manner that can be prioritized by developed and developing countries alike. This reframing is critical to CBD effectiveness because the vast majority of the world's biodiversity is located in the developing world (Myers et al. 2000). Without committed interest from developing countries, prospects for global biodiversity conservation are substantially limited.

Likely recognizing this, Djoghlaf worked to garner this interest by recasting biodiversity conservation from solely a passive recipient of climate impacts (Frame #1) to an active part of climate change solutions through, for example, adaptation potential (Frames #4, 7, and to a lesser extent 5). In particular, while discussions of climate impacts on biodiversity loss remain prevalent as a foundational justification for discussing the linkage at all, Djoghlaf's statements represented an effort to increase the political salience of biodiversity loss among those with more pressing development concerns. He did this by reframing biodiversity loss as a critical means to address the impacts of climate change on human communities.

Reiterating Finally, the Secretariat reiterated these human-focused framings (Frames #4 and 11, on adaptation and human security respectively) of biodiversity-climate overlap across a wide variety of forums. This aspect of the Secretariat's behavior is most clearly evident in ES

Djoghlaf's public statements in 2006 and 2007, when he carefully wove discussions of biodiversity-climate change overlap into his statements across a wide variety of venues. Indeed, informal interviews with CBD delegates suggest that in some instances the link between climate change issues and biodiversity loss was so peripheral to certain forums (e.g., the 2007 International Conference in Defense of the Quality of the Night Sky and the Right to Observe the Stars; Djoghlaf 2007b) that ES Djoghlaf's audience was left wondering why he was addressing the topic at all.

By means of comparison, between 2004 and 2005, climate-biodiversity overlap was substantively mentioned in only two of the sixteen statements delivered by Djoghlaf's predecessor Hamdallah Zedan, and the linkage was categorized as dominant in just one of them (which was delivered to the UNFCCC).[5] In contrast, despite no significant change in emphasis or frequency with respect to CoP/SBSTTA documents on the topic, Djoghlaf discussed biodiversity-climate overlap in 38 percent of his 2006 statements, and in 79 percent of those delivered in 2007 (2007a). Although Djoghlaf addressed climate-focused forums only twice in 2006 (of 47 total speeches analyzed) and four times in 2007 (of 75 total speeches analyzed), biodiversity-climate discussions appeared in his statements 86 times in 2006 and 472 times in 2007, an average of about 1.8 and 6.3 mentions per statement in 2006 and 2007 respectively.[6] The marked difference in emphasis between Djoghlaf and his predecessor, Zedan, points to the importance of leadership as another variable that likely conditions a secretariat's ability to influence politics. It remains to be seen how Djoghalf's successor, Braulio F. de Souza Dias, will engage this issue.

In summary, under Djoghlaf, the Secretariat influenced overlap management by strategically marketing discussions of biodiversity-climate overlap. It filtered specific constructions of this linkage in an effort to reframe the discourse surrounding biodiversity-climate overlap to one focused on the role of biodiversity in climate adaptation. Finally, Djoghlaf reiterated this new frame of the linkage across a wide variety of forums.

Change in Power Relations?   Although mechanisms of influence are observable in this case, in order to assert that the Secretariat actually did influence overlap management, we must first show that such mechanisms yielded impacts that reflect changes in power relations between member states. This section argues that the Secretariat's marketing campaign yielded such impacts in changing the way CBD states understood and subsequently managed biodiversity-climate overlap. Specifically, the Secretariat did this by introducing and emphasizing new frames of the relationship between biodiversity and climate change that shifted the discourse within the CBD on this issue. That is, the Secretariat's activities changed the way some CBD states understood and subsequently talked about this relationship, as reflected in their National Reports, post-marketing campaign decisions, and other documents. As explained in chapter 3, this impact changed productive power relations between states because it shaped norms and ideas that are important to regime operation.

Recall from the above analysis that, prior to the Secretariat's marketing campaign, CBD states largely discussed biodiversity-climate overlap in the context of how biodiversity will be impacted by climate change and its response measures (Frames #1 and 2), and the need for increased cooperation on the issue (Frame #8). This section examines how CBD states understood biodiversity-climate overlap *after* the marketing campaign by examining CBD CoP discussions and decisions in 2008 (CoP9) and 2010 (CoP10), as well as a sample of the CBD's first four National Reports.

At CoP9 in 2008, discussions of biodiversity and climate change focused on what some CBD delegates referred to as the "mitigation troika" of biofuels, ocean fertilization, and genetically modified trees (IISD 2008). Nevertheless, the human adaptation framing (Frame #4), which was emphasized by the Secretariat but absent from all CoP decisions prior to the marketing campaign, made it into the final CoP decision on biodiversity-climate overlap for the first time at this meeting (CBD CoP9 2008a). Specifically, the decision asks that future in-depth reviews of the CBD's programs of work should consider the "contribution of biodiversity to climate-change adaptation, and measures that enhance the adaptive potential of components of biodiversity" (CBD CoP9 2008a, paragraph 1(i)).[7]

This CoP decision also contains the terms of reference (ToRs) for a new AHTEG to address biodiversity and climate change issues. The ToRs explicitly recognize the *human adaptation* potential of biodiversity, specifically tasking the AHTEG with "highlighting case-studies and identifying methodologies for analy[z]ing the value of biodiversity in supporting adaptation in communities and sectors vulnerable to climate change" (CBD CoP9 2008a, Annex III, paragraph 3(b)). These two statements mark the first time that a human adaptation–oriented construction appears within a CBD CoP decision on biodiversity-climate overlap, suggesting that the Secretariat's marketing campaign was impacting state understandings of the issue as early as 2008.

We also saw the Secretariat's activities changing state practice at CoP10 in 2010. At this meeting, discussions of biodiversity-climate overlap focused on mitigation-oriented frames of geoengineering and REDD (IISD 2010b). However, the human adaptation benefits of biodiversity became increasingly integrated into CoP10 decisions on biodiversity-climate overlap. Specifically, CoP10's decision on "Biodiversity and Climate Change" encouraged states to consider the role of ecosystem management in helping humans adapt to climate change (Frame #4) right alongside the role of biodiversity in helping increase the resilience of biological systems (Frame #7) (CBD CoP10 2010b, paragraph 8(j)–(l)). Although human adaptation–oriented discussions remained secondary to mitigation-oriented discussions at this meeting, particularly as related to REDD and geoengineering, these CoP decisions indicate that the Secretariat's marketing efforts have nonetheless had an impact on the way states understand and address biodiversity-climate overlap.

Finally, CBD National Reports also provide preliminary support for the argument that the Secretariat's marketing campaign changed productive power relations between states. Specifically, analysis of a sample of the CBD's First (1997–1999), Second (2001–2005), and Third (2005–2007) Reports, all produced before the marketing campaign, revealed very little, but temporally increasing, discussion of climate change. However, the Fourth National Reports (2008–2010), produced after the marketing campaign, suggest that the Secretariat-introduced frames have percolated into the national discourse surrounding biodiversity-climate overlap (table 5.4).[8]

Following Djoghalf's marketing campaign, these reports begin to reflect the active role of biodiversity in adaptation (Frames #4 and 7) and human security (#11). Although India and Germany mentioned the human security dimensions of the linkage and the active role of biodiversity in adaptation, respectively, in their Third Reports, dominant framings at this time were limited to the core scientific frame (Frame #1) and those focused on biological adaptive capacity (Frame #3) and general cooperation (Frame #8). Of the eight sample countries that had submitted their Fourth National Reports by the time of writing, all (except Germany) discuss biodiversity as an adaptation tool, with Kenya and India becoming the first countries to refer to biodiversity's *human* adaptation benefits (Frame #4). India, Kenya, Indonesia, and Germany all

Table 5.4
CBD Fourth National Reports

Frame # (% of total discussion)	Frame Description
1 (46%)	Climate change causes biodiversity loss
11 (14%)	Climate change → (biodiversity loss) → security concerns
8 (12%)	General cooperation
3 (10%)	Adaptive capacity of biological systems to climate change
5 (7%)	Conservation contributes to mitigation
7 (7%)	Conservation contributes to ecosystem (or unspecified aspects of) adaptation

emphasized the security implications of biodiversity-climate overlap. For example, India's report commented, "agro-biodiversity deserves special attention to ensure conservation of valuable germ plasm for posterity, sustainable development, livelihood security and to deal with potential climate change impacts" (Government of India 2009, 28).

Although the appearance of Secretariat-emphasized frames in the Fourth National Reports following the marketing campaign suggests a change in the way states are managing overlap domestically, it is too early to comprehensively investigate and support this claim empirically. More data is needed to convincingly make the case that the marketing campaign has definitely impacted what states are doing to manage biodiversity-climate overlap. Nevertheless, this preliminary evaluation shows that albeit limited, the appearance of Secretariat-emphasized frames of biodiversity-climate overlap in CBD CoP decisions and, to a lesser extent, National Reports, indicates that the CBD Secretariat's marketing activities are beginning to change the way member states (especially developing countries) understand the issue—reflecting a change in productive power relations between states.

Alternative Explanations? It is, of course, possible that member states utilized human-focused frames of biodiversity-climate overlap for reasons other than the Secretariat's convincing them to do so. The content analysis above presents strong evidence that these frames did not emerge from the CBD CoP, the SBSTTA, or the scientific community—as we might expect if member states had developed the human-focused frames themselves. The most plausible alternative explanation is that member states began discussing the role of biodiversity conservation as a human adaptation strategy because adaptation discussions under the UNFCCC, rather than the CBD Secretariat, identified this as an important strategy.

However, external influence from the UNFCCC is unlikely for two reasons. First, within the UNFCCC, when biodiversity is discussed, it is generally in the context of REDD (IISD 2005, 2007a, 2007b, 2008, 2009, 2010a, 2011, 2012a).[9] REDD emerged in UNFCCC politics in 2005 as a way to operationalize Articles 2 and 3 of the Kyoto Protocol, which require parties to preserve carbon sinks—including forests—in meeting their emission reduction requirements (Holloway and Giandomenico 2009). The original language of the Kyoto Protocol therefore delineated the way forest conservation would be framed in the UNFCCC: as a mitigation issue, not an adaptation issue. That is, forest conservation is largely framed as a way to reduce greenhouse gas emissions,[10] not as a way to help humans adapt to impacts of climate change.

Second, prior to the Secretariat's marketing campaign in 2007, UNFCCC member states did not discuss adaptation in the context of biodiversity. This is evidenced in key documents wherein UNFCCC member states discuss adaptation issues, such as their National Adaptation Programmes of Action (NAPAs) and in the reports from technical workshops held under the Nairobi Work Programme on Impacts, Vulnerability, and Adaptation. In their NAPAs, UNFCCC member states nearly exclusively discussed biodiversity in the context of either climate impacts on biodiversity (Frame #1) or the human security impacts that emerge from this relationship (Frame #11) (table 5.5).

In contrast, if we look at how UNFCCC member states framed biodiversity-climate overlap after the CBD Secretariat's marketing campaign (post-2007), a different pattern emerges. After the marketing campaign, conservation as a tool in human adaptation made up 18 percent of the discussions on biodiversity-climate overlap (table 5.6).

Table 5.5
Emphasis of NAPA Frames, 2004–2006

Frame # (% of total discussion)	Frame Description
1 (81%)	Climate change causes biodiversity loss
11 (19%)	Climate change → biodiversity loss → security concerns

Table 5.6
Emphasis of NAPA Frames, 2007–2011

Frame # (% of total discussion)	Frame Description
1 (38%)	Climate change causes biodiversity loss
11 (24%)	Climate change → biodiversity loss → security concerns
12 (9%)	Biodiversity cobenefits of climate change adaptation strategy
3 (3%)	Adaptive capacity of biological systems to climate change
5 (2%)	Conservation contributes to mitigation

The relatively prolific discussions on the overlap of biodiversity, climate, and human security (Frame #11) within the UNFCCC suggests that UNFCCC discussions may be responsible, rather than the CBD Secretariat, for guiding how CBD members understood the human security implications of climate-biodiversity overlap. However, prior to 2007, UNFCCC members' adaptation plans did not mention biodiversity as a tool in adaptation (Frame #4) at all, and thus it is unlikely that CBD member states were influenced by UNFCCC discussions on this issue.

The UNFCCC's Nairobi Work Programme outlines a five-year plan to help countries make informed decisions on adaptation activities. The Nairobi Work Programme provides a particularly good metric for state understandings of biodiversity-climate overlap because it coincided with the CBD marketing campaign, holding three workshops between 2007 and 2009, and producing a 2008 technical paper (UNFCCC 2008) titled "Integrating Practices, Tools and Systems for Climate Risk Assessment and Management and Strategies for Disaster Risk Reduction into National Policies and Programmes." As such, if biodiversity conservation was seen in the UNFCCC as a promising tool for human adaptation, we would expect to see this framing (Frame #4) featuring prominently in these discussions. However, examination of the various workshop reports and the technical paper reveals that the relationship between biodiversity and adaptation is not discussed.[11] When biodiversity-climate overlap *was* discussed, it was only in the context of the impacts that climate change will have on biodiversity (Frame #1)—not in relation to biodiversity's role in adaptation. This provides strong evidence that the Secretariat's emphasis on the biodiversity benefits of human adaptation (Frame #4) did not originate in the UNFCCC, as this frame is completely absent from the key UNFCCC discussions of adaptation under review.

Although the above evidence suggests that the change in CBD member states' understanding of climate-biodiversity overlap is not attributable to developments under the UNFCCC, it is also possible that nongovernmental organizations (NGOs) may have influenced CBD states in this regard. Any such influence is comparatively minor, however, because these organizations tend not to emphasize the human adaptation benefits of biodiversity. This is evidenced through UNFCCC side events, where NGOs often present ideas to UNFCCC member states (Hjerpe and Linnér, 2010; Schroeder and Lovell 2012). Participant observation of more than fifty UNFCCC side events at four UNFCCC CoPs between 2006 and 2011 suggests that the human adaptation frame played a relatively minor role in NGO discussions of this topic. If conservation NGOs *were* pushing this construction during the study period, we would expect it to show up prominently at these side events. NGOs and UNFCCC politics are therefore, at best, secondary contributing influences on CBD member states' understanding of biodiversity-climate overlap.

In summary, it is unlikely that the observed changes in state power relations can be attributed to actors other than the Secretariat in this case. This supports the chapter's central argument, therefore, that the CBD Secretariat did influence overlap management by carrying out a marketing campaign that is beginning to change state understandings of biodiversity-climate overlap and their surrounding practice. Specifically, the Secretariat strategically framed biodiversity-climate overlap to emphasize the role that biodiversity conservation can play in human adaptation and security. This shift is important because it reframed biodiversity from the developed country priority of conservation to adaptation, a concern of central importance to developing countries.

As reflected in CoP discussions and National Reports, the Secretariat's marketing efforts are beginning to change some states' understandings of the biodiversity "problem" and thus the way they envision and formulate solutions to that problem—an impact that reflects *moderate* influence as defined in chapter 3.

Why Was the Secretariat Able to Exert Influence?

CBD member states' moderately solidified preferences coupled with the low substitutability of Secretariat functions help to explain why the CBD Secretariat was able to moderately influence overlap management in this case.

Preference Solidification   In addition to problem characteristics such as newness, other characteristics of state mandates can help us to understand the degree of state preference solidification surrounding biodiversity-climate overlap during the study period. As explained in chapter 3, state mandates that are administrative and restrict the secretariat's activities reflect strongly solidified preferences, those that are analytical and allow the secretariat flexibility in interpretation (i.e., open-ended) reflect weakly solidified preferences, and those that are analytical but restricted reflect moderately solidified preferences (see table 3.3). The more strongly solidified state preferences are, the less likely a secretariat will be able to influence overlap management (see table 3.5).

In this case, the Secretariat carried out its marketing campaign not merely in response to specific mandates from CBD member states, but proactively under its broad treaty-defined authority "to coordinate with other relevant international bodies" (Convention on Biological Diversity 1992, Article 24). In the absence of a specific evolving mandate to manage overlap, the Secretariat proactively created room for itself to maneuver by choosing to justify its marketing campaign under its open-ended mandate as contained in the treaty text (Convention on Biological Diversity 1992, Article 24). This mandate is open-ended in that it does not specify *how* the Secretariat should "coordinate," leaving room for both administrative and analytical Secretariat activities. Moreover, because it was so broad in its scope, it would be difficult to make the case that the Secretariat did anything that extended beyond its legal mandate. Rather, the Secretariat creatively interpreted the mandate to justify and design its biodiversity-climate marketing campaign—an activity that was certainly analytical in nature. These open-ended and analytical mandates reflect weakly solidified state preferences.

Specific CBD CoP decisions on "biodiversity and climate change" suggest that state preferences were, at best, moderately solidified until after the study period. These early decisions, taken between 2004 (CoP7) and 2006 (CoP8), called on the Secretariat to carry out a combination of open-ended analytical and administrative functions. They asked the Secretariat to gather information, such as case studies, to better understand the relationship between climate change and biodiversity. In identifying which cases to include and make available to member states, the Secretariat's mandate took on both administrative and analytical qualities.

Over time, however, CoP decisions on this issue become increasingly restrictive, articulating specific activities and goals. Later decisions (for example, those taken at CoP9 (2008) and CoP10 (2010)) are much more restrictive in nature. These decisions call on the Secretariat to carry out many functions, including meeting with specific organizations to compile and synthesize specific pieces of information and to consider particular reports in conducting analyses. In this way, these mandates were far more restrictive than those that came in the first part of the study period, suggesting that state preferences became increasingly solid over time.

As state preferences solidified over time, the Secretariat struggled to influence climate-biodiversity discussions. This is evidenced, for example, in state discussions surrounding a 2005 overlap management proposal, known as the global partnership on biodiversity (CBD Secretariat 2005a, Add.1). In contrast to the earlier more exploratory, information-gathering state discussions that surrounded the blueprint in the mid 1990s (see chapter 4) (IISD 1994), discussions surrounding the partnership reflected deep state engagement with the intricate details of the issue (IISD 2012b). However, because Secretariat influence in this case is largely constitutive (yielding changes in productive power relations), there is a time lag in assessing impacts. Evidence that *ideas* have changed is slower to accumulate than the clear changes to the rules and institutions we observed in chapter 4. As such, it is still too early to assess *recent* changes in Secretariat influence. Nevertheless, with REDD and bioengineering emerging as the dominant ways to frame climate-biodiversity issues within the CBD, state discussions appear to be more strongly influenced in recent years by what is happening in the UNFCCC.

As reflected in their increasingly restrictive and administrative mandates, state preferences appear to be solidifying over time. Whereas very early mandates were open-ended and analytical, reflecting weak state preferences, later mandates quickly became more restrictive and a mix of analytical and administrative in nature, reflecting moderately solidified preferences. As the more recent decisions are more numerous and specific to CBD overlap with climate—as opposed to overlap management more broadly—state preferences are categorized as moderately solidified in this case. It should be noted, however, that as state preferences solidified over time, Secretariat influence correspondingly decreased.

Substitutability The substitutability of the Secretariat's overlap management functions is also important in understanding secretariat influence. When secretariats enjoy deeper access to decision-making forums than other actors, and competition to perform overlap management functions is absent, secretariat functions enjoy the lowest degree of substitutability. Secretariat substitutability increases as their access relative to that of other actors decreases and competition to carry out overlap management functions increases (see table 3.4). The more substitutable secretariat functions are, the less likely the secretariat will be able to influence overlap management (see table 3.5).

Although this case study focused on one overlap management function carried out by the CBD Secretariat (i.e., marketing ideas), the Secretariat actually carried out a host of other overlap management functions related to climate-biodiversity overlap as well. These nonmarketing functions are reflected in CoP mandates under the agenda item "biodiversity and climate change," and almost always require the Secretariat to consult and cooperate with various other organizations such as other Biodiversity and Joint Liaison Groups, the IPCC, and the Global Environment Facility (GEF). These mandates give external actors increased access to CBD decision-making forums, and greatly increased the competition the Secretariat had in carrying out all of its overlap management functions (for examples, see CBD CoP9 2008a; CBD CoP10 2010b). As such, although not systematically analyzed in this study, these mandates indicate that, in general, Secretariat substitutability on "biodiversity and climate change" overlap management was high, and suggest influence would be unlikely in this case.

What is really interesting about this case, however, is the way that the Secretariat circumvented the limitations presented by having competition from other outside actors. It used its open-ended mandate for overlap management, as contained in the Convention text itself, to justify additional overlap management activities (i.e., marketing activities) beyond those articulated in CoP decisions on "biodiversity and climate change" specifically. In doing so, the Secretariat managed to carve out an overlap-management niche in which it enjoyed both deeper access than many other external actors and far less competition from those actors.

These efforts were largely carried out by the former executive secretary Ahmed Djoghlaf, who occupied a highly specialized position in biodiversity-climate politics. As the executive head of the CBD, Djoghlaf had agenda-setting capabilities not enjoyed by any other actors. He used this deep participation access to regularly address CBD parties about biodiversity-climate overlap in his opening remarks at many key CBD meetings. He further accepted invitations to address state actors in a wide variety of forums external to the CBD. Although this study does not systematically analyze the invitations extended to other actors, several interviewees noted that Djoghlaf regularly used these pulpits to market biodiversity-climate overlap in ways that other actors did not.

Djoghlaf also faced limited competition from external actors to perform this marketing function. The Secretariat's fixed mandate does not require the Secretariat to consult with other actors in managing overlap, nor does it give overlap management authority to any other actors. Although not explicitly addressed in the framework, competition was also likely low because Djoghlaf possessed highly specialized expertise relevant to biodiversity-climate overlap. His curriculum vitae reflects far-reaching expertise on biodiversity as well as climate change issues. Not only was he central to the original negotiations of the CBD as a Special Advisor at the UN Conference on Environment and Development (UNCED), where the CBD was originally agreed, but he has also held several prominent climate-related posts. For example, he served as vice-chairman of the Intergovernmental Negotiating Committee of the UNFCCC, as well as chairman of one of the subcommittees that negotiated the Preamble, the Objective, and the Principles of the UNFCCC. These positions give Djoghlaf a certain amount of credibility, which, although not impossible for other actors to replicate, certainly reduces their likelihood of doing so.

The Secretariat's overlap management functions, therefore, enjoyed mixed degrees of substitutability. With respect to overlap management functions carried out in response to evolving mandates contained in CoP decisions, the framework suggests a moderate to high level of substitutability of Secretariat functions (i.e., because access was equal and competition was moderate to high). However, with respect to the overlap management functions empirically examined in this study (i.e., Djoghlaf's marketing campaign), which were carried out under the authority of its fixed mandate in the Convention text, rather than the evolving "biodiversity and climate change" mandates, the Secretariat's functions enjoyed low levels of substitutability (i.e., because its access was deeper and competition was low).

In summary, state preferences were moderately solidified for the majority of the study period, but the Secretariat's substitutability and thus its capacity for influence—as predicted by the framework developed in this study—varied depending on which mandates one examines. Analysis of the CoP mandates on "biodiversity and climate change" shows that Secretariat substitutability was moderate to high. The study's framework would thus predict that secretariat influence was possible to unlikely (see table 3.5). However, empirical observation indicates that in

Table 5.7

Summary of Findings—CBD Biodiversity-Climate Overlap Management

Cases	Preference Solidification	Substitutability	Predicted Influence	Observed Influence
CBD Secretariat	Moderate	Low* Moderate/high+	Likely* Unlikely+	Moderate

* Based on fixed mandate
+ Based on evolving mandate

carrying out its marketing campaign the Secretariat was nonetheless able to influence overlap management, albeit modestly. It did this by utilizing not the specific evolving mandate under the "biodiversity and climate change" agenda items, but its much broader open-ended fixed mandate as contained in the Convention text itself. In contrast to its other overlap management functions, the Secretariat faced low competition from other actors in its marketing efforts justified under this broad mandate, and enjoyed deep access to decision-making forums. The Secretariat thereby effectively decreased its substitutability, creating an environment of low substitutability. Accordingly, the Secretariat increased its capacity to influence overlap management in this case.

The Secretariat's low substitutability coupled with states' moderately solidified preferences on this issue during the study period suggest that CBD Secretariat influence is likely in this case (see table 3.5). This prediction corresponds with the empirical finding of moderate Secretariat influence in this case (table 5.7).

Conclusions

Empirical evidence suggests that the CBD Secretariat moderately influenced biodiversity-climate overlap management by shaping the way states understood this relationship and discussed it in their National Reports—impacts that reflect changes in structural and productive power relations between states. This finding is surprising because states' moderately solidified preferences coupled with the high substitutability of the Secretariat's mandated overlap management functions as contained in CoP decisions (i.e., evolving mandates) suggest that the CBD Secretariat was unlikely to influence overlap management in this case. Nevertheless, the Secretariat *did* exert influence by creatively using its fixed mandate as contained in the Convention text to justify additional overlap management activities and lower the substitutability of its overlap management functions. Specifically, it designed and carried out a marketing campaign to shape how states understood and formulated solutions to issues at the intersection of biodiversity and climate change. This suggests that delegation is not as simple as previous scholarship suggests, and demonstrates how secretariats can creatively interpret mandated functions to extend beyond what is formally intended by states.

Recognized previously for its strong normative and limited cognitive influence when examined across all areas of its work (Siebenhüner 2009, 284), overlap management appears to be an area where the CBD Secretariat also exhibits a moderate amount of cognitive influence in shaping knowledge and belief systems. Preliminary analysis of National Reports and recent CoP decisions indicate that some of the frames constructed and strategically emphasized by the Secretariat have already begun to seep into the discourse and practice of some countries, in particular developing ones. This suggests that the Secretariat's marketing campaign is beginning to shift the incentive structure for countries with overriding development and adaptation concerns by making it more attractive for them to consider conservation as a tool in addressing those more pressing issues—in this case, adaptation and human security issues. The Secretariat has thus influenced the way these states understand problems and possible solutions at the climate-biodiversity interface—an impact that reflects changes in productive power relations.

Executive leadership also emerges in this case as a new and potentially important variable warranting future study. In the absence of Djoghlaf's strategic maneuvering around the Secretariat's restrictive CoP mandates on "biodiversity and climate change," it is unlikely that the Secretariat would have had any influence on overlap management at all. The impact of leadership likely has as much to do with a particular leader's cache of expertise as it does with his or her understanding of a secretariat's appropriate role in international affairs. Across treaty regimes, secretariat staff and state delegates interviewed for this study described executive secretaries in a variety of ways. Whereas some executive secretaries were seen to take an entrepreneurial approach in the secretariat's work, others were seen as much more conservative—reflecting a role for secretariats that is more in line with IR theory. The marketing campaign explored in this case is indicative of the former characterization and reflects the emerging domain of secretariat politics as "norm entrepreneurs" (Nadelmann 1990; Finnemore and Sikkink 1998).

Djoghlaf's approach clearly reflected entrepreneurial leadership. The content analysis above reveals that Djoghlaf strategically aimed to sell states conservation-focused solutions to climate adaptation issues. His expertise across CBD and climate politics coupled with his previous leadership position at the GEF suggest that he likely recognized how his framing of the linkage could attract additional resources for CBD implementation. That is, if CBD member states frame their conservation projects as adaptation projects, they also open themselves up to additional funding resources—including from the GEF and various mechanisms to fund adaptation in developing countries such as the UNFCCC's Adaptation Fund.

Although it is difficult to ascertain precisely how the CBD Secretariat would have influenced the overlap management politics (if at all) in the absence of its entrepreneurial leader, this case suggests that leadership conditions secretariat influence. While his predecessor, Zedan, initiated discussion on many of the frames that Djoghlaf brought to completion, the difference in marketing efforts and political uptake between these two leaders is remarkable. It remains unclear how the new executive secretary, Braulio F. de Souza Dias, will engage in CBD decision making in the years to come. Because the CBD Secretariat has historically made most, if not all, speeches given by its executive secretaries publicly available, this case is fertile ground for a future study on the importance of leadership in conditioning secretariat influence.

Finally, this case enriches our understanding of overlap management politics. Importantly, it highlights that overlap management is not just about the apolitical process of "maximizing synergies" and "minimizing conflicts" between regimes; rather, overlap management is a highly political process that creates winners and losers. The paths we choose, and who defines those paths, matter. The way in which overlap is framed has implications for which policy options states ultimately pursue. The CBD Secretariat encouraged states to develop climate adaptation projects that capitalized on the conservation benefits of adaptation. Although this focus presumably accrues benefits for conservation, it is unclear whether conservation-based adaptation is the best way to use growing, yet insufficient, adaptation funds. That is, if the primary goal of adaptation funding is to minimize impacts on human systems, it is unclear that allocating those funds for conservation projects maximizes progress toward that goal. Thus, marketing this particular framing of biodiversity-climate overlap may have net-negative impacts on human adaptation if those funds could have been used more efficiently. The dynamic of this case—in which a particular framing was marketed that prioritizes regime objectives, potentially over the aggregate interests of those states particularly vulnerable to climate change—highlights the role of secretariats as political actors who work to advance specific political interests.

6

Trade-Environment Politics at the WTO

Juridification has put the Secretariat in an impossible position. De jure they are not even players but facilitators of the play of others. That, of course, is a comforting nonsense.
—Former WTO panelist Joseph Weiler (2001, 205)

Overlap between trade and environmental issues hinges on the fact that trade liberalization contributes to environmental degradation.[1] More trade means more development and more consumption and, as a result, more resource use and more waste. Managing overlap is politically difficult because both environmental protection and economic development are laudable normative objectives, yet their relationship is colored by this underlying empirical tension. Further compounding this difficulty are the diverging policy approaches we have chosen to manage issues of trade and environmental protection across institutions (i.e., sanctions vs. environmental incentives) and the urgency demanded in both arenas. For example, over 1 billion people still live in "extreme poverty" (UN General Assembly 2012, 5), greenhouse gas concentrations recently surpassed 400 ppm over the Arctic (NOAA 2012), and we are expected to lose 50 percent or more of all species by the end of the twenty-first century (Myers 1993, 75).

States have made great efforts in recent years to manage and reconcile what has become a complicated terrain of overlapping rules and norms. For example, market mechanisms (e.g., emissions trading), which aim to achieve environmental objectives at the lowest possible cost, are now a central feature of many global environmental policies. Further, states have placed great stock in "sustainable development," and more recently "green growth," as grand compromises to reconcile the competing objectives of economic growth and environmental protection. These trends are reflected in the core themes of the 2012 Rio+20 Summit, wherein greening the economy was identified as the best way to reconcile these overlapping and rival interests (UN General Assembly 2012, 3).

As the quintessential brick-and-mortar face of global trade liberalization, the World Trade Organization (WTO) has been pulled, sometimes grudgingly, into the management of environmental issues. The WTO's approach to managing overlap with environmental issues is largely informal, internal, and in most areas quite limited. As highlighted in its Appellate Body decisions, it is far more normative than practical.[2] That is, rather than working with environmental organization partners to articulate concrete solutions in specific areas of overlapping concern, the WTO is figuring out *internally* how it understands its relationship to, and interaction with, environmental issues.

Among the many normative and procedural barriers to effectively mainstreaming environmental concerns into WTO politics is a stark ideological division among both WTO members[3] and Secretariat staff about the WTO's appropriate role in such issues. Highlighting these divisions within the Secretariat, one staff member interviewed for this study noted his divergence in opinion from Pascal Lamy, the recently replaced director general, who was an advocate of "triple-win" approaches to trade, environment, and development: "Lamy has a strong commitment to intergovernmental organizations (IGOs). He is a French socialist; he believes in global governance. I think this is a bunch of rubbish. In an economic context, it is the antithesis of what a market needs to function properly. Maybe it's useful in environmental issues, but I'm an economist, I don't know much about that." Despite the Secretariat's fractured understanding of its appropriate role in global governance beyond the trade realm, its ongoing activities within the Organization are slowly shaping the way trade-environment politics are understood and discussed within and outside the WTO.

The most visible and contentious site of trade-environment overlap management has long been the WTO's dispute settlement system. For example, the 2006 EC-Biotech case was a landmark decision with respect to clarifying how the WTO will legally approach its overlap with other bodies of international law (WTO Dispute Settlement Body 2006). In explicitly addressing the legal relationship between multilateral environmental agreements (MEAs) and the WTO for the first time, the WTO panel hearing the dispute asserted the primacy of international trade over environmental regimes. In short, the panel decided that it need not consider the provisions of the Convention on Biological Diversity's (CBD) Cartagena Protocol in evaluating the legality of the European

Community's regulations restricting biotech trade because not all parties to the WTO dispute were also parties to the Protocol.[4] This surprising decision, which undercut EU obligations under a key MEA, highlights both the significant role the WTO is playing in managing trade-environment overlap, as well as how little we know about the process by which these decisions are made.

As is detailed in the sections that follow, apart from the WTO's dispute settlement system, overlap management also occurs in at least two other less visible WTO forums: negotiations and discussions within the Committee on Trade and Environment in regular (CTE) and special sessions (CTESS), and the Trade-Related Aspects of Intellectual Property Rights (TRIPs) Council. For example, CTESS delegates consider possible tariff reductions on environmental goods, and the TRIPs Council addresses the relationship between WTO intellectual property rules and the protection of traditional knowledge as required under the CBD.[5]

This chapter explores how the WTO Secretariat participates in these processes. Although the seemingly endless Doha Round of trade negotiations and the Dispute Settlement Body's notoriously opaque processes make impacts particularly difficult to analyze in this case, this chapter argues that the WTO Secretariat influences trade-environment politics, albeit modestly, within the Organization. In managing overlap between trade and environmental issues, the Secretariat brokers knowledge and builds capacity in ways that enable certain countries to engage more effectively in trade-environment politics. In doing so, the Secretariat changes the structural and productive power relations between states.

Scholars have observed some of these impacts previously. Shaffer (2001, 18), for example, notes: "On the basis of their expertise, impartial reputation, inside information, and close contacts with trade diplomats, secretariat members can, at least at the margins, help shape knowledge, frame issues, identify interests, facilitate coalition-building, and thereby affect outcomes." However, as this chapter will show, these activities are not "marginal" as posited by Shaffer. Rather, they are important to WTO politics in their potential to redistribute authority between actors. Although these impacts are particularly difficult to measure due to data constraints, this chapter argues that they are most likely the result of Secretariat influence.

The remainder of the chapter is organized as follows. The subsequent section provides a brief organizational overview of the WTO, including a description of the Secretariat. The chapter then provides a summary of the politics surrounding trade-environment issues before delving into the Secretariat's role with respect to overlap management in two subcase studies of overlap management within the WTO. The analysis that follows applies the analytical framework presented in chapter 3 to evaluate whether the Secretariat influenced overlap management and tests the framework for explaining such influence in this case.

WTO: A Brief Overview

The WTO was established in 1995 following the Uruguay Round of trade negotiations as the organization responsible for housing and servicing not only a revamped version of its predecessor, the General Agreement on Tariffs and Trade of 1947 (GATT), but also a host of new international trade and trade-related agreements. There are sixteen such multilateral, and four plurilateral, agreements that emerged from the Uruguay Round covering such areas as trade in goods, dispute settlement, and rules for intellectual property protection, which the WTO is charged with overseeing. The primary function of the WTO is to provide a forum for trading partners to negotiate and settle disputes within the context of a set of binding rules aimed at liberalizing international trade in a nondiscriminatory manner.

The core of the organization is its membership. The WTO's 153 members negotiate and drive the policies that govern at least 95 percent of international trade (WTO Secretariat 2012).[6] The chief policy-making body is the Ministerial Conference, which consists of a representative from each member state and meets approximately every two years to make decisions on any matter related to any of the WTO agreements. Just below the Ministerial Conference is the General Council, also made up of one representative from each member state, which is responsible for the operation of the WTO in between Ministerial Conferences and makes all decisions by consensus. The General Council operates as the Dispute Settlement Body (DSB), administers the Trade Policy Review Mechanism, and oversees operation of all councils and committees including those established under the Ministerial Conference.

The General Council delegates responsibility for the day-to-day operation of the Organization to three councils on Goods, Services, and Trade-related Aspects of Intellectual Property Rights. These councils in turn establish committees to discuss the various aspects of their work. In 2001 the General Council established the Trade Negotiation Committee and various additional subcommittees in "special session," as well as groups to negotiate the various mandates contained in the Doha Development Agenda.

The WTO Secretariat services WTO members' needs by organizing meetings, taking minutes, and providing technical support. Its 646 regular staff, representing more than 70 nationalities, includes economists, trade lawyers, and other specialists in international trade. It is headed by a director general who oversees the Secretariat's 24 divisions and Appellate Body. The WTO's staff size and budget dwarf those of any of the biodiversity secretariats. In 2012, the WTO Secretariat's annual budget was CHF 189,962,500 (approximately USD 205,403,650), in comparison to the CBD's 2012 General Trust Fund (core) budget of USD 13,162,631 (WTO Secretariat 2012; CBD Secretariat 2012).[7]

The WTO's role in overlap management is diverse, as trade liberalization touches on countless other social issues, such as environment, labor, and development. Some "trade-plus" issues have been subsumed into the organization through specific legal agreements (e.g., intellectual property), while others, such as the environment, remain more peripheral. Overlap between trade and environmental rules and norms plays out primarily through the WTO's dispute settlement process and the ongoing Doha Round of negotiations. On the former, some WTO agreements (e.g., the GATT and the Agreement on Sanitary and Phytosanitary Measures) contain provisions that attempt to reconcile potential conflicts between trade liberalization and environmental protection. These provisions, however, do not provide clear direction and have been interpreted many times by the WTO's dispute settlement system. On the latter, the Doha Declaration—which guides the contemporary round of WTO negotiations—mandates members to negotiate on specific environmental issues (e.g., possible tariff reductions for environmental goods). These negotiations have remained stalled for quite some time.

Like United Nations (UN) Secretariats, the WTO Secretariat also has fixed and evolving mandates. Its fixed mandate is contained in Article VI of the Marrakesh Agreement establishing the WTO (WTO 1994). As with the UN secretariats, states expect the WTO Secretariat to be structured hierarchically, international in character, and responsible for meeting the evolving needs of member states. The mandate remains silent, however, on Secretariat functions—leaving those to be determined by the Ministerial Conference.

The fixed mandate is also silent on any overlap management functions for the Secretariat. Instead, the WTO Secretariat's capacity to influence overlap management between the WTO and various environmental regimes is built into the Secretariat's organizational structure. The WTO Secretariat has a division specifically dedicated to supporting work on issues of overlap between trade and environmental issues (i.e., the Division on Trade and Environment (DTE)). The DTE does not have an individualized fixed mandate; its work on overlap management is largely determined by its informal evolving mandates from member states.

The Politics of Trade-Environment Overlap at the WTO

The WTO's treatment of trade-environment overlap has a long history. The organizers of the 1972 UN Conference on the Human Environment asked the GATT (1947) Secretariat to draft a paper analyzing the trade impacts of environmental policies. GATT contracting parties subsequently established the Group on Environmental Measures in International Trade (EMIT) to examine the issue in more detail. However, the group didn't convene until the early 1990s when the European Free Trade Association requested that EMIT be convened for the first time in order to make a contribution to the upcoming UN Conference on Environment and Development (UNCED, or the "Rio Earth Summit") (WTO Secretariat 2013c). As such, in its early days, overlap management between trade and environmental issues within the WTO was predominantly characterized by concerns that environmental policies were being used as a smoke screen for protectionism (i.e., green protectionism).

In the lead-up to EMIT's first meeting, however, the classic divisions between developed and developing countries surrounding trade-environmental politics was beginning to take shape. For example, at the 1982 Ministerial meeting, several developing countries expressed concern about developed countries exporting domestically banned hazardous products to developing countries, and in 1991 US environmental activists expressed outrage over the outcome in the famous tuna/dolphin case. In the latter, a GATT panel had ruled in favor of Mexico, striking down a US environmental policy aimed at dolphin conservation—although never adopted, this case set the tone for environment-related dispute settlement for the next decade (WTO Secretariat 2013b).

The next milestone in trade-environment politics was the creation of the CTE in 1994 to consider the effects of environmental policies on trade, the relationship between MEAs and the WTO, and the transparency of environmental policies that impact trade (WTO Secretariat 2013c). Although the CTE's mandate more deeply integrates trade and environmental issues, the CTE has made little progress. WTO members have resisted incorporating environment-friendly policies into the trade regime, and the CTE has also been stymied by the fundamental divisions between developed and developing countries over the appropriate role of environmental issues within the WTO. For example, the United States and European Union have long resisted developing country demands for reductions in their agricultural subsidies, and also disagree with developing countries on the appropriate mode of liberalizing trade in environmental goods and services (Hoda and Gulati 2008). Further, as Neumayer (2004, 7) points out, the "nearly unanimous" opposition to environment-friendly WTO policies from the developing world can be explained in part by concerns about green protectionism, but ultimately they derive from deeper concerns that the distribution of WTO benefits is strongly skewed toward the developed countries.

WTO Secretariat Participation in Overlap Management

This section examines two subcases of overlap management within the WTO. Specifically, it examines how the WTO Secretariat participates in overlap management within environment-related negotiations and dispute settlement.[8] The subsequent section evaluates whether, and if so, how, these overlap management activities impact trade-environment politics by identifying any instances where such activities shaped power relations between states. In such instances, the Secretariat can be said to have influenced trade-environment politics.

WTO Subcase #1: The Secretariat Division on Trade and Environment
Paragraph 31 of the 2001 Doha Declaration outlines the WTO's first negotiating mandate on trade-environment overlap.[9] It mandates negotiations on the relationship between WTO rules and specific trade obligations set out in MEAs; procedures for information exchange between MEA secretariats and relevant WTO committees, along with criteria for granting observer status; and reducing or eliminating tariff and nontariff barriers to environmental goods and services. The CTESS negotiates these issues, and the Secretariat's DTE was assigned responsibility to service this new negotiating body—placing it at the center of WTO politics surrounding trade-environment overlap management.[10]

This section examines how the DTE carries out this work. It explains how the DTE participates in trade-environment politics at the WTO by providing negotiation support, hosting workshops, speaking at MEA conferences, and managing the WTO's public image.

The DTE's functions during CTESS meetings are rather banal—essentially limited to taking minutes and responding to direct requests from members.[11] However, as most WTO delegates are not experts on environmental politics, many of these requests ask the DTE to produce background documents on trade-relevant MEAs. As one interviewee explained, "We write documents for members informing them of issues from an environmental perspective, such as why the Montreal Protocol has a trade embargo on certain substances, or why the Basel Convention does what it does, or how the CBD rules fit within TRIPs." As of November 2007, the DTE had submitted 41 out of 119 (34 percent) documents to the CTE/CTESS on MEA-overlap issues, whereas all other IGOs collectively made 74 submissions (62 percent), and members made only 3 submissions (2.5 percent).[12]

The WTO Secretariat's DTE also works in less formal settings during negotiating rounds. State and Secretariat interviewees noted that informal communication makes up the bulk of many members' contact with the Secretariat. Informal communication includes undocumented interactions or requests made outside of CTESS meetings, often via phone or "in the corridors." Describing the informal communication between the Secretariat and members, one Secretariat interviewee reported: "In the context of a committee, we provide members with information; they can ask me about anything informally. [It] could be my personal opinion if I've heard anything lately about what is going on in CITES [Convention on International Trade in Endangered Species], or it could be a technical question about the history of negotiations."

The DTE also organizes regional technical assistance workshops. These workshops aim to increase the negotiation capacity of developing countries by helping capital-based trade delegates better understand trade-environment politics. Specifically, the workshops are designed to "raise awareness on the linkages between trade, environment and sustainable development and to promote greater dialogue between trade and environment policy-makers at national levels."[13] In addition to making their own presentations for members, the Secretariat typically invites IGOs such as the United Nations Environment Program (UNEP) or the UN Conference on Trade and Development (UNCTAD) to attend these workshops and present on issues related to the environment or sustainable development. The DTE organized approximately twenty-eight such workshops between February 1999 and December 2007 in various regions.

The DTE also participates directly in environmental conferences. It regularly attends MEA conferences to make formal presentations to member states and to host less formal side events. At the MEA conferences, many MEAs that use trade measures as a means to achieve their objectives have a standing item on their negotiating agenda that addresses their relationship with the WTO.[14] The DTE often attends these meetings to update delegates on what the WTO is doing of relevance to the specific MEA, and to clarify misunderstandings about these processes. For example, at a 2007 CITES Standing Committee meeting in Geneva, the WTO responded to CITES delegates' agitation regarding the MEAs' inability to secure permanent observership in the CTE/CTESS. The DTE explained that CTESS delegates do not necessarily object to granting observer status to MEAs on principle; rather, they cannot do so because of an overall freeze in observership approvals by the General Council resulting from a political dispute over the official status of other organizations such as the League of Arab States (personal observation 2007; Motaal 2002).

The Secretariat participated in eleven side events at MEA forums between 2002 and 2005, including the Rotterdam Convention, CITES, and the Basel Convention (WTO Secretariat 2007b). These events tend to focus on educating external actors about WTO politics. At the climate change Conference of the Parties (CoP) in Nairobi in December 2006, for instance, a representative of the DTE participated in a nongovernmental organization (NGO)/government coorganized side event, entitled "Trade, Climate Change and the Sustainable Energy Transition: Framing the Debate." The WTO Secretariat's presentation was primarily informative in character, summarizing the CTESS discussion of environmental goods with an emphasis on the negotiating process, member positions, and those goods which have been proposed for listing based on climate-friendly characteristics.

Finally, in the face of harsh criticism from environmental and labor groups, the DTE participates in managing the WTO's public image. For example, the Secretariat now makes many previously internal documents available on the WTO website and hosts online public "chat" sessions with former Director General Lamy. In addition, the Secretariat has produced various documents to make the WTO processes more accessible to the public, such as a book of one-page summaries of WTO disputes[15] and a matrix describing WTO/MEA overlap.[16]

In summary, the DTE participates in trade-environment politics at the WTO in five key ways: providing formal and informal negotiation support, hosting workshops, speaking at MEA conferences, and managing the WTO's public image.

WTO Subcase #2: The Secretariat's Role in Dispute Settlement

This final WTO case illuminates the Secretariat's role in supporting dispute settlement. It focuses on how the DTE supports environment-related disputes (GATT 1947, Article XX) at the panel level (as opposed to the Appellate level).[17] Although most panel disputes are appealed, which dilutes Secretariat influence, the unappealed EC-Biotech case cited above demonstrates that the Secretariat's role at the panel level can nonetheless be quite important.

Dispute settlement at the panel level begins with allocating Secretariat staff members to a case and selecting panelists (i.e., justices) to hear that case. Three Secretariat staff members are assigned to each case brought to the WTO: two from the Legal Affairs Division and one from the specialized division most relevant to the dispute in question. For example, the DTE supports panels in all environmental, or GATT Article XX, disputes. The Secretariat's activity in this regard is delegated via mandate: "the Secretariat shall have the responsibility of assisting panels, especially on the legal, historical, and procedural aspects of the matters dealt with, and of providing secretarial and technical support."[18] Within this mandate, the Secretariat's functions in supporting the settlement of panel-level disputes fall into four categories, corresponding to the phase of the dispute: panel formation, selection of panelists, informational support, and drafting decisions.[19]

First, once a member requests the formation of a panel, the Secretariat begins to perform its purely administrative tasks. These tasks include coordinating communication and meetings between parties to the dispute, notifying them of deadlines, and collecting and distributing all information submitted related to the dispute. In addition, at this phase of the dispute (as well as in any other phase), the director general can facilitate mediation between parties to foster a settlement.

The second phase of dispute settlement involves the selection of panelists. Panelists are selected on an ad hoc basis from a roster of experts nominated by WTO members. These nominees are people the members consider competent to serve on any panel at some point (i.e., names are not submitted for a specific dispute). The Secretariat compiles these names and maintains the roster, which contains approximately 200 names.[20] The Secretariat then nominates three people from the roster to serve as panelists for a particular dispute. The parties to the dispute can then accept the proposed panel or, if a "compelling reason" (WTO 2007, Article 8.6) exists, reject the Secretariat's proposed slate. If, within twenty days of the establishment of the panel, there is no agreement on panelists, either party can request that the director general compose the panel and, after consulting with the chairman of the Dispute Settlement Body and of the relevant council or committee, can choose a slate of people whom she or he considers "most appropriate" (WTO 2007, Article 8.7).

While the dispute settlement section of the WTO's 2007 Annual Report states that "the DSB has the sole responsibility to establish dispute settlement panels,"[21] the WTO website and most Secretariat-produced documents do not document how the DSB established specific panels (WTO 2007c, 1–172). Although this pattern makes it difficult to assess definitively how many Article XX dispute panels were composed by the director general's suggestion in recent years, studies of early disputes report that between 1995 and 2000 the director general selected panelists 40 percent of the time, and this number is on the rise (Davey 2002, 502; 2004). This is supported by interviews with staff within the DTE, who said that most, if not all, panels for Article XX disputes have been selected by the director general. Indeed, one interviewee noted: "parties rarely agree on the Secretariat's initial nominations, leaving the director general with the de facto final decision in the matter."[22]

During the third phase of dispute settlement, the Secretariat advises panelists by providing them with information related to the specific dispute they are hearing. This information takes the form of both interpretive legal guidance and technical information about specific cases. On the former, for example, one Secretariat staff member said: "We provide a fact sheet that explains what has been decided in the past regarding Article XX. ... We bring order to case law and present it in a user-friendly manner. We provide the panelists with a table, a complete picture of the case law but we never say what it means. We look at a variety of definitions of 'necessary' for example, from the dictionary and the ways it has been interpreted in the past. The Secretariat's role is really helping the panel understand the facts of the case." On this final point, panelists often rely on the Secretariat for guidance on technical matters, in part due to the sheer volume of information that accompanies most disputes. For example, in reference to a recent dispute, one Secretariat interviewee noted:

The first thing the Secretariat does is look at all the submissions that come in. There is way too much paper for the panelists to dig through. For example, you would need a dump truck to move all the paper that came in with the recent [X] dispute. We disentangle and summarize all the documents. We get input from both sides regarding what the panel should look at and we ask them to tell us what more analysis they want us to do. The panel has two sources of information, us and the parties involved in the dispute.

Finally, in phase four of dispute settlement, panelists often rely on the Secretariat to aid in drafting decisions. Although interviews suggest that the Secretariat plays an important role in this regard, interviewees were resistant to providing much detail about the Secretariat's role in the drafting process—most likely because the stakes of dispute settlement are so high. Nevertheless, former Secretariat staff member Petros Mavroidis has noted that the "Secretariat plays a much more active role than meets the eye that is confined to a reading of the DSU: essentially, almost all panel reports are being drafted by the WTO Secretariat, panelists reacting to a draft received" (Mavroidis 2005, 4).

Understanding Secretariat Influence

As detailed above, the WTO Secretariat performs a wide variety of activities in its efforts to manage overlap between trade and environmental issues. This section evaluates whether such activities impacted trade-environment politics by shaping power relations between states. If Secretariat activities did yield such impacts, then the Secretariat can be said to have influenced overlap management politics at the WTO. This chapter ultimately argues that secretariat influence was different with respect to developed countries, developing countries, and panelists. Developing countries relied on the DTE to a greater extent when preparing for dispute settlement than did the developed countries: thus, the Secretariat had weak and no influence, respectively. It also argues that the DTE shapes panel decisions by providing panelists themselves with information used for decision making and by drafting decisions, and thus exerts moderate influence with respect to panelists.

Did the Secretariat Exert Influence?

This book argues that secretariats influence overlap management when mechanisms of influence (e.g., knowledge brokering, capacity building, marketing, negotiation/litigation facilitation) are empirically observable and can be traced to changes in power relations between states, and alternative explanations for such changes can be eliminated. For a review of the three-step process used to assess whether the Secretariat was able to exert influence, see chapter 3 (figure 3.1).

Mechanisms of Influence?   Two closely related mechanisms of influence are evident in both subcases: knowledge brokering and capacity building. In servicing the CTESS (Subcase #1), the Secretariat's DTE engages in five key activities: formal and informal negotiation support, organizing workshops, speaking at MEA conferences, and managing the WTO's public image. In carrying out all of these activities, the DTE brokers knowledge about trade-environment issues. Importantly, these activities build capacity among its membership to engage on environmental issues. For example, the DTE provides WTO members with background information on such things as negotiation process and history. The Secretariat also engages in capacity building through its workshops and by speaking at MEA conferences, and provides external organizations with information about the status of environmental politics within the WTO.

Moreover, the Secretariat brokers knowledge that facilitates litigation (Subcase #2). For example, it filters and frames information that reaches panelists from parties and interested observers. The Secretariat also facilitates litigation through its central role in selecting panels to hear individual disputes and, critically, in helping those panelists to draft decisions (Mavroidis 2005).

Change in Power Relations?   The mere presence of mechanisms of influence, however, does not mean that influence occurred. In order to confirm influence, we must first determine whether the mechanisms of influence identified in the above discussion yielded impacts that reflect changes in power relations between states. This section argues that the Secretariat's overlap management activities did yield such impacts. In particular, the Secretariat's role in shaping the flow and availability of information shapes the way that *some* states understand trade-environment issues and, in doing so, changes the relative capacities of developed and developing countries to engage in overlap management. As explained in chapter 3, because these impacts shape shared norms and ideas that, in turn, restructure relationships between developed and developing countries, they reflect changes in productive and structural power relations respectively.

This section examines how the Secretariat's DTE changes power relations between member states within negotiations and dispute settlement respectively. Because most of the WTO's work happens behind closed doors (Weiler 2001), tracing impacts through document analysis is much more difficult than in the other cases explored in this book. However, insider accounts (e.g., Jawara and Kwa 2004; Weiler 2001; Mavroidis 2005) and interviews provide strong evidence that the WTO Secretariat is indeed shaping the shared norms and ideas surrounding overlap management.

DTE Negotiations (Subcase #1)   Decision-making structures are important in understanding how the Secretariat's DTE shaped power relations in WTO negotiations. WTO negotiations are consensus-based and operate within the framework of the "single undertaking" in that "nothing is agreed until everything is agreed." Negotiations are also characterized by a pattern of reciprocal concessions that reflect the dynamic of a zero sum game or Pareto efficiency, wherein, for any individual actor, gains on one issue typically correspond with losses on another. This does not preclude the neoliberal assumption that all actors benefit from trade liberalization. Rather, it suggests that these benefits are not distributed evenly, but are a function of actors' relative capacity to reap those benefits.

Due to the technical nature of trade politics, including their relation to environmental issues, expertise is a good proxy for a state's capacity to reap benefits. Therefore, changes in the distribution of expertise between members can have important impacts on the ability of members to reap regime benefits. If such increases in capacity are evenly distributed, then structural power relations are not implicated because relative capacities remain unchanged. If, however, changes in capacities aid some states more than others, structural power relations are implicated because the recipient states' capacities increase relative to those states who do not receive such assistance.

The Secretariat's knowledge-brokering and -building activities are central in enhancing state expertise. The Secretariat's workshops and informal consultations with members provide member states with background information, such as negotiation histories and technical advice. Capacity-building workshops are clearly aimed at developing countries specifically, and several interviewees noted that the Secretariat's informal information provision activities are also much more important for developing countries than for developed ones. As one Secretariat interviewee explained: "Many new delegates rely on the Secretariat to ask about where the negotiations are at, at a particular point in time. But this depends on the countries. Developing countries rely on us more than developed countries, who tend to have very clear positions and tend to ask us for more clerical assistance." In providing this information, the Secretariat arms underresourced member states with information necessary to better negotiate trade-environment issues. Because this changes the *relative* capacities between states, this impact reflects a structural change in power relations between developed and developing countries.

In supplying WTO member states with such information, the Secretariat likely shapes the way states understand trade-environment issues. For example, previous scholars have reported that the Secretariat drafts informal documents that later form the basis of consensus texts (Shaffer 2002a, 377). Although these activities may seem to involve straightforward transfers of information, there is considerable variation in simple— yet central—ideas, such as how members understand what it means for an environmental issue to be "trade-relevant."[23] These background documents and draft texts help to frame discussions within the CTE/CTESS by determining which MEAs are relevant, how they intersect with the WTO, and how the WTO can, has, or should address this overlap.

Although Secretariat staff interviewed for this study characterized its knowledge-brokering and capacity-building activities as "neutral," some of the state actors interviewed said that the Secretariat's preferences for negotiation outcomes frame these events. Some ministers of African countries have even described a Secretariat capacity-building workshop as an "attempt at manipulation" (Hormeku 2001, 2). This speaks to Neumayer's point noted above that trade-environment politics are undergirded by distrust among developing countries about the distribution of benefits under the WTO.

In summary, therefore, the DTE's activities impact countries in different ways. That developing countries are more reliant on Secretariat support is not entirely surprising but is nonetheless quite important, because by enabling these countries to negotiate more effectively, the Secretariat both changes the relative capacities between developed and developing countries and possibly steers states (intentionally or not) toward specific negotiating preferences. In doing so, the DTE changes both the structural and productive power relations between states.

DTE Dispute Settlement (Subcase #2) A similar dynamic is at play in dispute resolution, wherein developing countries also have less capacity to engage in disputes than do developed countries (Urpelainen 2012, 705). This can be explained in part by the exorbitant costs involved in dispute settlement (Bown and Hoekman 2005). Developing countries, therefore, rely more heavily on external sources of free support, including the Secretariat (Jones 2010). As described above, the Secretariat helps these countries to build litigation capacity by, for example, providing them with information about how GATT Article XX has been interpreted in the past, technical information about the environmental issue being considered, and/or with more general legal assistance. As Weiler (2001, 205) explains, "In dispute settlement the Secretariat is meant to be a purveyor of objective legal advice and legal services to Panels. *De facto,* inevitably and importantly, they are a repository of institutional memory, of horizontal and temporal coherence, and a long term hermeneutic strategy—all things that the Panel system ... should be but is unable to be." Because developing countries are more reliant on Secretariat expertise than developed countries are, the Secretariat shapes power relations in dispute settlement in the same way it did in negotiations. That is, it changes the relative capacities of countries to engage in dispute settlement—an impact that reflects structural power.

Secretariat influence also shapes power relations between states by changing the way panelists rule on disputes and, accordingly, how rules and norms surrounding environmental issues are understood within the WTO. These impacts reflect changes in structural and, arguably, institutional power relations between states.

As discussed above, the director general plays a central role in deciding who will serve as panelists for each WTO dispute. The inconsistent interpretation of certain GATT Article XX provisions underscores the intuitive notion that outcomes partly depend on who is making the decisions.[24] The Secretariat also plays a central role in filtering information for panelists and in drafting dispute settlement decisions (Mavroidis 2005). Because panelists are ad hoc, often have full-time jobs elsewhere, and therefore most often have little time to spare, they often rely heavily on the Secretariat for organizing, framing, and prioritizing information (Mavroidis 2005). These activities impact the way panelists understand legal rights and obligations (Howse 2005), which in turn influences how panelists decide on environmental cases and shapes broader understandings of these issues among member states. As described by former panelist Professor Joseph Weiler (2001, 206): "The Secretariat ends up giving (and pushing) 'objective' legal advice, which, inevitably, favors one of the parties over the other. This is an uncomfortable truth that members somehow prefer not to recognize. This advice has huge influence over Panelists." Howse (2005) comes to a similar conclusion, noting that

Secretariat documents may influence WTO panels' interpretation of legal rights and obligations in the WTO.

In summary, in shaping both how panelists are constituted and how they understand and make rules that shape broader WTO understandings of environmental issues, the Secretariat changes productive power relations between states, and possibly institutional power relations as well. More broadly, in managing trade-environment overlap, the WTO Secretariat shapes productive, and possibly institutional, power relations between states by brokering knowledge and building capacity. These activities impact how states understand issues within environmental negotiations and dispute settlement. When such activities also change the relative capacities of states to engage in these decision-making processes, the Secretariat also changes the structural power relations between states.

Alternative Explanations?   The WTO Secretariat enjoys a level of access to the WTO processes and membership not afforded to many outside organizations. The WTO is a notoriously closed organization (Weiler 2001), with little opportunity for formal input from outside actors. It is therefore unlikely that outside organizations are as important in building developing country capacity *within* the WTO. Further, because dispute settlement proceedings are typically closed to outside organizations, it is very unlikely that the Secretariat's influence on dispute settlement outcomes can be explained by interventions from another actor.

Nevertheless, there are several Geneva-based organizations, such as the South Centre and the UNCTAD, that do actively work to build developing country capacity on trade-environment issues. These capacity-building activities are likely most important in environmental negotiations and in helping developing countries to engage in dispute settlement. Thus, the Secretariat is likely only one of several actors to influence overlap management in these instances. Although this tempers the Secretariat's ability to shape productive power relations (i.e., because other actors are competing to shape shared understandings), changes in structural power relations are only enhanced by additional outside support. That is, the Secretariat need not be the only actor changing relative capacities in order to be an important actor in changing relative capacities.

In terms of what this means for the strength of Secretariat influence, the DTE does not appear to influence developed countries in negotiations, because they do not tend to request analytical information from the Secretariat. In contrast, the DTE does provide such information to developing countries, but competes with NGOs in this regard. As explained in chapter 3, influence is considered weak in cases where the secretariat changes the flow and/or availability of information that some states use in decision making. As such, DTE influence on developing countries in negotiations is present, but *weak* and *absent* with respect to developed countries. Further, influence on developing countries may be especially weak in this case due to the competition from NGOs to provide this information.

A similar pattern of influence is evident in dispute settlement with respect to how developed and developing countries prepare for and engage in dispute settlement. Developing countries rely more heavily on the Secretariat than do developed countries for legal support and information—reflecting *weak* and *no influence*, respectively. However, because the Secretariat shapes panel decisions by providing panelists themselves with information used for decision making and, critically, by drafting decisions, the DTE exerts *moderate* influence on panelists and their decisions. As explained in chapter 3, moderate influence is that which shapes state practices; in this case, the Secretariat shapes state practice indirectly, by shaping dispute settlement outcomes to which states must (and do) respond.

Why Was the Secretariat Able to Exert Influence?

The framework presented in chapter 3 posits that secretariats are most likely to influence politics when the functions they perform enjoy low substitutability and state preferences are weakly solidified. This section tests this framework in the WTO context.

Preference Solidification   In evaluating the nature of state preferences, issue newness and state mandates are particularly instructive. Mandates give us a sense of how states cost preference development and/or unfavorable outcomes. As explained in chapter 3, state mandates that are administrative and restrict a secretariat's interpretive ability reflect strongly solidified preferences, whereas those that are analytical and allow for a secretariat to interpret how a mandate should be fulfilled (i.e., open-ended) reflect weakly solidified preferences. Mandates that are analytical but restrictive are understood as moderately solidified in this study (see table 3.3). The more strongly solidified state preferences are, the less likely a secretariat will be able to influence overlap management (see table 3.5).

In this case, the issues involved are not new; states have been discussing environmental issues within the WTO since the Doha mandate was agreed on in 1999. Further, dispute settlement on environmental issues predates the WTO itself, with some of the most contentious cases dating back to the early 1990s under the GATT. Environmental issues therefore are not new in the WTO context, making weakly solidified preferences unlikely.

Before turning to state mandates, it should be noted that state preferences on environmental issues within the WTO are widely understood as divided. States have strong normative opinions about whether environment-friendly policies should be included in WTO politics at all. Whereas developed countries generally support inclusion of these issues, developing countries are "nearly unanimously opposed" (Neumayer 2004, 7). We see these divisions playing out in WTO adjudication and negotiations on environmental issues.

With regard to adjudication, most GATT environment-related cases have pitted developed and developing countries against one another. Of the five GATT Article XX disputes that have been heard and concluded by the WTO since it was established in 1995, all but one (2001 EU-Canada Asbestos) have involved a dispute between developed and developing countries. In three of these cases, developing countries challenged a US environmental regulation as being under the banner of green protectionism (2001 India etc.-US Shrimp/Turtle, 1996 Venezuela-US Reformulated Gasoline, and 2012 Mexico-US Tuna/Dolphin). In all three cases, the United States lost because its policies were found to be discriminatory. One notable exception to this trend is the 2009 Brazil-EU Retreaded Tires case. In this case, the EU challenged a Brazilian environmental law, which was also struck down for being discriminatory. We see similar divisions in environment-related negotiations. For example, during the CTESS discussions surrounding environmental goods and services, developed and developing countries have been at loggerheads for many years about the right approach to trade liberalization in this area (Crosby et al. 2010; WTO CTESS 2006a, 2006b, 2007, 2008). These divisions characterize much of the WTO's environment-related disputes and negotiations, suggesting that state preferences are either moderately or strongly solidified in this case.

These direct empirical observations of state preferences support conclusions based on the framework presented in chapter 3. The framework posits that restrictive analytical mandates reflect moderately solidified state preferences. As detailed above, members often request that the

Secretariat produce analyses of trade-environment issues but limit those analyses in specific ways. For example, they have requested that the Secretariat analyze how the WTO overlaps with a list of specified MEAs (WTO Secretariat 2013a), and how the dispute settlement body has treated specific issues, such as the use of taxes for environmental purposes (WTO Secretariat 1997). These informal mandates are analytical yet restrictive because they articulate which data should be used to conduct the analyses. They therefore reflect moderately solidified preferences.

There is, however, variation among countries in terms of preference solidification in this case. Some WTO Secretariat staff interviewees noted, for example, that developing countries' preferences are less well developed (i.e., more weakly solidified) with respect to informal channels of information provision on trade-environment issues than are those of developed countries. One interviewee said that developing countries often request analytical support, such as negotiation and/or litigation analyses, whereas developed countries' requests tend to be more administrative in nature. This difference is not surprising and is supported by accounts of the capacity constraints related to developing countries' participation in the WTO more broadly (Jawara and Kwa 2004). This suggests that whereas some developing countries may have moderately solidified preferences, developed countries' preferences are actually strongly solidified.

Finally, we must also evaluate the preferences of dispute resolution panelists who are also recipients of the Secretariat's knowledge-brokering activities. We cannot, of course, look to mandates per se, since panelists do not give mandates. Rather, we must look to practice—what the Secretariat actually does to support panelists. Former Secretariat staff indicate that almost all panel decisions are initially drafted by the Secretariat (Mavroidis 2005)—a highly analytical and open-ended mandate. This provides strong evidence that panel preferences are, at best, moderately solidified in this case and possibly even weakly solidified. It is difficult to make this determination definitively due to a lack of access to data, such as specific mandates, so this study conservatively categorizes panel preferences as moderately solidified.

Preference solidification is thus variable in this case depending on which group of actors we are evaluating. Whereas informal mandates suggest that developed countries' preferences are strongly solidified on trade-environment issues, they simultaneously suggest that developing country preferences are only moderately solidified. Further, the nature of

Secretariat participation in dispute resolution reveals that panelist preferences are also at most moderately solidified on these issues. This variation is important in highlighting how secretariat influence can change depending on who the object of influence is.

Substitutability If secretariat overlap management functions could not have been carried out by another available actor, then those functions enjoy low substitutability and secretariat influence is more likely. As explained in chapter 3, substitutability decreases as secretariat access to key decision-making forums increases relative to the access of other actors, and competition from outside actors decreases (see table 3.4). Both access and competition can be qualitatively evaluated by examining participation rules and practice. As with preference solidification, substitutability of the WTO Secretariat's overlap management functions varies in this case. Although access remains constant in both negotiations and dispute settlement, competition varies across these forums.

Within WTO politics, the Secretariat has deep access to decision-making forums, both in negotiations and in dispute settlement. In negotiations, observers are permitted into CTESS discussions only on an ad hoc basis and are given little opportunity to contribute to the discussion through verbal or written interventions. During dispute settlements, observers are not allowed inside the room at all, and panels are not required to consider written submissions that outside organizations may produce. In contrast, the Secretariat does enjoy these participation benefits. It is present at dispute settlement proceedings and CTESS negotiations, and can make submissions on a restricted basis to the latter. The Secretariat is also deeply involved in panel selection and support, as well as capacity building for both negotiations and dispute settlement. Based on these decision rules and practices regarding access, therefore, the Secretariat enjoys deep access rights in comparison to other outside actors.

Despite this deep access, the Secretariat faces strong competition from outside actors to broker knowledge to WTO member states. Competition is high for the Secretariat's knowledge-brokering activities during CTE/CTESS negotiations. There are several NGOs (e.g., International Center for Trade and Sustainable Development) and IGOs (e.g., United Nations Conference on Trade and Sustainable Development, South Centre) that specialize in trade-environment issues, regularly lobby governments, organize workshops and capacity-building activities, and produce papers and analyses on trade-environment politics within the WTO (Crosby et al. 2010). Although these organizations have limited formal access to key decision-making forums within the WTO, several interviewees noted the great efforts these groups make to provide knowledge-brokering services outside the WTO's walls, and Secretariat staff noted that they sometimes reach out to these organizations informally for their input. Based on the framework presented in chapter 3, therefore, the substitutability of the Secretariat's overlap management functions is moderate because competition is strong and access is deep.

On knowledge brokering for dispute resolution panelists, however, the Secretariat faces very low competition. Whereas interviews and previous research confirm that the Secretariat is often called upon to filter and frame information (e.g., technical information and/or past case law) for dispute resolution panels, panelists need not accept submissions from outside actors and tend not to request such submissions. Further, as noted above, the Secretariat enjoys far deeper access than outside organizations to dispute settlement proceedings. Therefore, competition for Secretariat functions is effectively absent in this instance. As such, because access is deep and competition is absent from outside actors in dispute settlement, the substitutability of the Secretariat's knowledge-brokering activities for panelists is very low.

In summary, preference solidification and substitutability vary within and across the subcases examined in this chapter (tables 6.1 and 6.2).

Table 6.1
Preference Solidification across Cases

	Developed Countries	Developing Countries	Dispute Resolution Panelists
Preference Solidification	Strong	Moderate	Moderate

Table 6.2
Substitutability across Subcases

	Developed Countries	Developing Countries	Dispute Resolution Panelists
Access	Deep	Deep	Deep
Competition	Strong	Strong	None
Substitutability	Moderate	Moderate	Very low

Table 6.3
Summary of Findings—WTO

Cases	Preference Solidification	Substitutability	Predicted Influence	Observed Influence
Negotiations/ Dispute Settlement (Developed Countries)	Strong	Moderate	Unlikely	**None**
Negotiations/ Dispute Settlement (Developing Countries)	Moderate	Moderate	Possible	**Weak**
Dispute Settlement (Panelists)	Moderate	Very low	Likely	**Moderate**

This variation in substitutability and preference solidification across subcases helps to explain the variation in secretariat influence observed across these cases and aligns with the general predictions of the framework presented in chapter 3 for predicting the likelihood of Secretariat influence (table 6.3).

Conclusions

Although its mandates are more restrictive in comparison to those of the CBD Secretariat examined in chapters 4 and 5, the WTO Secretariat still manages to influence trade-environment politics by shifting the structural and productive power relations between states. It shapes structural relations by building developing countries' capacity to engage on environmental issues, and shapes productive power relations by shaping the way states and panelists understand and respond to environmental issues.

It is important to underscore, however, that Secretariat influence in this case is variable across functions and depending on what the object of influence is. Importantly, in environmental negotiations, the Secretariat is able to weakly influence developing countries in negotiations through information provision, yet it is unable to influence developed countries in this context. Moreover, Secretariat influence is indirect in dispute settlement, with Secretariat activities impacting panel decisions, which in turn shape state behavior—reflecting moderate influence in this subcase.

The WTO case helps us to better understand how bureaucratic influence operates in global governance. The relationship between the Secretariat and WTO member states fits a standard principal-agent framework very closely. The WTO Secretariat largely responds to direct mandates from member states and does not actively seek to expand its zone of discretion. Yet differentials in capacity among principals create room for the Secretariat to shape power relations between states by enhancing underresourced states' capacity to engage in trade-environment politics.

This case also underscores arguments that institutional structures condition the ability of secretariats to influence politics. The WTO's consensus-based "single undertaking" approach to negotiations, as well as the ad hoc nature of dispute settlement, are critically important in understanding why the WTO Secretariat was able to exert influence. The "single undertaking" approach creates a zero sum game among negotiators. This structure magnifies the importance of the Secretariat's knowledge-brokering activities, because its influence increases developing countries' capacity to negotiate. The ad hoc nature of panels, coupled with the WTO's closed organizational culture, further enable Secretariat influence. These factors create conditions in which the Secretariat's overlap management functions have very low substitutability and, despite much outside expertise in trade-environment issues, the Secretariat faces low competition in performing its overlap management functions.

This case also yields important insights for the politics of overlap management. Importantly, WTO Secretariat staff asserted that cooperation failures between trade and environment ministries/departments at the domestic level are a significant barrier to effective overlap management at the international level. These interviewees explained that whereas some developed countries, such as the United States and United Kingdom, have relatively well-developed domestic networks for communication across trade and environmental ministries/departments, most developing countries lack institutions for cross-issue coordination. In the United States, for example, coordination occurs through an interagency task force on trade and environment. Such mechanisms are rare in developing countries, as is reflected in UNEP's ongoing work to build developing countries' capacity in this regard (UNEP 2004). This suggests that the degree of domestic (in)coherence between relevant ministries may be an important variable to consider in future studies of overlap management effectiveness.

Finally, and perhaps most importantly, this case highlights some major problems associated with secretariat influence in global governance.[25] On the one hand, the WTO Secretariat influence has important legitimacy-enhancing impacts such as increasing the transparency, information flow, and access to the Organization—all topics on which the WTO has been heavily criticized (Oxfam 2000). On the other hand, Secretariat influence also includes legitimacy-eroding impacts resulting from concerns about Secretariat accountability and bias. Indeed, accountability mechanisms are all but absent from the Secretariat's work.

A lack of Secretariat accountability in dispute settlement can be particularly problematic. The institutional design of the dispute settlement process results in panelists' overdependence on substantive support from the Secretariat, giving the Secretariat considerable influence at various stages of the process. Although this support is important for the reasons described above, Secretariat participation would benefit from transparency-enhancing mechanisms. For example, Weiler (2001) has suggested that Secretariat input to panelists be made available so that parties to disputes could comment on them directly. Deference to the Secretariat with respect to panel selection, wherein the Secretariat's specific role is rather opaque, could also benefit from transparency-enhancing reform.

Legitimacy concerns of a different nature also came to the fore through interviews with developing country delegates. The Secretariat is insistent on its neutral position in WTO affairs (Jawara and Kwa 2003), and the Secretariat's work to "level the playing field," through capacity-building workshops and informal consultations for example, may have some legitimacy-enhancing effects. However, some developing countries view the Secretariat's responsibility to equally serve all members as being in a state of tension. Although these countries are more reliant on the information provided by the Secretariat to build negotiation capacity, at least some developing countries feel that this information is biased against their interests (Jawara and Kwa 2003, 207). For example, some developing countries simultaneously rely on Secretariat expertise to build negotiation capacity and feel captive to the Secretariat's moral authority, which they feel tends to reflect developed countries' norms and positions. As explained by one interviewee: "The chair, with the Secretariat, is more open to doing what the United States and EC want—when they say no, it means no. When we say no, we still discuss [X]—we have to shout twice as loud sometimes to get a neutral outcome. This happens outside the CTESS as well."[26] Although the Secretariat's intentions may well be to level the playing field, some members believe that in attempting to do so, the Secretariat further entrenches developed countries' interests. The Secretariat may thus inadvertently be amplifying the central tension underlying trade-environment and WTO politics more broadly: developing country concerns that the benefits of trade liberalization are asymmetrical, favoring developed country interests.

7

The Limits of Secretariat Influence: CITES and the Protection of Commercially Exploited Aquatic Species

The Secretariat is our servant!
—CITES delegate, CoP14, 2007

This final case examines how the Convention on International Trade in Endangered Species (CITES) Secretariat managed overlap with the UN Food and Agriculture Organization (FAO). CITES and FAO overlap in their work surrounding governance of marine and freshwater species that have commercial value, or as they are commonly referred to by both organizations, "commercially exploited aquatic species." Whereas CITES aims to protect aquatic species that are threatened due to international trade, FAO is primarily interested in developing fishing industries to support economic development. At their core, therefore, FAO's mission is anthropocentric, whereas CITES is primarily concerned with conservation of the nonhuman world. Although these objectives do not necessarily conflict, in practice this normative divergence has made overlap management between these two organizations difficult and, at times, quite contentious.

The centerpiece of overlap management between CITES and FAO is a memorandum of understanding (MoU) on commercially exploited aquatic species (FAO and CITES 2006). A key feature of the MoU is a formal mechanism for FAO to provide advice to CITES parties on their proposals to list (i.e., protect) aquatic species under the Convention. Whereas the CITES Plants and Animals Committees tend to provide scientific advice on species management issues once species are protected under CITES, the Secretariat has historically been the primary source of scientific advice on *proposals* to protect individual species under the Convention in the first place.

CITES Secretariat advice takes the form of formal written recommendations on all party proposals to protect species under one of the

Convention's three appendixes.[1] The Secretariat's recommendations are either appended to each proposal in a section entitled "Comments from the Secretariat" or contained in a separate document that accompanies all such proposals submitted by parties to the Conference of the Parties (CoP) for consideration. Secretariat advice is not pro forma. The Secretariat evaluates each proposal against a set of listing criteria (CITES Secretariat 2009b). If the Secretariat concludes that the proposed species meets the conditions for listing laid out in the listing criteria, then it will support that proposal. If, on the other hand, it concludes that the proposed species does not meet the conditions of the listing criteria, it will provide a rationale for why the proposal should be amended or rejected. CITES parties can certainly evaluate proposals domestically as well, and CITES summary records reflect that they do so for the species they are most interested in. However, with an average of thirty-eight species listing proposals voted on per meeting between 2000 and 2013,[2] not all parties can comprehensively evaluate all listing proposals all the time. Therefore, parties have mandated that the Secretariat evaluate these proposals for them (CITES 1973, Article XV, paragraph 2).

The strong correlation between Secretariat recommendations and CITES voting outcomes suggests that CITES parties consider Secretariat evaluations seriously for most species (table 7.1). For example, CITES parties followed Secretariat recommendations on 75 percent of all proposals for nonaquatic species listings between CoP11 (2000) and CoP16 (2013). We see some unusual variation, however, with respect to how parties follow the Secretariat's advice on commercially exploited aquatic species. Whereas Secretariat influence on these proposals appeared to wane over time from 67 percent in 2000 to 14 percent in 2010, at CoP16 in 2013, parties followed the Secretariat's advice 100 percent of the time. This chapter will, in part, explain this variation.

Although it is possible that Secretariat advice is actually developed on the basis of state (i.e., CITES party) preferences, this is very unlikely, as proposals require a two-thirds majority of all CITES parties present and voting to pass. Therefore, in order to base its recommendations on aggregate party preferences, the Secretariat would have to coordinate its positions with a minimum of 116 of CITES's 175 parties for each proposal under consideration at each meeting. Because the Secretariat is already significantly underresourced to carry out its mandated work program, this type of time-intensive coordinating exercise would be prohibitively difficult (IISD 2007a).

Table 7.1

Percentage of CoP Decisions that Follow Secretariat Recommendations*

	Year	Aquatic Species	Nonaquatic Species
CoP11	2000	67%	77%
CoP12	2002	67%	83%
CoP13	2004	60%	66%
CoP14	2007	40%	89%
CoP15	2010	14%	54%
CoP16	2013	100%	80%
Total		60%	75%

* Calculations exclude proposals where no CoP decision was taken, and proposals that were withdrawn or on which the Secretariat recommendation was inconclusive. For example, although CoP14 reviewed seven proposals on aquatic species listings, two were withdrawn before the CoP made a decision on these species. Similarly, three proposals were withdrawn at CoP16 on the basis of Rule 23.6 which states that if two or more proposals related to the same species are submitted, the CoP must decide first on the proposal that is likely to have the least disruptive impact on trade. If the adoption of the first proposal negates the need for another proposal, all other proposals on the species are automatically withdrawn. If the Secretariat did not recommend adoption or rejection of the proposal, it was categorized as inconclusive and not counted toward or against the percentages of CoP decisions that followed Secretariat recommendations.

Together, these factors suggest that the CITES Secretariat has historically impacted voting decisions by brokering knowledge about which species qualify for protection and which do not. Although it is certainly not the sole influence on these decisions, voting records suggest that parties consider the Secretariat's advice on these issues at least some of the time. Accordingly, Secretariat influence has historically impacted decisions about which species are protected under the Convention and which are not—an outcome that reflects changes in institutional power relations because it results in a change in Convention rules.

The Secretariat's advising role was challenged, however, during the negotiation and implementation of the CITES-FAO MoU. Although the Secretariat had historically played a central role in advice provision on listing decisions, the Secretariat had limited influence when it came to managing commercially exploited aquatic species. This chapter traces the process of MoU negotiation and implementation, focusing on the Secretariat's role therein. In contrast to the previous cases explored in this book, the CITES case explores cross-institutional overlap management. Whereas the Convention on Biological Diversity (CBD) cases focused on unilateral overlap management and the World Trade Organization (WTO) cases address overlap management with diffuse external interests and organizations, the CITES case explores how a secretariat manages overlap when an issue is actively being addressed in more than one political forum (i.e., CITES and FAO). In this type of case, the politics are inherently more complicated as turf battles and forum shopping come into play.

This story is told through the lens of the CITES Secretariat as opposed to that of the FAO. Although parallel decision-making processes on commercially exploited aquatic species were underway at FAO during the study period, this study is most interested in how a single secretariat manages overlap in the face of direct competition from outside organizations. Although the chapter traces CITES parties' activities within FAO, it does not reflect on how the FAO Secretariat may have influenced FAO's decision making, nor does it analyze how the FAO Secretariat may have influenced the CITES listing process. The strong correlation between CITES decisions and FAO recommendations suggests, however, that the latter is quite likely—raising interesting questions about secretariat influence across organizations. Further, the FAO Secretariat did not respond to several interview requests. As such, FAO's perspective on the debate is limited to what can be gleaned from meeting reports, FAO submissions to CITES meetings, and other documents, such as secondary accounts of the debate within CITES about how to manage overlap with FAO.[3]

This debate was hashed out within CITES between 2000 and 2013 as the CITES-FAO MoU was negotiated and key provisions were implemented. This chapter examines how the CITES Secretariat participated in this debate. It argues that the CITES Secretariat was unable to influence overlap management. Although state preferences were only moderately solidified, the Secretariat was a highly substitutable actor: it faced strong competition and did not enjoy deeper access to key decision-making forums than did FAO. Further, some CITES parties preferred FAO's advice on proposed listings for commercially exploited aquatic species because it aligned with their economic interests; these parties only followed the Secretariat's advice on the matter when aligned with FAO recommendations. Therefore, despite the presence of several mechanisms of influence, this case demonstrates the limits of secretariat influence, because the CITES Secretariat was unable to use those mechanisms to impact overlap management politics in any substantive way.

The chapter is organized as follows. The next section provides a brief overview of CITES, including an overview of its Secretariat. Then it gives a description of the political context surrounding the protection of commercially exploited aquatic species under CITES and the role of the FAO. The analysis that follows applies the analytical framework presented in chapter 3 to help us better understand why the CITES Secretariat failed to influence overlap management in regard to commercially exploited aquatic species, despite its active participation in overlap management.

CITES: A Brief Overview

Among the oldest multilateral environmental agreements (MEAs), CITES was drafted following an International Union for the Conservation of Nature (IUCN) General Assembly resolution adopted in 1963 calling for "an international convention on regulation of export, transit and import of rare or threatened wildlife species" (Wijnstekers 2001). The treaty was opened for signature in 1973, entered into force in 1975, and at the time of writing has 180parties.

CITES aims to ensure that international trade in specimens of wild animals and plants does not threaten their survival. It tracks species trade through an extensive system of trade permits and certificates, and identifies species to be tracked through a listing system. CITES currently lists over 30,000 species in three appendixes, with each providing a different level of protection. Appendix I species, which include tigers and humpback whales, are "all species threatened with extinction which are or may be affected by trade" (CITES 1973, Article II.1). Appendix I species cannot be traded for "primarily commercial" purposes, and noncommercial trade is permissible only when accompanied by import/export permits and, inter alia, scientific confirmation that trade in the species will not be detrimental to its survival (i.e., a nondetriment finding).[4]

Appendix II lists those species "which although not necessarily now threatened with extinction may become so unless trade in specimens of such species is subject to strict regulation" (CITES 1973, Article II.2). Appendix II species include some seal and orchid species, and require an export permit and, inter alia, a nondetriment finding before trade is permitted. Finally, Appendix III species are those that are protected in at least one country that has asked other CITES parties for assistance in controlling trade in that species.[5]

The Convention establishes two operational bodies, the CoP and the CITES Secretariat. The CoP is the decision-making body for the

Convention. It currently meets every three years to perform functions such as setting the Secretariat's budget, reviewing amendments and additions to the appendixes, and negotiating the Convention's Strategic Plan. In the absence of consensus, CITES business is decided upon by a vote, requiring two-thirds of all parties present and voting to pass. Although nonstate actor participation is common at CITES CoPs, only member states are allowed to vote.

The CoP later established subcommittees, including the Standing Committee (SC) and the Plants and Animals Committees. The SC was established on the advice of the Secretariat, to provide guidance on the implementation of the Convention (Reeve 2002). It meets in between CoP meetings to oversee operation of the Convention, and is composed of representatives from CITES's six regions, Switzerland (the depository government), and representatives from the countries hosting the most recent and proximate meetings of the CoP. The Plants and Animals Committees are the technical committees for the Convention, composed of experts nominated and elected by member states. They meet twice between each CoP, largely to conduct reviews to assure that species are categorized appropriately within the appendixes.

The CITES Secretariat has the most far-reaching mandate of all the secretariats examined thus far in this book. Like the CBD Secretariat, the CITES Secretariat is administered by the United Nations Environment Program (UNEP) and its fixed mandate is short on structure. Further, like all the mandates examined thus far, the CITES Secretariat mandate contains language leaving room for interpretation and change as states' needs evolve over time. The CITES mandate is unique, however, in that it enumerates various specific activities that the Secretariat can engage in, many of which are central to regime operation.

The CITES Secretariat is mandated to "undertake scientific and technical studies" relevant to regime operation. Whereas its predecessors from older biodiversity conventions were permitted only to gather and distribute information to states, the CITES Secretariat is explicitly mandated to produce such information on its own. Further, in being mandated to review party reports and request additional information as needed, the CITES Secretariat is also given a role in enforcement. Finally, the Secretariat is mandated to make recommendations to parties regarding implementation of the Convention. This might include, but is not limited to, suggestions for which species should be protected under the Convention, or evaluations of how well a particular country is doing in meeting its obligations.

The CITES Secretariat has historically used this mandate to play a technical and advisory role on overlap management. For example, rather than submitting proposals of its own as does the CBD Secretariat, the CITES Secretariat typically comments on proposals submitted directly by parties to the CoP for consideration. However, CITES's approach to overlap management may be changing. Whereas previous overlap management efforts have largely been species-focused, more recent discussions have focused on strategic political issues instead. The current CITES Secretary General, John Scanlon, who took office in May 2010, has strongly emphasized the importance of overlap management for CITES in reducing operational costs and securing outside funding for implementation (IISD 2011). It remains to be seen how CITES parties will respond to these proposed changes, but Scanlon's approach could mark a departure from CITES's past practice on overlap management and a stronger role for the Secretariat in this area.

Political Context of Aquatic Species Protection under CITES

CITES claims many conservation successes. For example, it has been instrumental in reducing illegal poaching of elephants by strictly controlling international ivory trade. Yet, when it comes to the conservation of legally traded commercially exploited aquatic species, CITES has struggled to meet its core objectives. The reason for this is obvious: large fishing nations are resistant to placing trade restrictions on commercially valuable species for fear of economic loss.

As one of the world's largest fishing nations, Japan has been central to CITES politics surrounding commercially exploited aquatic species. Japan's preference for FAO leadership on aquatic species issues is reflected in the long history of Japanese efforts to exclude marine species from regulation under CITES. This debate dates back to the 1973 preparatory negotiations for the treaty, wherein Japan attempted to exclude "introductions from the sea" from CITES out of concern that CITES might begin to regulate whaling (Franckx 2006, 224–225). Japan's concern arose because its enormous fishing industry dominates consumption of some of the world's most valuable marine species, including one, the bluefin tuna, that has been dubbed the "ultimate political fish" (Martínez-Garmendia and Anderson 2005, 18). Japan is the world's largest consumer of bluefin tuna, with a single fish fetching USD 1.7million ($3,500/lb) at a Japanese fish market in 2013 (BBC News Asia 2013).

Along with other FAO member states, Japan has cited concerns about CITES's bias against sustainable use of fisheries, its lack of mandate and expertise to effectively manage marine species, and the need for coherence in global fisheries management (Young 2011; IISD 2013). Japan has gone to great lengths to exclude commercially exploited aquatic species from CITES. To show its opposition, it served bluefin tuna to CITES delegates at a reception at its embassy the night before CoP14 (2007) voted on the proposal to list the species (Economist 2010). Observers have long suspected that Japan has used development aid to buy votes at CITES (Strand and Tuman 2013), and it has admitted to doing so in the International Whaling Commission (Brown 1999). The problem is particularly poignant for African and small island developing states because they rely on large donor nations, such as Japan, for bilateral funding for issues well beyond CITES alone (IISD 2013).

Within FAO, some states have voiced concerns that CITES protects species to prevent extinction rather than to promote sustainable use (FAO 2004a).[6] They argue that this normative bent could have negative implications for employment, income, and food security in developing countries—issues that are core to FAO's mission (FAO 2004b). States voiced further concerns within FAO about the CITES "look-alike" provision. Under this provision, unthreatened species that look like protected species can also be protected under CITES in order to ensure that threatened species are not taken inadvertently (FAO 2004b). Finally, states voiced concerns about CITES's scientific competence for reviewing listing proposals for commercially exploited aquatic species. Some CITES parties pointed to FAO's extensive scientific expertise on fisheries issues in comparison to CITES (CoP12, Doc. 16.2.1), and to CITES's inadequate use of the best available scientific information when evaluating listing proposals in the past (FAO 2001).

State submissions on the MoU reveal that, within CITES, the political debate on who is best suited to review listings has been cloaked in a discourse of expertise (e.g., CITES Secretariat 2002d; FAO 2001). This expertise-centered debate was a convenient proxy for the underlying economic one, allowing states to avoid the much thornier and long-contentious negotiations surrounding CITES's role as a sustainable use versus conservation-oriented convention. If it were oriented toward sustainable use, then cost-benefit analyses may be in order before listing species in the appendixes, as suggested by states within FAO (FAO 2004b). If it were conservation-oriented, these analyses would be irrelevant. It is clear why states with strong fishing interests would prefer the former construction. However, this debate over CITES's identity has long been intractable, and despite modest changes in enhancing principles of sustainable use under CITES, deep divisions remain between CITES parties on the issue (IISD 2007a). The political debate was therefore sterilized by framing it as a question about scientific competence rather than addressing the underlying economic issues directly. Thus, a discourse of advice provision on listing proposals was at the heart of the heated debate surrounding the negotiation and implementation of the CITES-FAO MoU.

Nevertheless, economic interests are the most obvious explanation for why the Secretariat was unable to influence overlap management in the governance of commercially exploited aquatic species. We would expect states with strong fishing interests to resist Secretariat recommendations to list commercially valuable species, because restricting trade in such species would have negative economic consequences for their fishing industries. Indeed, some of these states, including Japan, Iceland, China, and Argentina, strongly resisted the Secretariat's recommendations to list commercially exploited aquatic species in the CITES appendixes, in part for these reasons (IISD 2013).

Yet economic interests are not the determining factor for all fishing states. Notably, two of the largest fishing parties, the United States and the EU, have proposed the vast majority of these listings. Further, CITES voting records reflect that parties have historically been starkly divided on issues of commercially exploited aquatic species. Most proposals to list these species failed by a narrow margin, and some were actually supported by a simple majority of CITES parties present and voting, but failed to gain the two-thirds majority needed to pass. Finally, party positions shifted dramatically at CoP16 in 2013 when, for the first time, all four proposals to list commercially exploited aquatic species in Appendix II passed (table 7.2).[7]

As we can see, although economic interests played a role in preventing Secretariat influence, they do not fully explain the observed outcomes. Secretariat influence was also constrained by other factors.

CITES-FAO Cooperation on Commercially Exploited Aquatic Species

Overlap between CITES and FAO is primarily related to management of species that are relevant to both development and international trade, such as fish and timber species. Whereas formal cooperation surrounding timber species is only now emerging, CITES and FAO have been

Table 7.2
Voting Records for Proposals on Commercially Exploited Aquatic Species

Species Proposed	Proponent(s)	CITES Secretariat Recommendation	Votes to Adopt	Votes to Reject	Votes Needed	Pass (Y/N)
CoP14						
Porbeagle sharks	EU	Recommends	54 (59%)	37 (41%)	61 (67%)	N
Spiny dogfish	EU	Recommends	55 (49%)	58 (51%)	75 (67%)	N
Sawfish	US/Kenya	Recommends*	67 (69%)	30 (31%)	65 (67%)	Y
Corals	US	Recommends	61 (53%)	55 (47%)	77 (67%)	N
Eels	EU	Recommends*	93 (91%)	9 (9%)	68 (67%)	Y
CoP15						
Corals	US/Sweden	Recommends	64 (52%)	59 (48%)	82 (67%)	N
Bluefin tuna	Monaco	Recommends*	20 (23%)	68 (77%)	59 (67%)	N
Hammerhead sharks	US/Palau	Recommends*	76 (59%)	53 (41%)	86 (67%)	N
Oceanic whitetip sharks	US/Palau	Recommends*	75 (60%)	51 (40%)	84 (67%)	N
Porbeagle sharks	EU/Palau	Recommends*	84 (65%)	46 (35%)	87 (67%)	N
Spiny dogfish	EU/Sweden/Palau	Recommends	60 (47%)	67 (53%)	85 (67%)	N
CoP16						
Oceanic whitetip sharks	US/Brazil/Colombia	Recommends*	92 (69%)	42 (31%)	89 (67%)	Y
Hammerhead sharks	EU/Colombia/Costa Rica/Ecuador/Honduras/Mexico	Recommends*	91 (71%)	38 (29%)	86 (67%)	Y
Porbeagle sharks	EU/Brazil/Comoros/Croatia/Egypt	Recommends*	93 (70%)	39 (30%)	88 (67%)	Y
Manta rays	Brazil/Colombia/Ecuador	Recommends*	96 (81%)	23 (19%)	79 (67%)	Y

* FAO also recommended adopting proposal.

negotiating how to manage overlap between themselves on commercially exploited aquatic species since the late 1990s (FAO Secretariat 1998).

With its mission to ensure the "sustainable management and use of fisheries and aquaculture resources," governance of commercially exploited aquatic species is central to FAO's operations. FAO provides governments, regional fisheries management organizations (RFMOs), and other stakeholders with scientific and technical data that help them to better manage fish stocks. In 1965, FAO created a Committee on Fisheries (COFI) to review FAO's work on fisheries issues, including international fisheries-related problems and their possible solutions (FAO Secretariat 2013). In 1985, the Committee on Fisheries established a subcommittee on fish trade (COFI/FT) to provide a forum for consultations on technical and economic aspects of international trade in fish and fishery products, and to discuss suitable measures to promote international trade in these products (FAO Secretariat 2013). In this latter capacity, FAO's work has overlapped substantially with that of CITES for decades.

In contrast to FAO's long and active history on the issue, commercially exploited aquatic species have only slowly appeared in CITES politics (IISD 2007a). Although close to 100 aquatic species, such as sea cucumbers and giant clams, are listed on the CITES appendixes, few if any are considered commercially important (FAO 2008). CITES recognizes that "wild fauna and flora in their many beautiful and varied forms are an irreplaceable part … of the earth which must be protected for this and the generations to come" (CITES 1973, Preamble). However, the relative absence of commercially exploited aquatic species from the CITES appendixes reflects CITES parties' historical reluctance to protect species that have economic value. To take the example cited earlier, bluefin tuna—a species that is widely regarded as overexploited due to international trade (Webster 2011) and thus an obvious candidate for protection under CITES—was proposed for protection under the Convention in 1992 and 2010. The first time, Sweden withdrew its proposal to list the species, and the second time, CITES parties rejected the proposal, noting their preference to address management of commercially exploited aquatic species in other forums, including FAO and RFMOs, where less precautionary approaches tend to be favored (IISD 2010c).

It makes sense, then, that both organizations have explored ways to work together. Although informal cooperation has long existed between CITES and FAO on fisheries issues, some CITES parties—notably the United States and Japan—pushed for formalizing overlap management through an MoU in the early 2000s (CITES Secretariat 2002c, 2002d Add.). The process of formalizing this relationship has been extremely difficult. As one indication of this challenge, the United States originally proposed a formal overlap management relationship between the two organizations in 2000; however, the final MoU was not agreed until 2006, and implementation of the MoU continued to be debated into 2013. This process was difficult largely because CITES parties disagree about what roles FAO and the Secretariat should play in advising them on which aquatic species qualify for protection under the Convention, with diverging priorities guiding each of the organizations' evaluations.

Negotiation of the MoU

CITES parties began to explore their potential role in the protection of commercially exploited aquatic species at CoP10 in June 1997 (CITES Secretariat 1997a, 1997b). CoP10 made little progress on the issue, however, due to concerns about the existing CITES listing criteria (CITES Secretariat 2004c). These listing criteria are critical to CITES operation because they are used to evaluate whether or not a particular species qualifies for protection under the Convention. In evaluating species, the criteria focus on things such as population levels, threats, and rates of decline.

The discussion within CITES at CoP10 did not explicitly acknowledge the underlying normative tension between CITES and FAO regarding the conservation of commercially exploited aquatic species versus their sustainable use. Instead, CITES discussions on the topic were largely technical in nature. Central to the discussion, some CITES parties argued that the existing CITES listing criteria were inadequate for evaluating proposals to list aquatic species due to unique features in the biology of these species. Mirroring ongoing discussions within FAO, these parties argued that many exploited fish species have high productivity, a feature which allows their populations to rebound following drops to population levels lower than is permitted under the CITES criteria (FAO 2001). Accordingly, because the Plants and Animals Committees were already mandated to conduct a review of the listing criteria, including to develop taxon-specific guidelines, the aquatic species discussion was tabled, with the next CoP not scheduled for another three years (FAO 1998).

The FAO COFI/FT initiated overlap management activities on commercially exploited aquatic species in 1998. Adopting a proposal from South Africa, it created an ad hoc group "to make suggestions on how … scientific review [of the CITES listing criteria] might best be pursued, leading perhaps to proposals for amendment to and/or appropriate inter-pretation of the CITES criteria in the context of marine fish species" (FAO 1998). With this decision, FAO signaled its interest in being actively engaged in the Plants and Animals Committees' review of the CITES listing criteria, and in any future CITES decisions to protect aquatic species under the Convention that would be based on these revised listing criteria.

The first formal proposal under CITES to manage overlap with FAO came from the United States two years later at CoP11 in April 2000. Referencing FAO's relevant expertise, the United States recommended formalizing what had previously been an informal overlap management relationship between the two organizations. Importantly, the United States called for the Plants and Animals Committees to formally "liaise" with FAO in developing the terms of reference (ToRs) to review the CITES listing criteria (CITES Secretariat 2000c). This seemed to be a technical and apolitical proposal. However, because the listing criteria define the thresholds at which a species qualifies for protection, they involve inherently normative assumptions about acceptable risk. As we will see in the discussion below, the Secretariat and FAO held very different opinions on this issue. As such, the process by which the criteria were revised and who led that process as defined in the ToRs was a highly political decision.

The Secretariat's comments on the US proposal provided a first glimpse of the turf battle with FAO that was about to unfold (CITES Secretariat 2000c). Emphasizing that informal cooperation with FAO already existed, the Secretariat systematically explained why each of the United States's six recommendations was unnecessary. Importantly, it reminded parties that further liaison with FAO on the ToRs was not necessary because the Animals Committee had already drafted the ToRs[8] and would be presenting them to CoP11 for consideration. The Secretariat's strong resistance to the US proposal was somewhat curious because the proposal was silent on any hierarchical relationship between CITES and FAO. It used weak, open-ended language about FAO's role in the process, and even underscored the Standing Committee's recommendation that review of the listing criteria be a "CITES-driven process" (CITES Secre-tariat 1999c, 53).

Examination of the Animals Committee's proposed ToRs to CoP11 (as referenced by the Secretariat) explains why the Secretariat resisted the US proposal so strongly. Importantly, these ToRs were explicitly based on a proposal drafted by the Secretariat to the 41st Standing

Committee (SC41) the year prior (CITES Secretariat 2000d, paragraph 4). In 1999, SC41 adopted the Secretariat's proposed ToRs over a competing proposal from FAO, which would have given FAO a much more important role in the review process (CITES Secretariat 1999a, 1999b). As such, additional liaison with FAO on the ToRs, as suggested by the United States, would reopen the debate on this issue—a debate that the Secretariat had already "won" at SC41. Therefore, that the Secretariat recommended that the CoP note, but not adopt, the US recommendations suggests that the Secretariat was trying to ensure that FAO's participation in the review was not reopened for discussion. Ultimately, as suggested by the Secretariat and others, the CoP merely noted the document and adopted the ToRs as proposed by the Animals Committee (CITES Secretariat 2000a, 2000b).[9]

With the listing criteria review process now fully underway, CITES parties turned their attention to formalizing overlap management more broadly with FAO. The appropriate role for FAO in CITES listing decisions continued to feature prominently in this discussion. At CoP12 in 2002, parallel proposals on CITES-FAO overlap management were submitted by the United States and Japan (CITES Secretariat 2002c, 2002d Add; IISD 2002). The Japanese proposal attempted to move CITES out of fisheries issues entirely. Reflecting Japan's long-standing resistance to limits on fishing rights (Clapham et al. 2007), Japan affirmed that "FAO and ... [RFMOs] are appropriate intergovernmental bodies responsible for fisheries and fisheries management" (CITES Secretariat 2002c, 3). It further asserted that "in cases where there is no responsible fisheries management organization and where trade is having a significant negative impact on conservation, the listing of commercially-exploited fish species in the Appendices may temporarily serve a useful conservation purpose" (CITES Secretariat 2002c, 4). In contrast, the US proposal merely encouraged the CoP to pursue an MoU with FAO without presupposing any hierarchy in this relationship.

In its comments on the two proposals, the Secretariat steered clear of the underlying political debate about where fisheries governance should occur. This study asserts that the Secretariat instead focused its attention on providing legal advice to parties that would indirectly shape decision making in ways that reflected its own desired outcomes. If followed, the Secretariat's legal advice would result in decisions that would preserve CITES involvement in governance of aquatic species, and maintain the Secretariat's ability to evaluate proposals on these species independently from FAO. This legal advice was related to two issues: the legal format of the proposals, and the ways in which any future MoU must conform to existing obligations under the Convention itself.

On the proposals' legal format, the Secretariat argued that the US proposal was preferable because it anticipated a *decision* on the issue, whereas Japan's proposal anticipated a *resolution*. This difference in legal format is significant. Under CITES, a resolution is "intended to be of a more permanent nature, guiding implementation of the Convention over periods of many years" (CITES Secretariat n.d. (a)). In contrast, a decision is a short-term mandate that "contain[s] instructions to a specific committee or to the Secretariat. ... [Decisions] are to be implemented, often by a specified time, and then become out of date" (CITES Secretariat n.d. (b)).

It is clear why a decision was preferable to the Secretariat. The United States's proposed decision would create an iterative process of policy development, with multiple possible entry points for Secretariat input—both formally and informally. In contrast, Japan's resolution articulated a normative framework, based on agreed rules and norms, to guide Convention activities over the longer term. Importantly, in proposing to formally recognize FAO as the more appropriate forum for fisheries management, Japan's proposed resolution would severely curtail CITES's future long-term involvement in governance of commercially exploited aquatic species. The Secretariat therefore supported the proposal that simultaneously preserved CITES involvement in aquatic species governance and gave the Secretariat the strongest possibility for influencing decision making on this issue.

Addressing the legal obligations under the Convention, the Secretariat's comments on the US proposal said that the proposed MoU should address "the role of FAO in the evaluation of proposals ... concerning commercially-important aquatic species ... in the context of Article XV paragraph 2" (CITES Secretariat 2002d). Importantly, the Secretariat didn't engage Japan's competing proposal that argued for limited CITES involvement in aquatic species governance. Rather, the Secretariat's comments took future CITES involvement in fisheries governance as a given, and explained how FAO's role should be circumscribed.

At first glance, the Secretariat appears to be acquiescing to FAO expertise on this issue. However, examination of Article XV paragraph 2, cited by the Secretariat, illuminates a more strategic objective. Rather than acquiescing to FAO's superior expertise on fisheries issues, the Secretariat draws attention to its own legally mandated role to independently evaluate proposed listings. Specifically, Article XV paragraph

2(b) states: "For marine species, the Secretariat shall ... consult inter-governmental bodies having a function in relation to those species ... [and] communicate the views expressed and data provided by these bodies *and its own findings and recommendations* to the Parties as soon as possible" (emphasis added). This reference to the Convention text is critical to the debate surrounding FAO's involvement in aquatic species listings under CITES. It reminds parties that the Secretariat is formally mandated to provide its *own* advice on proposed listings, irrespective of whether such recommendations align with those of external organizations, such as FAO.

In the interim between CoP12 (2002) and CoP13 (2004), the MoU drafting process finally began, with FAO's COFI/FT and the CITES SC developing parallel drafts. Under FAO, a draft MoU was agreed in 2004 at the ninth meeting of the COFI/FT. This draft sought to solidify FAO's role in advice provision on proposals to list commercially exploited aquatic species under CITES. Asserting FAO's "primary role" in fisheries management, it further stated: "CITES cannot replace traditional fisheries management and the particular importance of consulting all relevant bodies associated with the management of the species when considering amendments to the CITES Appendices ... [and that] the CITES Secretariat will incorporate to the greatest extent possible the results of FAO's scientific and technical review of proposals to amend the Appendices" (CITES Secretariat 2004b, Annex). COFI/FT agreed that this draft should form the basis of the future MoU with CITES, and that any CITES additions would be considered but should not "weaken or diminish the FAO text" (CITES Secretariat 2004b, 2).

In parallel, the SC chairman, in consultation with the Secretariat, produced another draft MoU (CITES Secretariat 2003). Despite CoP12's instruction to "elaborate [on] provisions regarding future FAO involvement in the scientific evaluation of proposals for including exploited aquatic species" (CITES Secretariat 2002b), this draft punted on this issue (CITES Secretariat 2003). The chairman and the Secretariat delayed any definitive articulation of FAO's involvement, merely stating that such provisions would be developed in the future (Article 1). Unable to reach agreement on the draft, the parties continued their intercessional discussions, submitting comments on the draft which the Secretariat incorporated into a revised draft MoU.

At CoP13, Japan berated the Secretariat for its handling of the revision process (CITES Secretariat 2004b). Japan criticized the Secretariat (not the chairman) for not incorporating party comments into the revised draft of the MoU as it was instructed to do. In its comments on Japan's submission, the Secretariat defended its actions and reminded Japan that the draft was in fact prepared by the chairman. It wrote: "Contrary to what is stated in paragraph 7 above, the revised draft MoU prepared by the Chairman of the Standing Committee did take into account Parties' comments on the initial draft" (CITES Secretariat 2004b, 2). No additional explanation was given, just the assertion of Japan's error. Due, in part, to lingering objections to the CITES text from Japan and Iceland, no decision was taken at CoP13, and intercessional discussions continued (CITES Secretariat 2004a, paragraph 12.4).

Divisions among parties continued at SC53 in 2005 surrounding, among other things, MoU language articulating whether the Secretariat must "respect" or merely "consider" or "take into account" FAO's advice on proposed listings (CITES Secretariat 2005b). Japan and Iceland vociferously opposed the latter two formulations because they subordinated FAO in the process, rather than "reflecting the notion of equal partners working together" (4–5). Divisions among parties were also related to preambular language that similarly created a hierarchy between the two organizations (CITES Secretariat 2006, Annex). In the end, parties reached consensus on a compromise text, which was forwarded to FAO for consideration, adopted without amendment at COFI/FT's tenth meeting in June 2006, and finally signed at CITES SC54 in October 2006.

Ultimately, the agreed MoU text preserved CITES's involvement in aquatic species governance but formalized FAO's future involvement in evaluating proposals to list such species. However, the final text was vague about the extent to which the Secretariat must incorporate FAO's advice into its own formal recommendations on proposals to list commercially exploited aquatic species. The controversial preambular language recognizing FAO's "primary role" in fisheries management was removed, but the operational provisions of the MoU did not do much to clarify the relationship. The MoU states: "The CITES Secretariat shall communicate the views expressed and data provided from [FAO's] review and its own findings and recommendations, *taking due account* of the FAO review, to the Parties to CITES. … In order to ensure maximum coordination of conservation measures, the CITES Secretariat will *respect, to the greatest extent possible*, the results of the FAO scientific and technical review of proposals to amend the Appendices" (CITES Secretariat 2005a, paragraphs 5–6; emphasis added). In effect, following six years of debate on the topic, the heart of the controversy was left unresolved. No clear hierarchy between the two review processes was established.

Implementation of the MoU

With CITES's future involvement in governance of aquatic species secured, the debate now turned to the question of hierarchy between the Secretariat and FAO in the advising process. The MoU's vague direction on this topic was first tested at CoP14 in June 2007. In the lead-up to this meeting, FAO submitted to the Secretariat its recommendations on seven proposed listings for commercially exploited aquatic species that were to be considered by the CoP. In accordance with the MoU, the Secretariat was to "respect [FAO's recommendations] to the greatest extent possible." However, of the seven aquatic species evaluated by the Secretariat and FAO, the two organizations concurred on only two—even though both organizations based their recommendations on the identical set of listing criteria that had been revised with input from each of them (CITES Secretariat 2007b). The Secretariat claimed that six of the seven proposed listings qualified for protection, whereas FAO supported only two of them (CITES Secretariat 2007b).

The diverging recommendations sparked intense controversy at CoP14. As reflected in its submissions to CoP14 on the issue, the Secretariat fought hard to cement its role as the primary provider of advice to parties on listing proposals. In addition to its formal recommendations on the proposed listings, the Secretariat submitted a copy of its correspondence with FAO in the lead-up to CoP14 (CITES Secretariat 2007c). In this correspondence, FAO expressed strong concern about the diverging recommendations, accused the Secretariat of "bypassing" its own listing criteria, and asserted that the Secretariat's recommendations were neither "adequately substantiated," nor "based on sound and relevant scientific information." In its response, the Secretariat noted that it was also concerned about the diverging recommendations and defended its findings, arguing that "often in matters of science, there is no 'correct' answer—it comes down to a matter of judgment" (6).

In the end, despite the Secretariat's efforts to influence the party preferences through its comments on each proposal, CoP14's decisions on the seven proposed listings *all* aligned with FAO's recommendations.[10] This debacle sparked a long and heated debate about what had caused the divergence in the first place and how to fix the problem.

Prior to CoP15 in 2010, the Secretariat and FAO had met in March 2008 to discuss the cause of the diverging recommendations. The two organizations agreed that although they based their recommendations on the same set of listing criteria (CITES Secretariat 2004c), their recommendations did not align because they interpreted the criteria differently (CITES Secretariat 2009c). Whereas FAO interpreted the criteria as applying strict numerical guidelines for listing a species in Appendix II (CITES Secretariat 2007d), the Secretariat argued that the criteria leave room for flexibility and precaution in considering whether or not a species qualifies for protection under Appendix II (CITES Secretariat 2009a).

The listing criteria articulate that a species can be listed in Appendix II if it meets one of two conditions. First, the Appendix II listing must prevent the species from becoming eligible for an Appendix I listing in the near future. According to Appendix I, this can occur when a population experiences a "marked *decline*" (CITES Secretariat 2004c, Annex 1; emphasis added). The second condition under which a species may be listed in Appendix II is if the listing would avoid "*reducing* the population to a level at which its survival might be threatened" (CITES Secretariat 2009b, Annex 2a; emphasis added). Importantly, both of these conditions must be read in conjunction with the definitions contained in Annex 5 of the document. Whereas Annex 5 defines the term "decline" with a specific numerical threshold for evaluating populations of commercially exploited aquatic species, the word "reduce" is not defined at all (CITES Secretariat 2009b, Annex 5).

Therefore, the heart of the disagreement between FAO and the Secretariat was about whether the words "reduce" and "decline" could be interpreted as synonyms. If so, as FAO argued they *should* be, then the specific definition for the term "decline" would apply to Appendix II listings, and strict numerical thresholds for population levels would need to be met in order for a species to be protected under Appendix II. If the terms were not interchangeable, as argued by the Secretariat, then application of the (undefined) word "reduce" would leave room for flexibility in deciding whether a species qualifies for protection in Appendix II. Most importantly, FAO's interpretation requires that there be a measurable impact on a population prior to an Appendix II listing, whereas the Secretariat's interpretation allows for preemptive action before such impacts are quantitatively observed (CITES Secretariat 2009a).

The controversy continued in the lead-up to CoP15. In their recommendations to CoP15 on the six proposals to list commercially exploited aquatic species, the Secretariat and FAO disagreed on two (corals and spiny dogfish) and agreed on four (bluefin tuna, hammerhead sharks, oceanic whitetip sharks, and porbeagle sharks). Of the four proposals where the two bodies had the same recommendation, both the Secretariat and FAO recommended listing the species. In FAO's case, these recommendations were based on its evaluation that the species met its less precautionary interpretation of the "decline" criterion (CITES Secretariat 2007b, Annex 2). This suggests that FAO and the Secretariat agreed only in cases where precautionary action was not needed because impacts were already quantitatively observable. Despite agreement between the Secretariat and FAO on these proposals, however, the CoP rejected these recommendations to list commercially exploited aquatic species in Appendix II, suggesting that other factors were at play.

With respect to the two proposals on which FAO and the Secretariat disagreed (corals and spiny dogfish), the Secretariat recommended listing the species and FAO recommended against doing so in both instances. The diverging recommendations were attributed to their differing interpretations of the criteria as described above (CITES Secretariat 2007b). The CoP agreed with FAO in both cases. In light of the diverging recommendations on these species, CITES discussions turned to which interpretation was correct. The Secretariat sought direction on the issue from CoP15. In its submission to CoP15, however, the Secretariat exhibited a clear preference for what that direction should be (CITES Secretariat 2009a). Rather than merely asking parties for guidance, the Secretariat argued that the CoP should endorse a very specific interpretation of the listing criteria that reflected the Secretariat's interpretation of the term "decline" as discussed above.

In making this argument, the Secretariat attempted to define the debate in terms that capitalized on its own domain of authority relative to FAO's (CITES Secretariat 2009a). Rather than framing the issue as one of scientific substance (i.e., "reduce" and "decline" should be considered synonymous because this is what makes most sense scientifically), the Secretariat framed it as a legal issue. Whereas the scientific framing is an area of authority that more squarely falls within the FAO ad hoc Advisory Committee's wheelhouse, the legal framing is an area where this FAO Committee, which was made up predominantly of fisheries scientists, was more hard-pressed to engage (CITES Secretariat 2007e).

The Secretariat conducted an extensive analysis to support its position on this issue (CITES Secretariat 2009a, 2009c, 2010a), drawing on the minutiae of decades of CITES negotiations and hundreds of pages of CITES documents (e.g., CITES Secretariat 1994a, 1994b). The

Secretariat's analysis made two core arguments that were fundamentally legal in nature. These arguments hinged on the original intent of CITES parties in negotiating the text of the listing criteria, and on how CITES parties had historically applied the listing criteria. On the original intent, the Secretariat traced the evolution of the negotiations on the listing criteria, which began in 1994. Its analysis demonstrated that CITES parties explicitly decided not to define the term "reduce" when negotiating the original criteria in 1994, nor when revising them in 2004. Rather, the Secretariat presented evidence that parties considered this precise issue and explicitly decided to leave room for flexibility (CITES Secretariat 2009a, 2–3).

The Secretariat also reminded CITES parties how they had historically interpreted the listing criteria. It did this by analyzing and explaining how parties had justified their past proposals to list species in Appendix II. The Secretariat analyzed all proposals submitted between 1994, when the criteria were agreed, and 2004, when the revised criteria were adopted by CoP13. Based on this analysis, it argued that of the seventy-six proposals submitted by parties to include species in Appendix II, *none* interpreted the term "reducing" in line with the Annex 5 definition of "decline," as FAO argued it should be interpreted (CITES Secretariat 2009a, 3). Further, the Secretariat said this interpretation was uncontested, arguing that "in the proceedings of the Conference of the Parties concerned, there is no evidence of the above proposals to amend the Appendices being criticized because the species concerned had not undergone a decline as defined in Annex 5 … [and] there does not seem to be any evidence that Parties believed that the word 'reducing' should be assimilated to the word 'decline'" (3). Finally, the Secretariat noted that when the revised criteria were first applied in 2007 at CoP14, none of the proposals sought to justify inclusion or deletion of species in line with FAO's interpretation (4).

Ultimately, with deep divisions between parties on the issue, CoP15 was unable to offer clear direction on which interpretation should guide the Secretariat's recommendations on proposed listings. It did, however, reject the Secretariat's proposed draft decision, which would have given the Secretariat a leadership role in further evaluating the problem (CITES Secretariat 2009a, Annex). Instead, CoP15 asked for evaluations of the interpretation issue from the Secretariat, as well as from FAO and the IUCN and the monitoring network TRAFFIC. The Animals Committee was mandated to consider all three evaluations and recommend a way forward to the Standing Committee, which would in turn make a recommendation on interpreting the terms "reducing" and "decline" to CoP16.

Despite the comprehensive reports produced by all three organizations, the 26th Animals Committee and subsequently the 62nd Standing Committee did little to resolve the debate. Rather than endorsing one interpretation over the other, their recommendations said that when making and/or evaluating listing proposals, the Secretariat, FAO, and other parties should clearly articulate which interpretation they are applying (CITES Secretariat 2012a, 2012b). At CoP16, the Secretariat seemed defeated on the matter. In its official submission, the Secretariat noted that parties had signaled their disinterest in the science underlying this issue when they opposed all proposals to list commercially exploited aquatic species at CoP15. This sentiment was further entrenched at this meeting, with the CoP adopting the SC's recommendation, refusing to articulate a hierarchy between CITES and FAO in evaluating listing proposals (IISD 2013). The CoP's hedging on the matter effectively left the scientific issue unresolved, leaving room for both precautionary and impact-based assessments in considering proposals on these species into the future.

Notwithstanding the Secretariat's inability to convince parties to grant it prominence in advising on listing decisions, CoP16 took an abrupt empirical turn. It approved *all* seven proposals to list commercially exploited aquatic species in Appendix II (IISD 2013). Three of those proposals had previously been rejected at CoP15, despite FAO and Secretariat recommendations that they be listed in Appendix II at both meetings. It is unclear what caused CITES parties to change their positions on these three species in the interim between CoP15 and CoP16. However, since only those species that met FAO's less precautionary interpretation of the decline criterion were even proposed for listing at CoP16 to begin with, this change in position may reflect an underlying normative shift among CITES parties toward FAO's less precautionary approach to species listings—challenging the sphere of influence the Secretariat tried so hard to retain.

Understanding Secretariat Influence

This section evaluates whether the CITES Secretariat's overlap management activities identified above influenced overlap management politics in this case. It argues that, despite its active participation in overlap management, the CITES Secretariat failed to influence overlap management politics because such activities did not impact power relations between states. This failure can be explained by moderately solidified CITES state preferences surrounding commercially exploited aquatic species, coupled with the high substitutability of the Secretariat's overlap management functions.

Did the Secretariat Exert Influence?

Secretariats influence political outcomes when mechanisms of influence (e.g., negotiation facilitation) are empirically observable and can be traced to changes in power relations between states, and when alternative explanations for such changes can be eliminated. For a review of the three-step process used to assess whether the Secretariat was able to exert influence, see chapter 3 (figure 3.1).

Mechanisms of Influence? The CITES Secretariat has historically enjoyed an important role in CITES decision making. This is most visible when the Secretariat comments and makes recommendations on proposals considered by the CITES CoP and its subcommittees. As discussed above, parties rely on Secretariat recommendations at least some of the time, if not on a regular basis, to guide decision making. Therefore, the Secretariat has historically played an important role in knowledge brokering and negotiation facilitation within CITES politics.

In managing overlap with FAO on commercially exploited aquatic species, the CITES Secretariat participated in negotiations through these same mechanisms (i.e., negotiation facilitation and knowledge brokering). The Secretariat did this in three key ways: commenting on proposals, submitting formal documents to the CoP, and drafting decisions for the CoP. Its work in each of these respects demonstrates the Secretariat's role as a political actor that attempts to shape, rather than merely respond to, state preferences. As demonstrated below, the Secretariat has preferences of its own, which are reflected in these documents—it does not merely respond to state mandates but tries to shape them. Centrally, the Secretariat's preference to maintain its role as the primary advisor to CITES parties on proposals to list commercially exploited aquatic species was made clear through the documents it submitted to the CoP on the MoU.

The Secretariat's comments on the original US proposal to formalize overlap management with FAO at CoP11 (1997) are a good example of how it sought to maintain its autonomous advising role (CITES

Secretariat 2000c). In systematically advising parties to reject each of the United States' six recommendations, the Secretariat effectively urged parties not to reopen discussions on the ToRs for the listing criteria review process. Similarly, in the lead-up to CoP12 (2002) the Secretariat once again utilized legal finesse to argue that parties should reject Japan's proposal (a resolution that would severely restrict the Secretariat's ability to advise on listing proposals) in favor of one from the United States (a decision that was silent on the Secretariat's role). Although the underlying tension was about which forum (CITES or FAO) was more appropriate to address fisheries issues, the Secretariat steered clear of this thorny political debate. Instead, it advocated that Japan's proposal should be rejected, employing technical legal arguments related to the form of the proposals (i.e., resolution or decision) and to parties' existing legal commitments under the Convention.

The Secretariat's role in drafting decisions and other documents for the CoP served as another potential mechanism for Secretariat influence. The Secretariat drafted the ToRs for the review of the listing criteria—a document that was central to limiting FAO's role in this critical CITES governance process (CITES Secretariat 2000d). The Secretariat also played a role in drafting the MoU itself. However, it is difficult to ascertain exactly how much impact the Secretariat had on this process. For example, the Secretariat consistently reminded CITES parties that the chairman had drafted the document only "in consultation with" the Secretariat. Nevertheless, Japan's berating of the Secretariat, not the chairman, at CoP13 (2004) for not incorporating party comments into the revised draft of the MoU suggests that the Secretariat may have played a more substantive role in the drafting process than is suggested by its consultative mandate (CITES Secretariat 2004b).

In summary, the CITES Secretariat participated in overlap management with FAO in a variety of important ways. Many of the Secretariat's activities reflect the mechanisms of influence described in chapter 3—most importantly, knowledge brokering and negotiation facilitation.

Change in Power Relations? Despite the presence of several mechanisms of influence in this case, this section argues that, despite strong efforts to do so, the CITES Secretariat did not influence overlap management. The Secretariat's activities ultimately had limited impact on negotiation outcomes and, as such, did not shape power relations between states. Further, those outcomes that did reflect Secretariat preferences are not clearly attributable to Secretariat activities. For example, it is unclear why the United States withdrew its proposal to solicit FAO input on the ToRs at CoP11, and the passage of a decision rather than a resolution on the issue at CoP12 reflected both Secretariat preferences and those of at least one powerful state.

The Secretariat's limited ability to impact outcomes is reflected in the final text of the MoU. Despite the Standing Committee's agreement that the CITES chairman/Secretariat draft (CITES Secretariat 2003) would form the basis of negotiations on the MoU, ultimately, the final text looked much more like the draft produced by FAO in 2004 (CITES Secretariat 2004b, Annex). Perhaps the most striking example of the Secretariat's inability to impact outcomes transpired at CoP14 when parties voted against the Secretariat's recommendations, and instead in line with FAO's, on all of the proposed listings for commercially exploited aquatic species where the two organizations disagreed. A similar dynamic unfolded at CoP15, where parties voted against the Secretariat's recommendations on all six proposals to list commercially exploited aquatic species. It should be noted that states also voted against FAO on four of the six proposals, agreeing with FAO only when FAO disagreed with the Secretariat. Although FAO and Secretariat recommendations aligned more closely at CoP15, parties nevertheless rejected the Secretariat's proposed draft decision on the matter, which would have given the Secretariat the central role in sorting out the disagreement between the two organizations regarding interpretation of the listing criteria (CITES Secretariat 2010b). CoP16 similarly refused to give the Secretariat primacy on the matter, leaving any hierarchy between the two organizations on evaluating listing proposals ambiguous (IISD 2013).

Although the impacts are quite modest, there is one area where the Secretariat was able to impact outcomes. As indicated by the Animals Committee chairman, the ToRs for the listing criteria review process were drafted by the Secretariat (CITES Secretariat 2000d). Although important because it provided the foundation for a process central to CITES operation, the Secretariat's ability to affect the listing criteria review was not particularly remarkable because its recommendations were very closely aligned with the Standing Committee's preference for a "CITES-driven" review process (SC41 Summary Record). Therefore, the Secretariat did not shape power relations between states in this case.

What Factors Constrained the Secretariat's Ability to Exert Influence?

Preference solidification and substitutability help us to understand why the CITES Secretariat was unable to influence politics in this case.

Preference Solidification   Issue newness and the costs of unfavorable outcomes and/or preference development illuminate the degree of preference solidification in this case. CITES-FAO overlap management is not a new issue. The two organizations have been cooperating on commercially exploited aquatic species since the late 1990s. As such, CITES parties have had a long time to develop preferences on the listing of these species, suggesting that preferences were moderately to strongly solidified. In addition, because the species under consideration in this case are by definition commercially valuable, we can assume that costs of unfavorable outcomes were moderate to high. Moreover, with the United States and Japan constantly at the center of debates on the issue, these costs were likely concentrated within a small number of large fishing states. In addition to the lack of newness, these empirical observations also suggest that preferences were at the very least not weakly solidified in this case.

To get a more accurate measurement of preference solidification, however, we can look to the mandates that states gave the CITES Secretariat on commercially exploited aquatic species. Mandates are particularly important in this case because they are agreed by all states, not just those who take center stage in the debates. Thus, mandates help to temper the effect of particularly vocal states (here, the United States and Japan) in evaluating the intensity of CITES state preferences as a whole. As explained in chapter 3, mandates that are analytical and open-ended reflect weakly solidified preferences, those that are administrative and restrictive reflect strongly solidified preferences, and analytical yet restrictive mandates reflect moderately solidified preferences (see table 3.3).

The most important mandates in this case are those contained in the CITES listing criteria related to how the Secretariat should evaluate proposed listings. The CITES listing criteria lay out highly analytical but very restrictive guidelines for how the Secretariat should evaluate each proposed listing. For example, the Secretariat can determine that a population is in "decline" only if "the long-term extent of decline is the total estimated or inferred percentage reduction from a baseline level of abundance or area of distribution. The recent rate of decline is the percentage change in abundance or area of distribution over a recent time period. The data used to estimate or infer a baseline for extent of decline should extend as far back into the past as possible" (CITES Secretariat 2009b, Annex 5). Indeed, much of the debate surrounding the diverging CITES and FAO recommendations was focused on their different interpretations of this precise mandate. This highly analytical but highly restrictive mandate suggests that CITES state preferences as a whole were moderately solidified in this case, despite clearly strong preferences by one or two key states.

Substitutability   Substitutability is also important in evaluating a secretariat's capacity for influence. When overlap management functions can be performed by other available actors, secretariat substitutability increases. This study measures substitutability through an evaluation of a secretariat's comparative access rights in key decision-making forums and the level of competition a secretariat faces in providing overlap management functions. As detailed in chapter 3, deep access rights coupled with no competition results in very low substitutability for secretariat overlap management functions. As a secretariat's relative access decreases and competition to perform overlap management functions increases, secretariat substitutability correspondingly increases. When this happens, the Secretariat's capacity for influence declines (see table 3.4).

Substitutability is particularly important in this case because the Secretariat's advising functions were easily substitutable with those of another actor (i.e., FAO). The CITES Secretariat faced strong competition from FAO to evaluate proposals to list commercially exploited aquatic species, and CITES parties granted FAO a deep level of access to key decision-making forums that was functionally on par with the Secretariat's access.

On competition, the Convention text and the CITES listing criteria *require* the Secretariat to seek input from external organizations, such as FAO, in developing its recommendations on aquatic species listing proposals (CITES 1973, Article XV2(b); CITES Secretariat 2009b). Evolving mandates related to the MoU mirror these requirements. For example, following the blowout at CoP14, parties mandated the Secretariat to consult with FAO on how to improve cooperation between the two organizations (CITES Secretariat 2007a). That parties repeatedly require the Secretariat to involve FAO in carrying out its overlap management functions (and that FAO agreed to do so) suggests that the Secretariat faced very strong competition from FAO to evaluate listing proposals.

These evolving mandates also speak to the deep access that FAO enjoyed to key CITES decision-making processes. For example, not only must the Secretariat consult with external bodies, such as FAO, on commercially exploited aquatic species listings, but it must also "communicate the views expressed and data provided by these bodies ... to the Parties as soon as possible" (CITES 1973, Article XV2(c)). In requiring the Secretariat to communicate FAO's recommendations to parties alongside its own recommendations, states granted FAO unprecedented access for an external organization to *the* central CITES decision-making procedure—for there is nothing more central to CITES politics than listing species on the appendixes. Granting FAO formal advisory participation rights is unusual not only in CITES politics but in global environmental politics more broadly, where observers are typically present but peripheral. The Secretariat's strong competition from FAO, coupled with FAO's deep access to key CITES decision-making forums, thus indicate that the Secretariat's overlap management functions were highly substitutable.

Factors not explicitly captured in this study's framework also help to explain why FAO enjoyed these privileges. For example, membership overlap is high between FAO and CITES, making FAO an attractive choice for outside advice. Moreover, some states likely favored FAO's advice because it arguably has more expertise on aquatic species issues than does the CITES Secretariat. This view is reflected in several party statements to this effect, FAO's specialized mission on the topic, and FAO's well-established networks with other fisheries management organizations (FAO Secretariat 2013). Finally, CITES parties may have preferred FAO's advice because they likely see FAO as a more legitimate purveyor of scientific advice than the Secretariat, in part because the COFI/FT is composed of state-nominated scientists rather than international bureaucrats. This sentiment was reflected during a plenary session at CoP14 (2007), when, in referencing FAO's COFI/FT, Argentina said, "the Secretariat is not a scientific body ... and should not discuss findings in the same way as an expert panel" (personal observation 2007). Therefore, although preference solidification was constant across organizations, FAO was able to exert influence in this case when the CITES Secretariat was not, in part because it was far less substitutable than the CITES Secretariat on this issue.

In summary, it is unsurprising that the CITES Secretariat was unable to influence outcomes in this case because state preferences were moderately solidified and Secretariat overlap management functions were highly substitutable. In these situations, this study's framework predicts that CITES Secretariat influence is unlikely. This prediction corresponds with the empirical finding in this case of no observed influence (table 7.3).

Table 7.3
Summary of Findings—CITES Secretariat

Case	Preference Solidification	Substitutability	Predicted Influence	Observed Influence
CITES Secretariat	Moderate	High	Unlikely	None

Conclusions

This case points to the limits of secretariat influence. Although the CITES Secretariat has impacted species listing decisions on many species in the past (see table 7.1), it was unable to do so with respect to important provisions in the CITES-FAO MoU that related to advice on proposals to list commercially exploited aquatic species.

Economic interests alone cannot explain the Secretariat's inability to influence the rules surrounding listing decisions in this case. As evidenced in their official statements on the issue, some powerful fishing states, such as Japan, had strong preferences that CITES not address fisheries issues at all. Yet other large fishing nations such as the United States and the EU were the primary proponents of most proposals to list aquatic species. CITES voting records also suggest that parties were relatively evenly divided on most proposals to list these species, rather than driven by economic interests alone.

Substitutability is particularly useful in helping us understand the Secretariat's failure to influence in this case. Whereas secretariats are often seen as merely administrators, FAO's COFI/FT was made up of state-appointed scientists, lending enhanced legitimacy to their advice provision on fisheries issues. As such, it is conceivable that for some parties, FAO was a preferable expertise provider, easily substitutable with the Secretariat.

This case reveals some important dynamics of bureaucratic politics. First, it highlights the limits of principal-agent frameworks for describing the state-secretariat relationship. It demonstrates that secretariats can be political actors who lobby for preferences that sometimes contradict those of their member states. The CITES Secretariat regularly disagreed with parties, for example, recommending that their proposals be rejected (e.g., CITES Secretariat 2000c) or simply asserting that a party's assessment of a given situation is incorrect (e.g., CITES Secretariat 2004b). This case further demonstrates how secretariats can actively work to shape state preferences, even though they are not always successful in doing so. Such an effort was most evident in the CITES Secretariat's submissions to the CoP about the divergence in interpretation with FAO on the listing criteria (e.g., CITES Secretariat 2009a). These documents did not simply inform parties about facts, but argued that parties should adopt specific policies. Importantly, the Secretariat used seemingly technical means to advocate for political ends. We saw this, among other issues, in the CITES Secretariat's use of legal advice to shape political decisions related to CITES-FAO cooperation at CoP12.

This insight raises questions about how secretariat preferences are formed in the first place. The CITES Secretariat's actions reflected its preferences to maintain both CITES involvement in governance of commercially exploited aquatic species and its own autonomy in evaluating listing proposals for these species. Rationalist frameworks of political behavior might suggest that the Secretariat was seeking to increase its own authority. However, observation of six CITES meetings between 2006 and 2009, coupled with interview data, suggest that this explanation is unlikely or at best incomplete. Rather, the CITES Secretariat's recommendations across all areas of CITES politics consistently reflect outcomes that would lead to an increase in problem-solving effectiveness as defined by the terms of the treaty. Whereas state interests tend to shift over time due to background political noise, Secretariat interests appear to be defined primarily by the treaty text. This case suggests that Secretariat preferences are rooted in their role as guardians of the treaties they service, a mantra that we heard in the WTO case as well.

Tracing the process by which the CITES Secretariat drafted the ToRs for the listing criteria review process reveals another important dynamic of secretariat politics: how secretariats construct their veils of legitimacy. Because CoP decisions are often made on the basis of recommendations from the Standing, Animals, and Plants Committees, the Secretariat masked its impact on political outcomes by filtering its ideas through lower level subcommittees first. These subcommittees took on Secretariat proposals as their own before presenting them to CoPs for consideration. Through this process, the Secretariat was able to shape decision-making outcomes from behind a veil of legitimacy as it relinquished credit for its ideas.

Finally, the case highlights the role that secretariats can play in ameliorating domestic incoherence. Interview data and summary reports of the FAO's COFI/FT meetings reveal that although membership overlap is high between CITES and FAO, state preferences are not consistent between the two organizations (e.g., FAO Secretariat 2002). Although less active on this topic than other secretariats examined in this study, the CITES Secretariat played a role in bringing issues of incoherence to the attention of state actors (FAO Secretariat 2002).

In addition to its insights on secretariat politics, this case also informs our understanding of overlap management politics. The CITES case is notable because it reflects an overlap management relationship that moved well beyond symbolic or practical cooperation on issues of common concern. Rather, CITES and FAO developed a deep overlap management relationship wherein an external organization was given a key role in core regime functions. In giving FAO the authority to evaluate and make recommendations on species listing proposals, CITES parties invited an unprecedented level of external involvement in CITES affairs. Determining the conditions under which states are willing to do this is a promising line of inquiry for future investigations into not only secretariat studies but overlap management politics as well.

The depth of FAO's mandated involvement in CITES decision making was particularly important because it created a mechanism for mission creep, enabling external norms and ideas that are central to CITES's core mission to be diffused within CITES. Although the CITES treaty text reflects a core mission of conservation (CITES 1973, Preamble), an underlying debate among CITES parties in recent years has been about whether the Convention's guiding norm is one of conservation or sustainable use (Young 2011). Whereas the Secretariat's evaluations tend to be precautionary in nature, FAO's tend to reflect a norm of sustainable use. In institutionalizing FAO's role in evaluating listing proposals, CITES parties incrementally moved the Convention's mission away from the former normative orientation of conservation and toward sustainable use.

8

Conclusions

As for the Secretariat, your reward may be in heaven.
—CBD delegate, January 2008

Secretariats are more than administrative lackeys; they shape global governance in important ways. This book argues that in the messy world of overlapping regimes, secretariats emerge not simply as state functionaries or appendages, but as actors in their own right. Fundamentally, the book shows that secretariats influence politics by changing power relations between states. Although secretariats may not enjoy the coercive strength to dictate their will against state preferences, they can influence political outcomes in ways that reflect constitutive forms of power. The book illustrates how secretariats can shape power relations between states by designing rules and institutions (institutional power), restructuring relative capacities and relationships between states (structural power), and shaping shared norms and ideas (productive power) (Barnett and Duvall 2005). By shaping state power relations in these ways, secretariats themselves can be powerful actors in global governance.

For example, the book shows how the Convention on Biological Diversity (CBD) Secretariat autonomously designed the core set of rules and practices that formed the foundation of overlap management governance within the biodiversity regime complex. This shaped institutional power relations between states by creating the institutional framework within which states continue to interact on this issue—it set the limits of what was institutionally possible within the CBD for decades. The book further demonstrates how the CBD Secretariat shaped the way CBD member states understood the relationship between biodiversity and climate change. This changed productive power relations between states by reframing biodiversity conservation as an issue with increased political saliency for developing countries, but also as an issue of interest to additional funding avenues that are otherwise earmarked exclusively for climate change projects. Finally, the book demonstrates how the World Trade Organization (WTO) Secretariat's capacity-building activities redistributed resources necessary for developing countries to engage effectively in trade-environment negotiations and dispute settlement. This changed power relations between states by redistributing relative capacities to engage in what is effectively a zero sum game in WTO politics. Paradoxically, as detailed below, some see this redistribution as markedly biased toward developed countries' interests.

In order to explain how secretariats shape power relations in these ways, the book builds a theory of secretariat influence—disentangling the relationship of influence to the related, yet analytically distinct, concepts of power and authority. It presents a new analytical framework for identifying secretariat influence and understanding the conditions under which it is likely to occur. This framework extends Biermann and Siebenhüner's (2009) typology of secretariat influence by identifying additional mechanisms (i.e., marketing and litigation facilitation) and enabling conditions of secretariat influence (i.e., low substitutability and weak preference solidification). Further, it builds on existing frameworks—which measure secretariat influence by looking for changes in state behavior (i.e., outcomes)—by instead looking for changes in rules, relationships, and norms (i.e., impacts) resulting from secretariat activities (i.e., outputs) (Biermann and Siebenhüner 2009). Specifically, the book looks for impacts that reflect changes in power relations between states, and illustrates how causal chains can be identified between such impacts and mechanisms of secretariat influence (e.g., knowledge brokering). It argues that a secretariat has influenced politics only when changes in state power relations can be empirically observed and attributed to specific mechanisms of secretariat influence through process tracing and counterfactual analysis.

Centrally, the book argues that when secretariat functions enjoy low substitutability and state preferences are weakly solidified, secretariat influence is more likely. That is, secretariats are more likely to influence governance when they play a highly specialized role that few other actors can easily fill, and when issues are relatively new and/or costs associated with preference development or unfavorable outcomes are high. These conditions can create a space for secretariats to maneuver in political decision making. The book tests these arguments in four empirical cases of secretariat participation in overlap management politics within the

Table 8.1

Summary of Findings

Case	Substitutability	Preference Solidification	Influence
CBD—biodiversity	Low	Weak	Strong*
CBD—climate	Low	Moderate	Moderate*
WTO—dispute settlement	Very low (panelists)	Moderate (panelists)	Moderate (panelists)
WTO—negotiations/ dispute settlement	Moderate (states)	Moderate (developing countries) Strong (developed countries)	Weak (developing countries) None (developed countries)
CITES	High	Moderate	None

*Decreased over time.

CBD, the Convention on International Trade in Endangered Species (CITES), and the WTO. It finds varied levels of influence across the cases, supporting the argument that influence is more likely (and stronger) when the aforementioned conditions are met (table 8.1).

These cases offer various insights for secretariat studies. First, they demonstrate that secretariat influence is not static, but changes over time as institutional, informational, and capacity constraints shift. We see this most clearly in the two CBD cases. In both cases, Secretariat influence decreased over time as CBD state preferences solidified. Further, the initial increase in secretariat influence observed in the CBD climate case points to a new and important insight about secretariat politics: secretariats can *themselves* alter their constraining conditions. Although the CBD Secretariat was faced with restrictive Conference of the Party (CoP) mandates on "biodiversity and climate change" and strong competition from other actors (i.e., high substitutability), the Secretariat nevertheless managed to create an environment of low substitutability, albeit for a short period of time. It did this by strategically negotiating a way around its restrictive CoP mandates in order to carry out additional overlap management functions (i.e., public speeches), in which it faced low competition from other actors. It isn't that the Secretariat was defying member states; rather, it created room for itself to maneuver within its broadly defined mandate as contained in the Treaty text itself. As one CBD

Secretariat staff member interviewed for this study emphasized, "we can always find a decision to justify what we want to do."

This example highlights that secretariat politics do not always fit neatly into principal-agent frameworks, which typically use delegation as a starting point for understanding how international organizations (IOs) operate. Rather, secretariats can creatively interpret mandated functions to extend beyond what is formally delegated by states. Similarly, although it was not explicitly delegated to make policy recommendations, in the CBD biodiversity case the Secretariat creatively interpreted its open-ended administrative overlap management mandate and, in the mid 1990s, designed the institutional structures for overlap management that remain in place over 20 years later. This dynamic is further reflected by the WTO Secretariat's informal advising—particularly for developing countries—and the CITES Secretariat's lobbying against specific state proposals related to commercially exploited aquatic species listings. Together, all cases explored in this book illustrate how secretariats can act in the absence of delegation, create room to maneuver, and sometimes even design their own mandates. This insight also raises questions about how secretariats form preferences to begin with. Although the CITES and WTO cases suggest that secretariat preferences reflect goals that enhance regime effectiveness, more systematic analysis is needed to fully answer this question.

Whereas the existing literature examines variation in secretariat influence across IOs and treaty regimes, this study suggests that secretariat influence can also vary across issue areas within a single organization, and as a function of who the target of influence is. On variation across organizations, the CITES case is most illustrative. CITES voting records coupled with Secretariat recommendations to the CoP suggest that the CITES Secretariat does influence state decision making on some issues. However, in the context of overlap management related to commercially exploited aquatic species, the Secretariat failed to exert any influence. As argued in chapter 7, this variation can in part be explained by variation in the substitutability of relevant Secretariat functions and in state preference solidification across various issues on the CITES agenda.

The WTO case is most illustrative of variation in influence depending on who the target of influence is. The WTO Secretariat's influence was stronger when the target of influence was developing countries or dispute resolution panelists, as opposed to developed countries. Not only do the latter rely less heavily on Secretariat support, but the WTO's closed-door culture makes competition less intense for the Secretariat's overlap management functions. These dynamics are intuitively clear but obscured analytically by the focus in other studies on structural variables (such as problem structure) in explaining secretariat influence. Examination of relational variables—such as substitutability and preference solidification—brings these new dynamics of secretariat politics into focus.

Executive leadership also emerges as a potentially important variable in understanding secretariat influence, in particular through the CBD climate case. Executive leadership in IOs is largely underexplored because IO scholars tend to conflate executive heads with the larger IO structure (Schroeder 2013). Further, the secretariat's "veil of legitimacy" (Depledge 2007) has made gathering empirical evidence to support such theory building difficult. Nonetheless, the CBD climate case along with other recent studies outside the environmental context (e.g., Schroeder 2013) suggest that executive leadership may be a fruitful line for future inquiry in better understanding the dynamics of secretariat influence and that of IOs more broadly.

The cases in this book also suggest that secretariat influence becomes less likely as the number of actors involved in overlap management increases. As governance objectives moved from unilateral policy development within the first CBD case to iterative cross-institutional cooperation between CITES and the Food and Agriculture Organization (FAO) in the final case, secretariat influence generally decreased. This waning influence likely occurs because opportunities for turf battles and forum-shopping increase as more institutions are involved in governance decisions, thus elevating competition among actors and substitutability in functions, and making secretariat influence more difficult (Oberthür and Stokke 2011).

Finally, although it is not particularly surprising that secretariats can influence politics when state preferences are weakly solidified, the CBD climate and WTO cases reveal that secretariat influence is possible even when state preferences are *moderately* solidified. This finding is important because it points to the central role that secretariats can play in helping states develop preferences on issues where political saliency is not necessarily low. That is, state preferences may be only moderately solidified on issues when such issues are new to a political forum or when other more pressing issues have usurped their attention at a particular point in time.

This is most visible in the first CBD case, wherein states identified overlap management as an important issue by including it in the treaty itself. However, due to overriding political issues related to securing developing country buy-in, early CBD discussions were focused else-where, on such areas as biosafety and finance. The Secretariat capitalized on this situation by broadly interpreting its open-ended mandates to define the institutional structures for overlap management, which CBD states who were preoccupied with other issues accepted nearly verbatim. These institutional structures continue to guide overlap management governance decades later, pointing to a critical observation of this study: even when modest, secretariat influence can have crucial impacts on governance because it can result in a path-dependent dynamic. This finding is fleshed out in more detail below in the section entitled "Does Secretariat Influence Matter?"

In addition to these new insights for secretariat studies, the book also has broader theoretical implications that are key for the study of IOs and overlap management. Most importantly, this study unfolds in close conversation with recent investigations into the influence of IOs and their secretariats in international affairs. Previous studies largely see secretariat behavior as either pathological—resulting in (un)intended negative outcomes—or depoliticized—resulting in (un)intended positive outcomes. Barnett and Finnemore's (2004) point of departure is that IOs create space to maneuver, which is problematic because it results in pathologies that might, for example, undercut their original mission. In contrast, Biermann and Siebenhüner (2009) present the positive implications of secretariat influence, largely looking at secretariats as depoliticized actors that can enhance regime function.

My findings concur with both of these previous contributions. They add some nuance, however, in demonstrating how secretariat influence can cut both ways—with positive implications and negative ones. For example, the second CBD case highlights how secretariat marketing activities can attract much-needed resources to the biodiversity regime by linking conservation to climate change adaptation. At the same time, syphoning scarce adaptation resources through conservation projects may not be the best use of these funds for ameliorating climate impacts on human communities. Similarly, in the WTO cases, Secretariat capacity-building efforts simultaneously enhances developing countries' ability to engage in WTO politics and yet, in the eyes of some interviewees, further entrenches developed-country biases. In other words, some observers see the Secretariat's capacity-building efforts as helping developing countries to engage, but only on developed countries' terms.

In addition to its primary focus on secretariat influence, the book further illuminates the terrain of overlap management in global environmental governance by looking at secretariat influence through the lens of overlap management. Because this topic is still in its analytical infancy, the book, like other recent contributions (e.g., Oberthür and Stokke 2011), takes an inductive approach to help us better understand how overlap is managed and, importantly, who is playing a role—sometimes a leading one—in this governance process. On how overlap is managed, previous work has largely focused on unidirectional single interactions between two organizations (e.g., Oberthür and Gehring 2006). This book sheds light on a wider array of overlap management strategies that range from unilateral efforts within a single treaty regime (i.e., the first CBD case) to cross-institutional approaches that require deeper, bidirectional, and iterative interactions between two or more treaties over time (i.e., the CITES-FAO case).

Centrally, the cases explored here demonstrate that overlap management is not necessarily structurally determined, but can also be redirected by political agents who can (re)define structural constraints and shape decision-making preferences. Although policy fields and governance level (i.e., horizontal versus vertical)[1] certainly affect overlap management outcomes, such structural constraints alone do not predetermine them. Rather, overlap management outcomes emerge from a combination of structural characteristics of regime overlap and agent-based decision making—i.e., "agent strategies" (Hawkins and Jacoby 2006).

There are, of course, also limits to this study's analytical reach. Additional cases reflecting greater variation in substitutability of secretariat functions would help us to better understand just how important this variable is in conditioning secretariat influence. Such additional cases could also shed light on the relative importance of substitutability and preference solidification, as well as on how these variables interact with one another. Further, in future investigations the framework could be applied to cases beyond the environmental realm. Although the WTO case suggests that secretariat influence may be generalized to other issues areas, how secretariat influence translates into other issue areas is not yet explained.

The question of how secretariat influence compares to that of other actors was also not taken up in this book. Secretariats are only one piece of the "division of labor" in overlap management (Gehring 2011). More research is needed to understand when secretariats should be called upon and when other actors might be better suited to the task. As Selin (2010) explains, in the diffuse nonhierarchical chemicals regime, coalitions between states, nongovernmental organizations (NGOs), and IOs can also play an important role in managing overlap. How secretariat influence compares to that of other actors in terms of strength, mechanisms employed, and enabling/constraining conditions warrants further attention.

In addition, although this study shows how secretariat influence can result in both positive and negative regime outcomes, additional research could uncover the conditions under which we might expect one type of outcome or the other. This analysis might investigate variables such as organizational structure and culture alongside political contexts, including varied constellations of interests among state actors and the degree of (in)coherence at the domestic level in key states. Additionally, the first CBD case suggests that leadership may also be important in this regard and should be investigated in future research on this topic.

Finally, the study raises questions about whether we should expect to see secretariat influence in other areas of secretariat work—beyond overlap management. The subsequent section takes up this question, offering some possible explanations based on the case studies explored in this book.

Why Are Secretariats Able to Influence Overlap Management?

This study suggests that secretariat influence in overlap management is a function of the problem structure of overlap management itself, coupled with secretariats' network position in international affairs. On structural factors, most states maintain a strong will to develop overlap management strategies, but lack the capacity to do so. As is reflected in the countless overlap management–related decisions, resolutions, and political statements examined in this study alone, states continue to reinforce the importance of overlap management and demonstrate their willingness to develop and engage in this political exercise. However, active and organized management of overlapping regimes is a relatively new phenomenon in international affairs. Although overlap management, in related forms, has long taken place in international politics—for example, wherein one state utilizes a linkage (i.e., a case of overlap) to advance its own political goals[2]—using such a linkage to advance broader regime goals through collective decision-making is relatively new. This suggests limited state experience and expertise in this area, and thus a window of opportunity for secretariats to influence decision making on this topic.

Further, the problem structure of overlap management is characterized by diffuse and unconnected state shareholders. At the domestic level, different government ministries or departments often manage separate but overlapping issues, and coordination between these institutions tends to be weak (IIED 2009; UNEP 2000; OECD 2009). For example, in the United States, the Fish and Wildlife Service leads negotiations under CITES, the Department of State leads negotiations on climate change, and the US Trade Representative leads negotiations on international trade. Although the United States goes to great lengths to coordinate positions on overlapping areas, interviews with those who had participated in such meetings indicated that coordination is imperfect and sometimes even pro forma. This problem is magnified for developing countries, where capacity constraints are larger (IIED 2009). Highlighting the importance of this issue, one biodiversity secretariat interviewee explained:

It is interesting to see the different views that come up from parties in the different biodiversity convention processes. There are cases where you have the same person, cases where you have a different minister in the same ministry, and cases where you have different ministries altogether. In cases where you have different people, one thing is quite clear: there is very little dialogue between focal points of different conventions—very little consultation regarding what's happening on one convention that can affect the outcomes in another. ... We all recognize it, but everyone is stretched; often the convention is only a small part of the work profile. Least-developed countries sometimes have one poor guy responsible for everything.

Another biodiversity secretariat interviewee added, "we can synergize until we're blue in the face, but unless countries do so at the national level, it's all for naught." Studies of issue coordination support this sentiment, in that they conclude that better coherence across domestic ministries/departments is a prerequisite for states' ability to effectively manage overlap across international institutions (UNEP 2000).

Taken together, these problem characteristics of overlap management (i.e., newness and diffuse shareholders) create a governance niche for nonstate actors, such as secretariats, to fill. Although there are many nonstate actors who could fill certain aspects of this role, secretariats' position in international affairs is key in understanding why secretariats are particularly well suited to manage overlap. First, there is a good fit between overlap management needs and secretariat authority. Overlap management requires cross-institutional knowledge, both to identify overlap management needs and opportunities, and to understand how policies can be designed to work in cross-institutional political and legal contexts. Further, overlap management requires practical cooperation across treaty regimes. This can be enhanced by long-view knowledge about previous stumbling blocks, points of leverage, and possible areas of political convergence. Secretariat authority derived from institutional memory and expertise is well suited to filling these needs.

As noted above, many state actors lack the capacity to coordinate across overlapping issue areas. In contrast, the secretariats examined in this study often have well-developed cross-regime networks, which can facilitate information flow that aids in the identification of overlap management needs and the development of overlap management strategies. For example, well-developed networks between the WTO Secretariat and the United Nations Environmental Program's (UNEP) Economics and Trade Branch result in the sharing of cross-regime expertise relevant to trade-environment politics that well equips these two secretariats to guide overlap management. Biodiversity secretariat interviewees further reported holding positions at various biodiversity treaty secretariats over the course of their careers. This experience gives them a unique opportunity to understand how overlap plays out on the ground, making practical and efficient management of overlapping issues more likely.

Secretariats are also well positioned to manage overlap because, when necessary, they are able to influence overlap management from behind a "veil of legitimacy" (Depledge 2007). As a result, secretariats can play a substantive role in political decision making without necessarily taking credit for their role. This happens through various mechanisms. As explained by Depledge (2007), secretariats often plant ideas with the chairs of international meetings behind the scenes. Chairs then legitimize these ideas by taking them on as their own. Several secretariat interviewees reported aiding states in drafting documents during dispute settlement or negotiations, for example. Yet secretariats often veil their suggestions to state decision-makers. As explained in chapter 4, in designing the CBD's overlap management architecture in the early 1990s, the CBD Secretariat often routed its ideas through a subsidiary body of the CoP called the Ad Hoc Open-ended Working Group on Review of Implementation (WGRI). Therefore, official recommendations on overlap management emerging from the Secretariat's ideas would be forwarded to the CoP from the WGRI rather than from the Secretariat itself. Similarly, one interviewee noted the importance of her network of states that tend to be sympathetic to secretariat input—"friends of the Secretariat"—in channeling secretariat ideas through formal political processes. "Veils" like these make it more likely that secretariat ideas will be accepted by states that, in principle, prefer a more limited secretariat role in governance decisions.

This fit between overlap management needs and secretariat characteristics suggests that overlap management is an area of politics where we would expect to see secretariat influence. As such, secretariats are likely to influence issues that share similar problem characteristics with overlap management, including issues that are new, that are important but peripheral to core regime goals, and that require specialized expertise and/or networks. Perhaps unsurprisingly, but nonetheless importantly, secretariats are likely to continue to influence governance in areas where states lack adequate capacity to manage issues themselves but have a strong willingness to manage them. Consequently, the cases suggest that secretariats are likely to influence politics not merely by responding to delegation, but by shaping what gets delegated to begin with.

Does Secretariat Influence Matter?

Despite the important role that secretariats play in overlap management, their influence is bounded. Secretariats do not always drive overlap management because they are, of course, less powerful than states. Although secretariat influence often shapes and sometimes even defines state interests, when state interests conflict with those of secretariats, there is little doubt about who ultimately calls the shots.

Albeit modest, secretariat influence is nonetheless important for three main reasons. First, secretariats can influence how states understand problems and thus the way they allocate resources to solve those problems. For example, the CBD Secretariat was able to catalyze a shift in the way member states understood the relationship between biodiversity and climate. It did so by marketing a strategic framing of the linkage that positioned biodiversity as an active player in climate adaptation solutions. Not only did this framing help overcome existing barriers to cooperation under the CBD by increasing the political salience of conservation for developing countries (i.e., by linking it to adaptation), but it is also beginning to shape the way financial resources, particularly those earmarked for climate change adaptation, can be (re)allocated to address conservation.

Second, secretariat influence has the potential to both enhance and erode equity in international politics. It can either help to level the playing field between developed and developing countries, or further entrench existing power dynamics between these groups. For instance, the WTO Secretariat supports developing countries' participation in trade-environment-related negotiations and dispute settlement through knowledge brokering and capacity building. On the one hand, these activities work to level the playing field by enhancing developing countries' capacity to engage in WTO politics. On the other hand, some developing country delegates interviewed for this study said that these capacity-building activities work to further advance developed countries' interests because the Secretariat gives preference to those perspectives in its knowledge-brokering and capacity-building activities.

Third, and most importantly, even when modest, secretariat influence can have significant governance impact as it can result in a path-dependent dynamic. Structural and issue-framing decisions made early in the history of a regime often persist and shape the operation of the regime long into the future. Because secretariats often play an important role in shaping the way issues are understood and addressed early on in the policy cycle, their actions can create institutions that guide policy making long after their initial level of influence has waned. Although secretariat influence is typically modest in international affairs, path dependence helps us to understand the conditions under which secretariat influence can continue to shape political decision making into the future. The remainder of this section considers this relationship.

At the most rudimentary level, path dependence means that "history matters." Institutions have a tendency toward inertia, and therefore past decisions enable or constrain future decision making (Greener 2005). Path dependence has strong explanatory power, especially when previous actions establish a pattern of self-reinforcing practices that benefit key decision makers. Pierson (2000) has referred to this as path dependence grounded in a dynamic of increasing returns, wherein "increasing returns" are benefits that continue to accrue to these decision makers as certain practices are repeated over time. In the context of secretariat politics, these benefits might include such things as political capital, financial resources, and/or regime-relevant problem-solving tools. Levi (1997) further suggests that when such benefits result from the use of entrenched institutions (i.e., widely adopted and difficult to change), any change in established practice is particularly difficult. Therefore, secretariat influence matters most when it results in impacts that benefit key decision makers and such benefits are institutionally entrenched. Under these conditions, secretariat influence can create a path-dependent dynamic, which magnifies the impacts of such influence.

The first CBD case is particularly illustrative in this regard because the Secretariat's "blueprint" constructed an overlap management policy architecture that resulted in a path-dependent dynamic. The blueprint both yielded benefits for key decision makers and was widely adopted and difficult to change (i.e., it was entrenched). In terms of benefits, the Secretariat's blueprint set in motion overlap management activities that have become central to CBD implementation. For example, it identified "lead implementation partners" to design and execute joint work programs to implement CBD objectives that cut across two or more biodiversity treaties. In this vein, the Secretariat works with the Ramsar Convention to coordinate work on wetland protected areas, and has similar overlap management collaborations with the Convention on Migratory Species (CMS), the World Heritage Convention (WHC), and CITES. Because the CBD is a normative and coordinating convention, rather than an implementing one, uprooting these well-established implementing programs would undercut much of the CBD's overall implementation capacity, which is effectively carried out by other multilateral environmental agreements (MEAs) through these overlap management arrangements. Therefore, these joint work programs yield important implementation benefits for CBD member states.

In terms of entrenchment, the majority of the Secretariat's overlap management proposals contained in the blueprint have been officially adopted by CBD member states. These proposals included regular meetings between the executive heads of the various biodiversity secretariats, joint work programs between biodiversity secretariats, and coordination of CoP agendas (CBD CoP/2/INF/2). By the early 2000s, these tools were formally adopted not just within the CBD but also across the biodiversity regime complex. The executive heads of the biodiversity conventions met ten times between June 2004 and September 2011 to guide overlap management within the biodiversity regime complex, and by 2002, the CBD had formally agreed on joint work programs with CITES, CMS, and the Ramsar Convention.

Secretariat influence matters, therefore, to the extent that it shapes the way states understand issues, impacts equity dynamics in international affairs, and results in a path-dependent dynamic.

Should Secretariats Influence Politics?

The cases explored in this study also raise important questions about the broader implications of secretariat influence. On the one hand, secretariats are strengthening global governance regimes. Among other effects, their work enhances developing country participation through capacity building, streamlines complex governance tasks through knowledge brokering, and helps states to see and capitalize on otherwise hidden opportunities for interregime coordination through marketing. Their unique position in governance networks helps secretariats to deploy cross-regime expertise and institutional memory to develop policy tools that fit in a cross-institutional context—all functions that are of tremendous value given the increasingly scarce resources and complex, cross-sectoral policy issues that characterize global environmental governance. On the other hand, secretariat influence raises important questions about whose interests are represented in secretariat politics. Secretariat influence can be problematic if it privileges one set of norms/ideas over others. Further, it raises questions about whether bureaucrats, with thin accountability to the people impacted by their activities, should be substantively participating in political decision-making processes at all.

These questions are familiar to scholars of US public administration, who have been theorizing about domestic bureaucracies in this regard for decades. Central to scholarly discussions about domestic bureaucratic accountability and legitimacy is the question of how bureaucracies are *controlled*. The debate over bureaucratic control turns on the balance between technical decisions made by experts on the one hand, and political processes and power on the other. It addresses how much discretion bureaucracies should have, and the appropriate mechanisms for controlling them (Blau 1963; Carpenter 2001; Gruber 1987; Wilson 1967). Moreover, this literature reveals why controlling bureaucracies is so difficult. Gruber (1987), for instance, argues that plural understandings of terms such as fairness, access, coordination, and democracy underlie the problems we have in maintaining democratic control over bureaucracies. These variables are, of course, important at the international level as well, perhaps even more so with stakeholders even further separated from decision-making processes.

Blau (1963) highlights another challenge in this regard. He writes, "Our democratic institutions originated at a time when bureaucracies were in a rudimentary stage and hence [democratic institutions] are not designed to cope with their control. To extend these institutions by developing democratic methods for governing bureaucracies is, perhaps, the crucial problem of our age" (265). Blau's statement is particularly relevant because it highlights the parallel challenges of bureaucratic control that we are beginning to see at the international level. As existing institutions struggle to keep pace with a rapidly evolving governance architecture and distribution of power in international politics, the limits of original bureaucratic design for handling complex overlapping environmental problems come to the fore.

So how much discretion should secretariats have, and how should it be controlled? The heart of these questions, and indeed of secretariat politics more broadly, lies in the ability of a secretariat to maintain its legitimacy in the eyes of states. If and when secretariats fail to do so, states are likely to rein in secretariat autonomy, and accordingly their capacity to influence politics. Decreasing secretariat activities is fairly easy for states to do because much of global governance proceeds on the basis of consensus. States can typically rein in secretariat discretion through mandate or by rejecting secretariat advice based on an objection by a single member state. In considering the legitimacy of secretariat influence, identifying mechanisms to control secretariats are therefore less important than establishing *when* control is needed. The latter question requires consideration of what constitutes legitimate secretariat behavior and what does not. Although a complete analysis of this question is well beyond the scope of this study, the US public administration literature lends some initial insight.

Carpenter (2001) argues that bureaucratic legitimacy must be rooted in reputational uniqueness and political multiplicity. That is, bureaucracies must show that they can create solutions that cannot be found anywhere else in the polity, and their interests must be grounded in multiple and diverse political affiliations. Reputational uniqueness roughly equates with nonsubstitutability in that it points to secretariats' distinct position in international politics that sometimes allows them to create solutions which cannot be found anywhere else in the polity. As the cases explored in this book demonstrate, substitutability shifts across issues, organizations, and time. As the first CBD case illuminates, secretariats can sometimes construct reputational uniqueness by designing rules and institutions that place themselves at the center of governance architectures.

Political multiplicity, in contrast, is core to secretariats' identity and "international character," as laid out in treaty texts and the United Nations (UN) Charter.[3] In order to maintain legitimacy, secretariats must keep this international character. As we saw in the WTO case, maintaining international character may not always be straightforward—in some cases, biases that favor some countries over others are entrenched into regime rules and norms. The emerging body of scholarship on third world approaches to international law engages with this tension directly in highlighting the role that IOs can play in perpetuating the interests of powerful countries within ostensibly legitimate processes (Chimni 2006;

Gupta 2012). The exclusion of large portions of the agricultural sector from tariff reductions under the WTO is a classic example of this dynamic (Gupta 2012).

Legitimate secretariat participation in international affairs is thus less about identifying mechanisms of control and more about evaluating metrics for bureaucratic legitimacy. Although further research is needed to flesh out a comprehensive framework, the US public administration literature suggests that a secretariat's ability to maintain political multiplicity and construct reputational uniqueness are important in evaluating when secretariats' influence in world politics is legitimate and when it may be better to rein them in.

Overlap Management 2.0

Governance of overlap management is evolving, and with it secretariats' role therein. Overlap management has been on the docket of many IOs since the mid 1990s, and states have gained a fair amount of experience with the overlap management mechanisms described in this book, such as joint work programs and intra-secretariat cooperation. These approaches have been important in integrating overlap management on the agendas of many treaty regimes. However, few major successes have been claimed, and problems of treaty congestion remain topics of discussion in many forums.

As such, states are now beginning to experiment with new approaches and institutional architectures. These new approaches are tailored to a range of governance needs and constructions of regime overlap, which can be multilevel and engage varying constellations of actors and coalitions. While some of these ideas tend to move state actors to a more central position in managing overlapping regimes, others create new "superbureaucracies" dedicated primarily to this new area of intersecting governance schemes.

Global chemicals governance is one area where overlap management has grown in innovative ways in recent years. As explained by Selin (2010), chemicals governance has evolved as a set of overlapping non-hierarchical treaties, each addressing various stages of the chemical's life cycle. Unlike many other regime complexes that have actual (e.g., UN Framework Convention on Climate Change) or de facto (e.g., CBD) framework conventions to guide overlap management, the chemicals regime lacks a central bureaucratic hub that might be a natural leader in managing overlap. Nevertheless, overlap management in the chemicals regime has emerged as an important issue, with treaty-clustering initiatives and joint meetings of the CoPs pushing overlap management in new directions (IISD 2010c). Of particular note, the emerging overlap management framework within the chemicals regime includes a Strategic Approach to International Chemicals Management (SAICM).[4] Adopted in 2006, SAICM is a voluntary program with its own secretariat (hosted by the United Nations Environment Program) set up to help the various chemicals conventions coordinate action to meet common goals, such as those identified at the 2002 World Summit on Sustainable Development.[5] SAICM represents a very different approach to overlap management than that developed by the CBD Secretariat in the mid 1990s.[6] Although it is still in its early stages of development, SAICM's "superbureaucracy" approach may, if successful, emerge as a new framework for overlap management in the years to come, potentially presenting increased opportunities for secretariat influence.

At the other end of the governance spectrum are proposals to refocus overlap management from international bureaucracies to state-level actors. Although not referring to overlap management precisely as envisioned here, Slaughter's (2004) call for the further cultivation and development of government networks has far-reaching relevance to overlap management. She argues that as contemporary governance problems such as terrorism and trafficking operate through networked actors, so too do government officials, including justices, bureaucrats, and legislators. Slaughter cites examples across policy fields, including environmental issues, wherein domestic-level actors cooperate across national borders to achieve policy goals on issues of common concern. It is not difficult to conceive of such a framework working to manage overlap between international regimes as well. That is, domestic-level bureaucratic networks could potentially fill the same governance niche that secretariats have primarily occupied for the past two decades.

The importance of overlap management in world politics is also evidenced by the fact that it has percolated up and is being integrated across UN agencies, both within and beyond environmental politics. Typically referred to as "coherence building" or "policy coordination" in this context, several high-profile overlap management initiatives are now under way in the UN. As one example, the UN's "Delivering as One" approach, currently being piloted in eight countries, seeks to manage overlap at the country level across development, humanitarian assistance, and the environment. This approach mirrors but is even more far-reaching than the recent initiatives within the chemicals regime in its goal of "one leader, one programme, one budget, and where appropriate, one office" (UN General Assembly 2013). The Chief Executives Board for Coordination (CEB) under the UN is another important example. Made up of the heads of twenty-nine UN agencies and some extra UN IOs, the CEB seeks to enhance coordination across agencies on a host of issues including climate change, gender equality, and financial issues (UNCEB 2013). This approach further underscores the natural fit between overlap management and international bureaucratic expertise as well as an actor's position in international governance networks.

It remains to be seen which (if any) of these approaches will ultimately form the foundation for the next era of overlap management governance. However, with treaty congestion and regime complexity as dominant characteristics of contemporary global governance within and beyond environmental politics, overlap management will likely remain an important area of policy development in world politics. Further, as suggested by their placement at the center of contemporary cutting-edge overlap management initiatives—such as the SAICM and the CEB—secretariats will continue to play a central role in overlap management for years to come.

Appendix A: Case-Specific Methods

This book elucidates the inner workings of secretariats by providing the first book-length study of these bodies based on extensive document analysis (process tracing, coding, and content analysis) and ethnographic fieldwork (seventy-five interviews, sixty-three person-days of participant observation at international meetings, and four months working within a secretariat office). It analyzes four cases of overlap management within three treaty secretariats. The first two cases examine the Convention on Biological Diversity (CBD), the third World Trade Organization (WTO) case is divided into two subcases reflecting negotiations and dispute settlement in parallel but separate analyses, and the final case examines the Convention on International Trade in Endangered Species (CITES).

Cases of overlap management were selected based on evidence of regime overlap (i.e., without overlap, there is no need for overlap management); the nature of the relationship between overlapping policy field(s);[1] availability of resources for fieldwork; variation in types of overlap management activities; and critically, access to interview subjects and data. Case selection on the basis of these criteria allowed for unprecedented depth in the study of these veiled organizations.[2] However, as explained in chapter 1, it also required different data collection methods across cases. These case-specific data collection methods are described below.

Chapter 4 chronicles the evolution of overlap management within the CBD through an extensive process-tracing exercise covering over seventeen years of CBD negotiations. Where possible, it triangulates this data through my observation of two CBD meetings between 2007 and 2008, and fifteen semistructured interviews with Secretariat staff (CBD, Convention on Migratory Species, Ramsar, and CITES) and member states. These interviews were used to better understand how the biodiversity secretariats managed overlap under the CBD, and what role the CBD Secretariat specifically played in that process.

Chapter 5 employs document and content analysis to examine how the CBD Secretariat framed the biodiversity-climate linkage, and uses process tracing to illuminate where these framings originated (i.e., member states or elsewhere). I analyzed official CBD documents produced by the Secretariat and by CBD member states related to climate-biodiversity linkages between 2000 and 2007. I identified discussions of the biodiversity-climate linkage in each document, and coded each discussion according to one of eleven distinct frames identified through preliminary analysis of the data. In total, I coded 160 documents constituting 1,286 pages of data that discussed in part or in whole the policy-relevant linkages between biodiversity and climate change.[3] Finally, chapter 5 triangulates these findings with approximately fifteen interviews that I conducted in June 2006 at the CBD Secretariat headquarters in Montreal, Canada, and my observation of two CBD side events at UNFCCC meetings between December 2006 and December 2007.

Chapter 6 relies more heavily on interviews, participant observation, and secondary sources to understand how the WTO Secretariat participates in overlap management. I conducted 34 semistructured interviews with WTO Secretariat staff and delegates, as well as five interviews with nongovernmental organization (NGO) and intergovernmental organization (IGO) staff members who work with the WTO Secretariat on environmental issues, between September and December 2006 in Geneva, Switzerland. Interviewees were asked to explain and evaluate the Secretariat's participation in WTO affairs related to environmental issues. This chapter also employs participant observation, including four months I spent working on trade-environment issues within the United Nations Environment Program's Economics and Trade Branch, and my attendance at the WTO's 2006 Public Forum and various environmental treaty CoPs where the WTO Secretariat spoke and/or hosted a side event on trade-environment issues.

Finally, chapter 7 illuminates the CITES Secretariat's role in overlap management by employing a combination of document analysis, interviews with key informants, and participant observation. I analyzed all publicly available formal documents related to cooperation between CITES and the UN Food and Agriculture Organization (FAO) produced between 1997 and 2013. These included all formal documents prepared for the CITES and FAO meetings where cooperation between the two organizations was discussed, the official summary records following each meeting, and the *Earth Negotiations Bulletin* reports of these meetings (when available). The formal CITES documents prepared for each meeting were particularly instructive in shedding light on secretariat behavior because the CITES Secretariat formally comments, in writing, on all proposals submitted to CITES parties for consideration. As such, the Secretariat's activities and preferences are unusually transparent. The document analysis was supported by ten interviews with Secretariat staff, relevant NGOs, and state delegates to CITES,[4] as well as by observation of all six CITES meetings between October 2006 and March 2009.[5]

Appendix B: Details of Coding Procedure Used in Chapter 5

My coding procedure was designed to understand how the biodiversity-climate linkage is framed by each actor type (i.e., Secretariat, CoP, scientists, and the Subsidiary Body on Scientific, Technical, and Technological Advice [SBSTTA]) in the aggregate. Ultimately, I was interested in understanding whether the Secretariat's management of the linkage is simply directed by the Convention on Biological Diversity (CBD) CoP, SBSTTA, and relevant scientists, or is autonomously constructed, suggesting that the Secretariat influences governance of overlap management.

I categorized all documents as either Secretariat-produced "outputs" or member state–produced "inputs." Output documents included 117 public statements given by former CBD Executive Secretary Djoghlaf between 2006 and 2007;[1] the sixteen publicly available statements delivered by Djoghlaf's predecessor, Hamdallah Zedan, between 2004 and 2005;[2] the Secretariat-authored foreword to the CBD ad hoc technical expert group's (AHTEG) first two reports on Biodiversity and Climate Change; Djoghlaf's contribution to Gincana 2 on Biodiversity and Climate Change, and to a Joint Liaison Group report on linkages between the Rio conventions; and the CBD Secretariat–produced Global Biodiversity Outlook (GBO) 1 and GBO 2.

Input documents included CBD CoP decisions (V/21, V/3, V/4, VI/20, VII/26, VII/15, IX/16, IIX/30) and SBSTTA recommendations (VI/7, IX/11, X/13, XI/14, XII/5) on "Biodiversity and Climate Change" and "Cooperation." In addition, because the CBD CoP often instructs the Secretariat to make a recommendation on the basis of specific pieces of scientific information, I also examined scientific input documents as a second possible input source. I examined those sources of scientific information which should in theory be driving Secretariat behavior, as identified by the CBD CoP in numerous CoP decisions over time (table B.1).

Table B.1

Scientific Inputs

Year	Document Title
2001	IPCC Assessment Report (AR) 3 Synthesis Report
2002	IPCC Technical Series V: Climate Change and Biodiversity
2003	CBD Technical Series 10: Interlinkages between Biological Diversity and Climate Change (Main Text)
2005	Millennium Ecosystem Assessment: Ecosystems and Human Well Being: General Synthesis
2005	Millennium Ecosystem Assessment: Ecosystems and Human Well Being: Biodiversity Synthesis
2006	CBD Technical Series 25: Emerging Issues for Biodiversity Conservation in a Changing Climate (Main Text)
2007	IPCC AR 4 Synthesis Report
2007	Gincana 3 Biological Diversity and Climate Change

I then examined each document for discussion of the biodiversity-climate linkage, and coded each discussion as one of eleven distinct discursive frames of the linkage.

Next, I categorized each discussion of the linkage as a dominant, secondary, or tertiary frame, before scaling this system up to understand emphasis in the aggregate for each actor type. Due to the varied nature of the documents in terms of length and substance, my procedure for categorizing dominant frames for individual documents varied slightly across data sources. When analyzing relatively short Secretariat input documents (about one to five pages long), I categorized a frame as dominant if it reflected the main point(s) of the discussion of the linkage, or if it was repeated more than three times.[3] On CoP and SBSTTA decisions, dominance was assigned on the basis of both the location of the frame (i.e., a frame in the main text was given more weight than one in the preamble), and by the percentage of the decision/recommendation that was dedicated to a particular frame. Regarding the much longer scientific reports, dominance was determined on the basis of both how much space in the report was dedicated to discussion of a particular framing and how much space was dedicated in comparison to alternative framings. Because this study is aimed at identifying broad trends of emphasis, identifying the dominant frame(s) was a fairly straightforward process for all documents examined.

Identification of secondary and tertiary frames was more complicated. Simple quantification of the number of times a frame was used does not adequately capture the importance of a particular frame. For example, it does not allow differentiation between one in-depth discussion and multiple passing mentions. As such, I began by identifying tertiary frames as those that were mentioned in passing and were not used to support the dominant frame(s). For example, if the dominant frames in a document are that climate change and mitigation measures cause biodiversity loss (Frames #1 and 2), then an unconnected or isolated mention of general cooperation (Frame #8) would be classified as tertiary. All frames that were neither dominant nor tertiary were categorized as secondary frames. That is, secondary frames either were used to substantively support dominant frame(s) and/or were otherwise substantively discussed in the document.

Finally, to determine aggregate emphasis for each actor type, I applied a point system to each data set (i.e., data sets produced by the Secretariat, CoP, SBSTTA, and scientists). This system allocated points on the basis of the number of times a particular frame showed up as dominant (5 points), secondary (3 points), and tertiary (1 point) across each data set, and excluded any frame that earned less than 3 points. The number of points allocated to each frame was then divided by the total number of points allocated across the entire data set in order to provide an indication of the relative emphasis of each (percentage of points allocated).

Because the process of ordering these frames involves an inherent amount of subjectivity, I analyzed the data in three different ways, yielding nearly identical results for dominant and secondary frames. Specifically, I dropped any points allocated on the basis of tertiary mentions of a particular frame. When analyzed in this way, dominant and secondary frames remain the same across all data sets. The third way I analyzed the data was simply according to how many times a frame showed up as dominant in each data set. When analyzed in this way, most frames remain in place with the following exceptions: adjacent frames 7 and 11 switch places for the Secretariat data set; and adjacent frames 2 and 5 switch order in the SBSTTA data set. As such, while the system of determining relative emphasis is not perfect, it is adequately robust for the purposes of comparing the extent to which the Secretariat mirrors stated discussions of the biodiversity-climate linkage.

Notes

Chapter 1

1. IR scholarship has greatly contributed to scholarship on international organizations (IOs). However, most of this scholarship tends to conflate secretariats with the IOs of which they are part. Further, this study focuses on treaty secretariats rather than those of larger IOs, such as the World Bank, that have been the focus of most of this scholarship. This rationale is discussed in the "Methodological Approach" section below.

2. For an in-depth review of the IO literature, see Simmons and Martin (2002).

3. See, for example, Biermann and Bauer (2005); Downs (2000); Miles et al. (2002); Mitchell (1994, 2003); Von Moltke (2001); Young (1991, 1994, 2002); and Young et al. (2008).

4. See, for example, Betsill and Correll (2008); Biermann and Pattberg (2012); Biermann and Siebenhüner (2009); Cashore, Auld, and Newsom (2004); Clapp and Fuchs (2008); Falkner (2003); Gulbrandsen and Andresen (2004); Haas (1990); Newell (2000); and Selin (2010).

5. This definition follows Krasner's (1983) classic definition of the term.

6. Recent scholarship suggests that such conflicts are less common than previously thought. See Oberthür and Gehring (2006).

7. See Jinnah (2012) for a discussion of this case.

8. See, for example, Gehring and Oberthür (2000, 2009); Jinnah (2010, 2011a, 2011b); Oberthür (2009); Oberthür and Stokke (2011); Rosendal (2001a, 2001b); Selin and VanDeveer (2003); Stokke (2000, 2004); Young (1996, 2002); and Young et al. (2008).

9. Practitioners use a variety of terms to refer to the process, including interregime cooperation or collaboration, coherence building, triple-win policy scenarios, and synergy capture.

10. See, for example, Barnett and Finnemore (2004); Biermann and Siebenhüner (2009); and Jinnah (2010, 2011b).

11. See, for example, Brack and Btanczik (2004); Charnovitz (2003); Conca (2000); Esty (2002); Jinnah (2011a); and Shaffer (2002a).

12. The details of the WTO's environmental mandates are discussed in chapter 5.

13. Oberthür and Gehring (2006) employ a similar approach in their study of institutional interaction, in which multiple cases of interaction are studied within a single institution.

14. However, CITES interviewees were also the most generous with their time and willing to maintain an iterative relationship over time.

15. See chapter 2 for a detailed discussion of this issue.

16. The IMF refers to its secretariat as an "international civil service." See International Monetary Fund (n.d.).

Chapter 2

1. As quoted in Ranshofen-Wertheimer (1945), 391.

2. Even scholars who see IOs as potentially independent and/or autonomous actors understand secretariats as mere technical administrators. See, for example, Abbott and Snidal (1998), 9.

3. Personal observation, 2007.

4. See Mathiason (2007) for a discussion of why states see secretariats as "invisible."

5. Joanna Depledge (2007) coined this term to describe a similar relationship between the United Nations Framework Convention on Climate Change (UNFCCC) Secretariat and chairpersons at the climate change negotiations.

6. See, for example, Carpenter (2001).

7. According to Marx (1957), some trace the bureaucratic form back to the mid 1700s and the French economist Vincent de Gournay. Others, such as Kilcullen (1996), argue that bureaucracies can be traced back to the royal clerks of the Middle Ages who traveled by horseback with their kings and, because they were literate, had the responsibility of carrying the writing implements and official records for the party.

8. There is a rich literature on domestic bureaucracies. One particularly relevant strand for this study is that on bureaucratic control. See, for example, Blau (1963); Gruber (1987); and Wilson (1967).

9. The IMF doesn't technically refer to its administrative staff as a "secretariat." Rather, it uses the term "international civil service." This study understands these terms as essentially synonymous. Although there are important differences in empirical function, state expectations for the norms of behavior are quite similar. For example, the IMF's code of conduct is very similar to that of the UN Staff Rules discussed below (International Monetary Fund 1998).

10. Secretariats also employ a large number of part-time, short-term consultants and unpaid interns. These short-term hires impact secretariat culture. Many of the nonsalaried employees interviewed for this study in Geneva were dissatisfied with their positions, feeling exploited and underpaid. Due to UN rules

limiting the term length of any single consultancy, they were often forced to bounce around between short-term posts, hoping for the opportunity to apply for a permanent full-time salaried position. These problems are compounded for consultants from many developing countries who, due to strict Swiss immigration policies, must grapple with obtaining visas to stay in Geneva between consultancies.

11. See chapter 1.

12. As Ranshofen-Wertheimer (1945) explains, governments were divided on this issue when negotiating the structure and makeup of the League of Nations Secretariat.

13. See chapter 2 of Biermann and Siebenhüner (2009) for a comprehensive review of this literature.

14. Gutner (2005) and Barnett and Finnemore (2004) point to this dynamic in arguing that IOs can be both agents and principals.

15. Barnett and Finnemore (2004), 5.

16. Interview with CBD Secretariat staff member, June 2006.

17. Interviews with WTO delegates, September-December 2006.

Chapter 3

1. Others have described these concepts as "power resources." See, for example, Hall (1997).

2. See chapter 2.

3. See Huber and Shipan (2002).

4. See chapter 2 for a discussion of fixed and evolving mandates.

5. For more on the relationship between worldviews and environmental governance, see Clapp and Dauvergne (2005, 1–18).

6. For examples of academic literature, see Eglin (1995); Juma (1989); Motaal (2002); and Tamiotti and Finger (2001). For an example of a technical report, see WTO Secretariat (2007d); for a working paper, see Valentini (2005); and for an analysis, see Auboin (2007).

7. On regime effectiveness, see Young (1994).

8. See Betsill and Corell (2008, 25), for a closely related definition and discussion of influence as it relates to their analysis of nongovernmental organizations (NGOs).

9. Interviews with WTO and biodiversity secretariat staff suggest, however, that states are unlikely to bring solidified domestic preferences to international forums on overlap management because it is also a fairly new issue at the domestic level. This is also evidenced by requests for best practices on this issue within the WTO and in the experimental overlap management strategies utilized in some countries for cross-treaty biodiversity governance. See IISD (2007a).

Chapter 4

1. "Biodiversity-related" refers to all treaties classified under the subject headings "nature," "species," and "habitat."

2. The CoP has established one open-ended ad hoc intergovernmental committee for the Nagoya Protocol on ABS and four working groups to consider the following topics: Article 8(j) (traditional knowledge), access and benefit sharing, review of implementation (and coordination), and protected areas.

3. CBD CoP4 (1998b), Annex I, paragraph III.7.

4. See the "Thematic Programmes and Cross-Cutting Issues" page on the official website of the CBD, available at http://www.cbd.int/programmes/ (updated March 10, 2011; accessed November 15, 2013).

5. These numbers are approximated using the Staff list on the CBD website.

6. INF documents are typically produced by the Secretariat and circulated electronically to the parties, as well as made available via the Convention website, prior to each meeting. They, along with official documents, are also made available to the parties in hard copy at each meeting.

7. See "Conference of the Parties," CDB website, http://www.cbd.int/cop/ (accessed March 13, 2012).

8. The document indicates that there are eight such areas, but it subsequently proceeds to identify only seven.

9. More recent MoCs have taken upward of five years to negotiate.

10. By 2004, the Secretariat had finalized more than seventy MoCs.

11. This group was established by the Secretariat in cooperation with the SBSTTA during the intercessional period.

12. The Secretariat had by this time formalized over 175 "partnerships" (CBD Secretariat 2006b, paragraph 51).

13. See also IISD (2005) (Summary of WGRI1).

14. A review of the *Earth Negotiations Bulletin* report of this meeting suggests that this idea was not incorporated into the draft decision by a party but was indeed contained in the original decision the Secretariat had drafted on this matter (IISD 1996).

15. This particular cooperative relationship, i.e., that between Ramsar and CBD, is considered by both secretariats to be one of their most successful cooperative endeavors.

16. There is, however, a joint initiative between UNEP, GEF (Global Environment Facility), and UNEP-WCMC (UNEP Conservation Monitoring Centre 2013) to create a joint reporting system for the Rio Conventions. See "Integrated Reporting to the Rio Conventions," UNEP World Conservation Monitoring Centre, http://www.unep-wcmc.org/integrated-reporting-to-the-rio-conventions_675 .html, accessed February 12, 2014.

Chapter 5

1. An earlier version of this chapter was published in *Global Environmental Politics* (Jinnah 2011b).

2. See chapter 4 for a more detailed account of these early political debates.

3. See appendix B for a detailed description of how the content analysis was carried out.

4. Although some of the scientific bodies are not state actors per se, all scientific bodies examined are those that were identified by CBD member states as sources of information upon which the Secretariat should base its work. As such, information from these scientific bodies implicitly reflects state preferences on this issue.

5. See appendix B for a detailed explanation of the coding procedure, including how frames were categorized as dominant.

6. No change in emphasis was observed before and after International Biodiversity Day in 2007 when the theme was "Biodiversity and Climate Change."

7. In separating out a second clause related to the adaptive potential of *biological* systems (i.e., after the comma), the implication is that the first clause (i.e., before the comma) implicitly refers to *human* adaptive potential.

8. This study examined the National Reports of a sample of CBD member states that had submitted at least three of the four CBD National Reports to date in English, and with an aim to capture both geographical representation and variation with respect to proximity to biodiversity hotspots (Myers et al. 2000). The analysis includes the National Reports submitted by Brazil, China, India, Indonesia, Kenya, Malaysia, the Philippines, Germany, Sweden, and Turkey. Each report was coded for framings of biodiversity-climate overlap using the same method used above for analyzing CoP, SBSTTA, scientific, and secretariat-produced documents. Appendix B contains a detailed account of the coding procedure.

9. In December 2008, REDD came to be known as REDD+, with "plus" incorporating the inclusion of "conservation, sustainable management, and the enhancement of forest stocks" in its definition.

10. Forest conservation mitigates climate change because deforestation is a leading cause of greenhouse gas emissions.

11. Reports available at UNFCC, "Adaptation planning and practices," http://unfccc.int/adaptation/nairobi_work_programme/programme_activities_and_work_areas/items/3991.php (accessed April 30, 2012).

Chapter 6

1. An earlier version of this chapter was published in *Global Environmental Politics* (Jinnah 2010).

2. See, for example, WTO Appellate Body (1998) on "United States—Import Prohibition of Certain Shrimp and Shrimp Products." In this decision, the Appellate

Body felt it necessary to clarify that environmental issues should be "of significance" to WTO members, yet failed to offer any concrete instructions on how to reconcile the tensions between trade and environmental rules and norms, such as the protection of sea turtles, in practice.

3. See Najam (2004).

4. See WTO (2006), 335–336.

5. For more in-depth discussion on various aspects of trade-environment politics, see Clapp and Dauvergne (2005); Steinberg (1997); and Williams (2001).

6. See World Trade Organization website, http://wto.org/ (accessed November 25, 2013).

7. Arguably, this is because the WTO oversees maintenance of twenty agreements compared to the CBD's two.

8. The TRIPs Council and the associated Secretariat's Intellectual Property (IP) Division have been excluded from this study due to lack of access to sufficient data and because preliminary investigation made it clear that the IP issues warrant a study of their own.

9. I focus my analysis on the period after 2001 because, although most Secretariat staff I interviewed were able to speak about the period before 2001, most WTO delegates I spoke with were unable to do so.

10. See Shaffer (2002b).

11. Information from author's interview in fall 2006 with a United Nations Environment Program (UNEP) representative who regularly attends CTE/CTESS meetings.

12. See WTO Secretariat (2007a).

13. See WTO Secretariat (2007b), 3.

14. For example, CITES, the Basel Convention, and the Montreal Protocol all address this issue.

15. See WTO Secretariat (2007c).

16. See WTO Secretariat (2013a).

17. The Appellate Body is not examined here because it has its own Secretariat.

18. See WTO Dispute Settlement Understanding (DSU), Article 27 (WTO 2007).

19. In accordance with institutional requirements for protecting my interviewees' identifying information, I have written this section without mentioning specific cases. Although interviews were restricted to the Secretariat's participation in supporting chapter XX disputes, it is likely that the Secretariat influences panel-level dispute settlement in other areas as well.

20. See Huffbauer et al. (2005), 216.

21. See WTO Secretariat (2007d), 36.

22. See also Weiler (2001).

23. For example, members' opinions diverge on seemingly objective details such as which MEAs contain specific trade obligations.

24. See Jinnah (2003).

25. For a detailed discussion on the WTO's "legitimacy crisis," see Esty (2002).

26. I have omitted the subject matter under discussion in order to protect the identity of this interviewee.

Chapter 7

1. CITES protects plants and animals by placing trade restrictions on species that are threatened due to international trade. Parties place protected species in one of three appendixes depending on their level of threat.

2. My calculation includes the number of proposals for which the Secretariat made a recommendation, and does not include those proposals that were withdrawn or inconclusive.

3. Young (2010, 469), for example, provides such an account of this negotiation process from the perspective of an Australian delegate to FAO.

4. There are approximately 5,600 plant and 30,000 animal species listed in the CITES appendixes. See http://www.cites.org/eng/disc/species.php.

5. In contrast to the species listed in the other two appendixes that are decided upon by a vote, parties may make unilateral amendments to Appendix III.

6. FAO reports do not attribute statements to individual member states.

7. A proposal from Australia (CITES Secretariat 2013) to move the freshwater sawfish from Appendix II to Appendix I was also approved at CoP16.

8. This was done in cooperation with the Plants Committee.

9. Nevertheless, FAO continued to carry out its own independent review of the listing criteria. It produced a report on this issue in October 2001, which it submitted to CITES CoP12 in November 2002 (CITES Secretariat 2002e).

10. These seven include only those proposals for which the Secretariat recommended adoption or rejection. This means that the CoP agreed with the Secretariat only in the two instances when its recommendations were in line with FAO's.

Chapter 8

1. See Oberthür and Gehring (2006).

2. See, for example, Axelrod and Keohane (1985); Haas (1980); and Tollison and Willett (1979).

3. See chapter 2.

4. SAICM works in cooperation with the Inter-organization Program for the Sound Management of Chemicals (IOMC). Established in 1995, IOMC is one of the oldest overlap management institutions and serves as a meta-level overlap management organization between the UN agencies that deal with chemicals safety. See the IOMC website, http://www.who.int/iomc/en/.

5. See Selin (2010) for an in-depth discussion of linkages within the global chemicals regime, including the role played by SAICM in managing those linkages.

6. See chapter 4.

Appendix A

1. Gehring and Oberthür (2009) suggest that this is an important variable to consider when evaluating the impact of overlapping regimes.

2. Any information given to me specifically as a condition of my consultancy positions is confidential and is treated as such in this study.

3. A detailed account of this coding procedure can be found in appendix B.

4. I contacted FAO's representative to CITES meetings various times to request an interview and never received a response.

5. These meetings were CITES SC54, CoP14, PC17, PC18, AC23, and AC24.

Appendix B

1. Of the 135 statements available on the CBD Secretariat's website, 117 are available in English. The remaining 18 were excluded from this analysis.

2. Preliminary analysis of statements prior to 2004 revealed infrequent discussion of the linkage.

3. I was not looking for the main point of the document itself, just for the document's discussion of the climate-biodiversity linkage. More than one dominant frame was possible and common.

References

Abbott, Kenneth W., and Duncan Snidal. 1998. Why States Act through Formal International Organizations. *Journal of Conflict Resolution* 42 (1):3–32.

Adler, Emanuel, and Peter M. Haas. 1992. Conclusion: Epistemic Communities, World Order, and the Creation of a Reflective Research Program. *International Organization* 46 (01):367–390.

Allen, Adriana, and Nicholas You. 2002. *Sustainable Urbanization: Bridging the Green and Brown Agendas*. London: DFID, UN-HABITAT, and DPU Press.

Alter, Karen J., and Sophie Meunier. 2009. The Politics of International Regime Complexity. *Perspectives on Politics* 7 (1):13–24.

American Heritage Dictionary of the English Language. 2000. Boston: Houghton Mifflin.

Auboin, Mark. 2007. *Fulfilling the Marrakesh Mandate on Coherence: Ten Years of Cooperation between the WTO, IMF and World Bank*. Geneva: World Trade Organization.

Axelrod, Robert, and Robert O. Keohane. 1985. Achieving Cooperation under Anarchy: Strategies and Institutions. *World Politics* 38 (1):226–254.

Bachrach, Peter, and S. Baratz Morton. 1962. Two Faces of Power. *American Political Science Review* 56 (4):947–952.

Barnett, Michael, and Raymond Duvall, eds. 2005. *Power in Global Governance*. Cambridge: Cambridge University Press.

Barnett, Michael, and Martha Finnemore. 2004. *Rules for the World: International Organizations in Global Politics*. Ithaca: Cornell University Press.

Bauer, Steffen. 2006. Does Bureaucracy Really Matter? The Authority of Treaty Secretariats in Global Environmental Politics. *Global Environmental Politics* 6 (1):23–49.

Bauer, Steffen, Steinar Andresen, and Frank Biermann. 2012. International Bureaucracies. In *Global Environmental Governance Reconsidered*, ed. Frank Biermann and Philipp Pattberg, 28–44. Cambridge, MA: MIT Press.

BBC News Asia. 2013. Japan Bluefin Tuna Fetches Record $1.7m. British Broadcasting Corporation. January 13.

Bernstein, Steven. 2005. Legitimacy in Global Environmental Governance. *Journal of International Law and International Relations* 1 (1–2):139–166.

Bernstein, Steven. 2011. Legitimacy in Intergovernmental and Non-State Global Governance. *Review of International Political Economy* 18 (1):17–51.

Betsill, Michele M., and Elisabeth Corell. 2001. NGO Influence in International Environmental Negotiations: A Framework for Analysis. *Global Environmental Politics* 1 (4):65–85.

Betsill, Michele M., and Elisabeth Corell. 2008. *NGO Diplomacy: The Influence of Nongovernmental Organizations in International Environmental Negotiations*. Cambridge, MA: MIT Press.

Biermann, Frank, et al. 2009. Studying the Influence of International Bureaucracies: A Conceptual Framework. In *Managers of Global Change: The Influence of International Environmental Bureaucracies*, ed. Frank Biermann and Bernd Siebenhüner, 37–74. Cambridge, MA: MIT Press.

Biermann, Frank, and Steffen Bauer. 2005. Managers of Global Governance: Assessing and Explaining the Influence of International Bureaucracies. Global Governance Working Paper No. 15.

Biermann, Frank, and Philipp Pattberg, eds. 2012. *Global Environmental Governance Reconsidered*. Cambridge, MA: MIT Press.

Biermann, Frank, and Bernd Siebenhüner, eds. 2009. *Managers of Global Change: The Influence of International Environmental Bureaucracies*. Cambridge, MA: MIT Press.

Blau, Peter. 1963. *The Dynamics of Bureaucracy*. Chicago: University of Chicago Press.

Bodansky, Daniel. 1999. Legitimacy of International Governance: A Coming Challenge for International Environmental Law. *American Journal of International Law* 93 (3):596–624.

Bown, Chad, and Bernard Hoekman. 2005. WTO Dispute Settlement and the Missing Developing Country Cases: Engaging the Private Sector. *Journal of International Economic Law* 8 (4): 861–890.

Brack, Duncan, and Thomas Btanczik. 2004. *Trade and Environment in the WTO: After Cancun*. London: Royal Institute of International Affairs.

Brown, Paul. 1999. Japan Admits Using Aid to Build Pro-Whaling Vote. *Guardian*, November 11.

Busch, Per-Olof. 2006. The Secretariat of the Climate Convention: Making a Living in a Straitjacket. Global Governance Working Paper No. 22.

Bushey, Douglas, and Sikina Jinnah. 2010. Evolving Responsibility? The Principle of Common but Differentiated Responsibility in the UNFCCC. *Berkeley Journal of International Law Publicist* 28 (2): 1–10.

Butchart, Stuart H. M., et al. 2010. Global Biodiversity: Indicators of Recent Declines. *Science* 328 (5982): 1164–1168.

Calderwood, Howard B. 1937. The Higher Direction of the League Secretariat. *Arnold Foundation Studies in Public Affairs* 5 (3): 1–31.

Caldwell, Lynton K. 1984. *International Environmental Policy: Emergence and Dimensions*. Durham: Duke University Press.

Carpenter, Daniel P. 2001. *The Forging of Bureaucratic Autonomy: Reputations, Networks, and Policy Innovation in Executive Agencies, 1862–1928*. Princeton: Princeton University Press.

Cashore, Benjamin, Graeme Auld, and Deanna Newsom. 2004. *Governing through Markets: Forest Certification and Non-State Authority*. New Haven: Yale University Press.

CBD [Convention on Biological Diversity] CoP1. 1994a. Decision I/4. Selection of a Competent International Organization to Carry Out the Functions of the Secretariat of the Convention. November 28–December 9, Nassau, Bahamas.

CBD CoP1. 1994b. Decision I/5. Support to the Secretariat by International Organizations. November 28–December 9, Nassau, Bahamas.

CBD CoP1. 1994c. Decision I/9. Medium-term Programme of Work of the Conference of the Parties. November 28–December 9, Nassau, Bahamas.

CBD CoP2. 1995. Decision II/13. Cooperation with Other Biodiversity-related Conventions. November 6–17, Jakarta, Indonesia.

CBD CoP4. 1998a. Decision IV/15. The Relationship of the Convention on Biological Diversity with the Commission on Sustainable Development and Biodiversity-related Conventions, Other International Agreements, Institutions and Processes of Relevance. May 4–15, Bratislava, Slovakia.

CBD CoP4. 1998b. Decision IV/16. Institutional Matters and the Programme of Work. May 4–15, Bratislava, Slovakia.

CBD CoP5. 2000. Decision V/4. Progress Report on the Implementation of the Programme of Work for Forest Biological Diversity. May 15–26, Nairobi, Kenya.

CBD CoP6. 2002a. Decision VI/20. Cooperation with Other Organizations, Initiatives and Conventions. April 7–19, The Hague, Netherlands.

CBD CoP6b. 2002b. Decision VI/22. Forest Biological Diversity. April 7–19, The Hague, Netherlands.

CBD CoP6. 2002c. Decision VI/26. Strategic Plan for the Convention on Biological Diversity. April 7–19, The Hague, Netherlands.

CBD CoP7. 2004a. Decision VII/15. Biodiversity and Climate Change. February 9–20, Kuala Lumpur, Malaysia.

CBD CoP7. 2004b. Decision VII/26. Cooperation with Other Conventions and International Organizations and Initiatives. February 9–20, Kuala Lumpur, Malaysia.

CBD CoP8. 2006a. Decision VIII/16. Cooperation with Other Conventions and International Organizations and Initiatives. March 20–31, Curitiba, Brazil.

CBD CoP8. 2006b. Decision VIII/25. Incentive Measures: Application of Tools for Valuation of Biodiversity and Biodiversity Resources and Functions. March 20–31, Curitiba, Brazil.

CBD CoP9. 2008a. Decision IX/16. Biodiversity and Climate Change. May 19–30, Bonn, Germany.

CBD CoP9. 2008b. Decision IX/27. Cooperation among Multilateral Environmental Agreements and Other Organizations. May 19–30, Bonn, Germany.

CBD CoP10. 2010a. Decision X/20. Cooperation with Other Conventions and International Organizations and Initiatives. October 8–29, Nagoya, Japan.

CBD CoP10. 2010b. Decision X/33. Biodiversity and Climate Change. October 8–29, Nagoya, Japan.

CBD Secretariat. 1995. UNEP/CBD/CoP/2/INF/2. Cooperation with Other Biodiversity-Related Conventions. November 6–17, Jakarta, Indonesia.

CBD Secretariat. 1996a. UNEP/CBD/CoP/3/29. Activities Undertaken in Relation to Cooperation with Other Biodiversity-Related Conventions. November 4–15, Buenos Aires, Argentina.

CBD Secretariat. 1996b. UNEP/CBD/CoP/3/35. Relationship of the Convention with Other Conventions, Institutions and Processes: Modalities for Enhanced Cooperation with Relevant Biodiversity-Related Bodies. November 4–15, Buenos Aires, Argentina.

CBD Secretariat. 2002. UNEP/CBD/CoP/6/15. Cooperation with Other Bodies and Contribution to the 10-year Review of Progress Achieved since the United Nations Conference on Environment and Development. April 7–19, The Hague, Netherlands.

CBD Secretariat. 2005a. UNEP/CBD/WG-RI/1/INF/7. Report of the Third Meeting of the Biodiversity Liaison Group. Ad Hoc Open-Ended Working Group on Review of Implementation of the Convention. September 5–9, Montreal, Canada.

CBD Secretariat. 2005b. UNEP/CBD/WG-RI/1/7. Cooperation with Other Conventions, Organizations and Initiatives, and Engagement of Stakeholders in the Implementation of the Convention. Ad Hoc Open-Ended Working Group on Review of Implementation of the Convention. November 6–17, Jakarta, Indonesia.

CBD Secretariat. 2006a. CBD Technical Series No. 25. Guidance for Promoting Synergy among Activities Addressing Biological Diversity, Desertification, Land Degradation, and Climate Change. Ad Hoc Technical Expert Group on Biodiversity and Adaptation to Climate Change. Montreal, Canada.

CBD Secretariat. 2006b. UNEP/CBD/CoP/8/25. Cooperation with other Conventions, Organizations and Initiatives and Engagement of Stakeholders, including Options for a Global Partnership. March 20–31, Curitiba, Brazil.

CBD Secretariat. 2012. UNEP/CBD/QR/58–59. Biannual Report on the Administration of the Convention on Biological Diversity. February 29, Montreal, Canada.

CBD Secretariat. 2013a. MEA Cooperation: Cooperative Activities. http://www.cbd.int/cooperation/related-conventions/activities.shtml.

CBD Secretariat. 2013b. Harmonization of Biodiversity-Related Reporting. http://www.cbd.int/reports/harmonization.shtml.

CBD Secretariat. 2013c. Official website. http://www.cbd.int.

CBD Secretariat. 2013d. Thematic Programmes and Cross-Cutting Issues. http://www.cbd.int/programmes/.

Charnovitz, Steve. 2003. *Trade and Climate: Potential for Conflicts and Synergies*. Washington, DC: Pew Center on Global Climate Change.

Chatterjee, Pratap, and Matthias Finger. 1994. *The Earth Brokers*. New York: Routledge.

Chimni, Bhupinder S. 2006. Third World Approaches to International Law: A Manifesto. *International Community Law Review* 8 (1):3–27.

CITES [Convention on International Trade in Endangered Species]. 1973. *Convention on International Trade in Endangered Species of Wild Fauna and Flora*. Washington, DC: CITES

CITES CoP12. 2002. Decision 12.7. Establishment of a Memorandum of Understanding between CITES and the Food and Agriculture Organization of the United Nations. November 3–15, Santiago, Chile.

CITES Secretariat. N.d. (a). CITES Resolutions. CITES Secretariat, Geneva. http://www.cites.org eng/res/intro.php. Accessed February 28, 2014.

CITES Secretariat. N.d. (b). Decisions of the Conference of the Parties. CITES Secretariat, Geneva. http://www.cites.org/eng/dec/intro.php. Accessed February 28, 2014.

CITES Secretariat. 1994a. CoP9 Com.9.17 (Rev.). Draft Resolution of the Conference of the Parties—Criteria for Amendment of Appendices I and II. November 7–18, Fort Lauderdale, United States of America.

CITES Secretariat. 1994b. CoP9 Doc.9.41. Interpretation and Implementation of the Convention: New Criteria for Amendment of Appendices I and II. November 7–18, Fort Lauderdale, United States of America.

CITES Secretariat. 1997a. CoP10 Doc. 10.60. Interpretation and Implementation of the Convention: Establishment of a Working Group on Marine Fish Species. June 9–20, Harare, Zimbabwe.

CITES Secretariat. 1997b. CoP10 Doc. 10.61. Interpretation and Implementation of the Convention: Establishment of a Working Group on Marine Fish Species. June 9–20, Harare, Zimbabwe.

CITES Secretariat. 1999a. Doc. SC.41.19. Review of the Criteria for Amendment of Appendices I and II. February 8–12, Geneva, Switzerland.

CITES Secretariat. 1999b. Doc. SC.41.19.1. Summary Report of the Meeting of the FAO. Geneva, Switzerland.

CITES Secretariat. 1999c. Doc. SC41. Summary Report. Forty-first Meeting of the Standing Committee. February 8–12, Geneva, Switzerland.

CITES Secretariat. 2000a. CoP11 Com.I. 11.1 First Session. April 11, Nairobi, Kenya.

CITES Secretariat. 2000b. CoP11 Com.II. 11.2 Second Session. April 12, Nairobi, Kenya.

CITES Secretariat. 2000c. CoP11 Doc.11.14. Strategic and Administrative Matters: Synergy with the United Nations Food and Agriculture Organization. April 10–20, Gigiri, Kenya.

CITES Secretariat. 2000d. CoP11 Doc.11.25. Interpretation and Implementation of the Convention: Procedure for the Review of Criteria for Amendment of Appendices I and II. April 10–20, Gigiri, Kenya.

CITES Secretariat. 2002a. Resolution Conf. 14.2. CITES Strategic Vision: 2008–2013. April 9–20, Nairobi, Kenya.

CITES Secretariat. 2002b. CoP12 Doc. 12.7. Establishment of a Memorandum of Understanding between CITES and the Food and Agriculture Organization of the United Nations (FAO). November 3–15, Santiago, Chile.

CITES Secretariat. 2002c. CoP12 Doc. 16.2.1. Strategic and Administrative Matters: Cooperation with Other Organizations—CITES and FAO—Synergy and Cooperation between CITES and FAO. November 3–15, Santiago, Chile.

CITES Secretariat. 2002d. CoP12 Doc. 16.2.2. Strategic and Administrative Matters: Cooperation with Other Organizations—CITES and FAO. November 3–15, Santiago, Chile.

CITES Secretariat. 2002e CoP12 Inf.5. Interpretation and Implementation of the Convention Amendment of the Appendices. November 3–15, Santiago, Chile.

CITES Secretariat. 2003. SC49 Doc. 6.3. Strategic and Administrative Matters: Ad Hoc Expert Group on Listing Criteria for Marine Species under CITES (Cape Town, South Africa, November 20, 1998). February 8–12, Geneva, Switzerland.

CITES Secretariat. 2004a. CoP13 Com. II Rep. 10 (Rev. 1). Summary Report—Tenth Session. October 8, Bangkok, Thailand.

CITES Secretariat. 2004b. CoP13 Doc.12.4. Strategic and Administrative Matters: Cooperation with Other Organizations—Cooperation with the Food and Agriculture Organization of the United Nations. October 2–14, Bangkok, Thailand.

CITES Secretariat. 2004c. Resolution Conf. 9.24 (Rev. CoP13). Criteria for Amendment of Appendices I and II. October 2–14, Bangkok, Thailand.

CITES Secretariat. 2005a. SC53 Doc.10.1. Cooperation with the Food and Agriculture Organization of the United Nations. June 27–July 1, Geneva, Switzerland.

CITES Secretariat. 2005b. SC53. Summary Record (Rev. 1). June 27–July 1, Geneva, Switzerland.

CITES Secretariat. 2006. SC54 Doc. 10—Annex. CITES Issues with Respect to International Fish Trade and the CITES/FAO MoU. Committee on Fisheries, Sub-Committee on Fish Trade. May 30–June 2, Santiago de Compostela, Spain.

CITES Secretariat. 2007a. Com.II.7. Cooperation with the Food and Agriculture Organization of the United Nations: Draft Decisions of the Conference of the Parties. June 3–15, The Hague, Netherlands.

CITES Secretariat. 2007b. CoP14 Doc.68. Interpretation and Implementation of the Convention: Amendment of the Appendices—Proposals to Amend Appendices I and II. June 3–15, The Hague, Netherlands.

CITES Secretariat. 2007c. CoP14 Inf.26. Correspondence between the FAO and CITES Secretariats Concerning Proposals to Amend the Appendices. June 3–15, The Hague, Netherlands.

CITES Secretariat. 2007d. CoP14 Inf.64. The Interpretation of Annex 2 (a) (Criteria for the inclusion of species in Appendix II in accordance with Article II, paragraph 2 (a), of the Convention and Annex 5 (Annex 5: Definitions, Explanations and Guidelines) of Resolution Conf. 9.24 (Rev. CoP13) in Relation to Commercially-Exploited Aquatic Species). June 3–15, The Hague, Netherlands.

CITES Secretariat. 2007e. FAO Fisheries Report No. 833 FIMF/R833. Report of the Second FAO Ad Hoc Expert Advisory Panel for the Assessment of Proposals to Amend Appendices I and II of CITES Concerning Commercially-exploited Aquatic Species. March 26–30, Rome, Italy.

CITES Secretariat. 2007f. Resolution Conf. 10.4 (Rev. CoP14). Cooperation and Synergy with the Convention on Biological Diversity. June 3–15, The Hague, Netherlands.

CITES Secretariat. 2007g. Resolution Conf. 14.2. CITES Strategic Vision 2008–2013. June 3–15, The Hague, Netherlands.

CITES Secretariat. 2009a. CoP15 Doc. 63. Criteria for the Inclusion of Species in Appendices I and II. March 13–25, Doha, Qatar.

CITES Secretariat. 2009b. Resolution Conf. 9.24 (Rev. CoP15). Criteria for Amendment of Appendices I and II. March 13–25, Doha, Qatar.

CITES Secretariat. 2009c. SC58 Doc. 43. Interpretation and Implementation of the Convention: Amendment of the Appendices—Criteria for Amendment of Appendices I and II. July 6–10, Geneva, Switzerland.

CITES Secretariat. 2010a. AC25 Doc. 10. Criteria for the Inclusion of Species in Appendices I and II (Decisions 15.28 and 15.29). March 13–25, Doha, Qatar.

CITES Secretariat. 2010b. CoP15 Com.I Rec5 (Rev1). Summary Record. March 13–25, Doha, Qatar.

CITES Secretariat. 2012a. SC62 Doc. 39. Interpretation and Implementation of the Convention: Trade Control and Marking—Criteria for the Inclusion of Species in Appendices I and II. July 23–27, Geneva, Switzerland.

CITES Secretariat. 2012b. AC26 WG2 Doc. 1. Criteria for the Inclusion of Species in Appendices I and II (Decision 15.29). Twenty-sixth meeting of the Animals Committee. March 15–20, Geneva, Switzerland, and March 22–24, Dublin, Ireland.

CITES Secretariat. 2013. CoP16 Prop. 45. Consideration of Proposals for Amendment of Appendices I and II. March 3–15, Bankok, Thailand.

Clapham, Phillip J., et al. 2007. The Whaling Issue: Conservation, Confusion, and Casuistry. *Marine Policy* 31 (3):314–319.

Clapp, Jennifer, and Peter Dauvergne. 2005. *Paths to a Green World: The Political Economy of the Global Environment*. Cambridge, MA: MIT Press.

Clapp, Jennifer, and Doris Fuchs, eds. 2008. *Corporate Power in Agrifood Governance*. Cambridge, MA: MIT Press.

CMS [Convention on Migratory Species] CoP8. 2005. UNEP/CMS/ Resolution 8.11. Cooperation with Other Conventions. November 20–25, Nairobi, Kenya.

CMS CoP9. 2008. UNEP/CMS/Resolution 9.6. Cooperation with Other Bodies. December 1–5, Rome, Italy.

Colgan, Jeff, Robert Keohane, and Thijs Van de Graaf. 2012. Punctuated Equilibrium in the Energy Regime Complex. *Review of International Organizations* 7 (2):117–143.

Committee of Thirteen. 1930. *Report of the Committee*. Committee of Inquiry on the Organization of the Secretariat, the International Labour Office, and the Registry of the Permanent Court of Justice.

Conca, Ken. 1994. Rethinking the Ecology-Sovereignty Debate. *Millennium* 23 (3):701–711.

Conca, Ken. 2000. The WTO and the Undermining of Global Environmental Governance. *Review of International Political Economy* 7 (3):484–494.

Convention on Biological Diversity. 1992. Rio de Janeiro, June 5. United Nations Treaty Series 1760: 79.

Cox, Robert, and Harold Jacobson, eds. 1973. *The Anatomy of Influence*. New Haven: Yale University.

Cronin, B., and I. Hurd. 2008. *The UN Security Council and the Politics of International Authority*. New York: Routledge.

Crosby, Aaron, Soledad Aguilar, Melanie Ashton, and Stefano Ponte. 2010. *Environmental Goods and Services Negotiations at the WTO: Lessons from Multilateral Environmental Agreements and Ecolabels for Breaking the Impasse*. Winnipeg, Canada: International Institute for Sustainable Development.

Cutler, A. Claire, Virginia Haufler, and Tony Porter, eds. 1999. *Private Authority and International Affairs*. Albany: SUNY Press.

Dahl, Robert. 1957. The Concept of Power. *Behavioral Science* 2 (3):201–215.

Davey, William J. 2002. A Permanent Panel Body for WTO Dispute Settlement: Desirable or Practical? In *Political Economy of International Trade Law: Essays in Honor of Robert E. Hudec*, ed. Daniel Kennedy and James Southwick, 496–527. New York: Cambridge University Press.

Depledge, Joanna. 2007. A Special Relationship: Chairpersons and the Secretariat in the Climate Change Negotiations. *Global Environmental Politics* 7 (1):45–68.

DeSombre, Elizabeth. 2000. *Domestic Sources of International Environmental Policy*. Cambridge, MA: MIT Press.

Dickson, David, and Sian Lewis. 2010. More Research Needed into Biodiversity-Poverty Links. Science and Development Network. http://www.scidev.net/ global/ biodiversity/editorials/more-research-needed-into-biodiversity-poverty-links .html. Accessed May 25, 2010.

Djoghlaf, Ahmed. 2007a. Opening Statement of the Executive Secretary of the Convention on Biological Diversity. Statement delivered to the Annual Meeting of the United Nations Inter-Agency Support Group on Indigenous Issues. September 17, Montreal, Canada.

Djoghlaf, Ahmed. 2007b. Statement delivered to the International Conference in Defense of the Quality of the Night Sky and the Right to Observe the Stars. April 19, Montreal, Canada.

Djoghlaf, Ahmed. 2007c. Statement delivered on the Occasion of the Celebration of the International Day for Biological Diversity at the Millennium Seed Bank. May 22, Royal Botanic Gardens, Kew, UK.

Downs, George W. 2000. Constructing Effective Environmental Regimes. *Annual Review of Political Science* 3:25–42.

Economist. 2010. Eaten Away: A Ban on Trade in Bluefin Tuna Is Rejected. *Economist*, May 18.

Eglin, Richard. 1995. Trade and Environment in the World Trade Organization. *World Economy* 18 (6):769–779.

Esty, Daniel. 2002. The World Trade Organization's Legitimacy Crisis. *World Trade Review* 1 (1):7–22.

Falkner, Robert. 2003. Private Environmental Governance and International Relations: Exploring the Links. *Global Environmental Politics* 3 (2):72–87.

FAO [UN Food and Agriculture Organization]. 1998. FAO Fisheries Report No. 589. Report of the Sixth Session of the Subcommittee on Fish Trade. UN Food and Agriculture Organization, Rome.

FAO. 2001. Fisheries Report No. 667. Second Technical Consultation on the Suitability of the CITES Criteria for Listing Commercially Exploited Aquatic Species. UN Food and Agriculture Organization, Rome.

FAO. 2004a. Fisheries Report No. 746. Report of the Expert Consultation on Legal Issues Related to CITES and Commercially Exploited Aquatic Species. UN Food and Agriculture Organization, Rome.

FAO. 2004b. Fisheries Report No. 741. Report of the Expert Consultation on Implementation Issues Associated with Listing Commercially Exploited Aquatic Species on the CITES Appendices. UN Food and Agriculture Organization, Rome.

FAO. 2008. Financial Mechanisms for Adaptation to and Mitigation of Climate Change in the Food and Agriculture Sectors. Prepared for the High Level Conference on World Food Security: The Challenges of Climate Change and Bioenergy. June 3–5, Rome, Italy.

FAO and CITES. 2006. Memorandum of Understanding between the Food and Agriculture Organization of the United Nations (FAO) and the Secretariat of the Convention on International Trade in Endangered Species (CITES).

FAO Secretariat. 1998. COFI/99/Inf.16 Part II. Report of the Meeting of the FAO Ad Hoc Expert Group on Listing Criteria for Marine Species under CITES. November 20, Cape Town, South Africa.

FAO Secretariat. 2002. FI-709-08. COFI—Report on the Eighth Session of the Sub-Committee on Fish Trade. February 12–16, Bremen, Germany.

FAO Secretariat. 2013. About Us—Fisheries and Aquaculture Department. http://www.fao.org/fishery/en.

Finnemore, Martha, and Kathryn Sikkink. 1998. International Norm Dynamics and Political Change. *International Organization* 52 (04):887–917.

Folke, Carl, et al. 2004. Regime Shifts, Resilience, and Biodiversity in Ecosystem Management. *Annual Review of Ecology Evolution and Systematics* 35:557–581.

Franckx, Erik. 2006. The Protection of Biodiversity and Fisheries Management: Issues Raised by the Relationship between CITES and LOSC. In *The Law of the Sea: Process and Prospects,* ed. David Freestone, Richard Barnes, and David Ong, 210–232. Oxford: Oxford University Press.

GATT [General Agreement on Tariffs and Trade]. October 30, 1947. *United Nations Treaty Series* 55:194.

Gehring, Thomas. 2011. The Institutional Complex of Trade and Environment: Toward an Interlocking Governance Structure and a Division of Labor. In *Managing Institutional Complexity: Regime Interplay and Environmental Change,* ed. Sebastian Oberthür and Olav Schram Stokke, 227–254. Cambridge, MA: MIT Press.

Gehring, Thomas, and Sebastian Oberthür. 2000. Exploring Regime Interaction: A Framework for Analysis. Prepared for Final Conference of the Concerted Action Programme on the Effectiveness of the International Environmental Agreements and EU Legislation. Barcelona, Spain, November 9–12.

Gehring, Thomas, and Sebastian Oberthür. 2009. The Causal Mechanisms of Interaction between International Institutions. *European Journal of International Relations* 15 (1):125–156.

Giddens, A. 1984. *The Constitution of Society: Outline of the Theory of Structuration.* Cambridge, MA: Polity Press.

Government of India. 2009. *India's Fourth National Report to the Convention on Biological Diversity.* Ed. A. K. Goyal and Sujata Arora. New Delhi: Ministry of Environment and Forests.

Green, Jessica F., and Jeff Colgan. 2012. Protecting Sovereignty, Protecting the Planet: State Delegation to International Organizations and Private Actors in Environmental Politics. *Governance: An International Journal of Policy, Administration and Institutions* 26 (1):1–25.

Greener, Ian. 2005. The Potential of Path Dependence in Political Studies. *Politics* 25 (1):62–72.

Gruber, Judith. 1987. *Controlling Bureaucracies: Dilemmas in Democratic Governance.* Berkeley: University of California Press.

Gulbrandsen, Lars H., and Steinar Andresen. 2004. NGO Influence in the Implementation of the Kyoto Protocol: Compliance, Flexibility Mechanisms, and Sinks. *Global Environmental Politics* 4 (4):54–75.

Gupta, Joyeeta. 2012. Changing North-South Challenges in Global Environmental Politics. In *Handbook of Global Environmental Politics,* ed. Peter Dauvergne, 97–112. Cheltenham, UK: Edward Elgar.

Gutner, Tamar. 2005. Explaining the Gaps between Mandate and Performance: Agency Theory and World Bank Environmental Reform. *Global Environmental Politics* 5 (2):10–37.

Gutner, Tamar, and Alexander Thompson. 2010. The Politics of IO Performance: A Framework. *Review of International Organizations* 5 (3):227–248.

Haas, Ernst B. 1980. Why Collaborate? Issue-linkage and International Regimes. *World Politics* 32 (April):365.

Haas, Peter M. 1990. Obtaining Environmental Protection through Epistemic Consensus. *Millennium* 19 (3):347–363.

Haas, Peter M. 1997. Introduction: Epistemic Communities and International Policy Coordination. *International Organization* 46 (1):1–35.

Hajer, Maarten. 1995. *The Politics of Environmental Discourse: Ecological Modernization and the Policy Process.* Oxford: Oxford University Press.

Hajer, Maarten. 2003. Policy without Polity? Policy Analysis and the Institutional Void. *Policy Sciences* 36 (2):175–195.

Hall, Rodney Bruce. 1997. Moral Authority as a Power Resource. *International Organization* 51 (4):591–622.

Hall, Rodney Bruce, and Thomas J. Biersteker, eds. 2002. *The Emergence of Private Authority in Global Governance.* New York: Cambridge University Press.

Hardin, Garrett. 1968. The Tragedy of the Commons. *Science* 162 (3859): 1243–1248.

Hawkins, Darren G., and Wade Jacoby. 2006. How Agents Matter. In *Delegation and Agency in International Organizations,* ed. D. G. Hawkins, David A. Lake, Daniel L. Nielson, and M. J. Tierney. Cambridge: Cambridge University Press.

Hawkins, Darren G., David A. Lake, Daniel L. Nielson, and Michael J. Tierney, eds. 2006. *Delegation and Agency in International Organizations.* Cambridge: Cambridge University Press.

Held, David. 1995. *Democracy and the Global Order: From the Modern State to Cosmopolitan Governance.* Stanford: Stanford University Press.

Hjerpe, Mattias, and Björn-Ola Linnér. 2010. Functions of CoP Side-Events in Climate-Change Governance. *Climate Policy* 10 (2):167–180.

Hoda, Anwarul, and Ashok Gulati. 2008. *WTO Negotiations on Agriculture and Developing Countries.* Baltimore: Johns Hopkins University Press.

Holloway, Vivienne, and Esteban Giandomenico. 2009. Carbon Planet White Paper: The History of REDD Policy. Adelaide, SA: Carbon Planet Limited.

Hooper, David U., et al. 2005. Effects of Biodiversity on Ecosystem Functioning: A Consensus of Current Knowledge. *Ecological Monographs* 75 (1):3–35.

Hormeku, Tetteh. 2001. WTO Facing Crisis of Legitimacy, Needs Institutional Reforms. Paper presented at symposium for non-governmental organizations at the WTO, Geneva, Switzerland.

Howse, Robert. 2005. WTO Governance and the Doha Round. *Global Economy Journal* 5 (4):1–6.

Huber, John D., and Charles R. Shipan. 2002. *Deliberate Discretion? The Institutional Foundations of Bureaucratic Autonomy.* Cambridge: Cambridge University Press.

Huffbauer, Gary, Jeffrey Schott, Paul Grieco, and Yee Wong. 2005. *NAFTA Revisited: Achievements and Challenges.* Washington, DC: Institute for International Economics.

Hurd, Ian. 1999. Legitimacy and Authority in International Politics. *International Organization* 53 (2):379–408.

IIED [International Institute for Environment and Development]. 2009. *The Challenges of Environmental Mainstreaming: Experience of Integrating Environment into Development Institutions and Decisions.* London: IIED.

IISD [International Institute for Sustainable Development]. 1994. Summary of the Second Conference of the Parties to the Convention on Biological Diversity. *Earth Negotiations Bulletin* 9 (39): 1–10.

IISD. 1996. Third Session of the Conference of the Parties to the Convention on Biological Diversity. *Earth Negotiations Bulletin* 9 (65): 1–14.

IISD. 2002. Summary of the Twelfth Conference of the Parties to the Convention on International Trade in Endangered Species of Wild Fauna and Flora. *Earth Negotiations Bulletin* 21 (30): 1–16.

IISD. 2004. Summary of the Seventh Conference of the Parties to the Convention on Biological Diversity. *Earth Negotiations Bulletin* 9 (284): 1–18.

IISD. 2005. Summary of the First Meeting of the CBD Ad Hoc Open-Ended Working Group on Review of Implementation. *Earth Negotiations Bulletin* 9 (327): 1–16.

IISD. 2007a. Summary of the Fourteenth Conference of the Parties to the Convention on International Trade in Endangered Species of Wild Fauna and Flora. *Earth Negotiations Bulletin* 21 (61): 1–24.

IISD. 2007b. Summary and Analysis of the Thirteenth Conference of the Parties to the UN Framework Convention on Climate Change and Third Conference of the Parties Serving as the Meeting of the Parties to the Kyoto Protocol. *Earth Negotiations Bulletin* 12 (354): 1–22.

IISD. 2008. Summary of the Fourteenth Conference of the Parties to the UN Framework Convention on Climate Change and Fourth Meeting of the Parties to the Kyoto Protocol. *Earth Negotiations Bulletin* 12 (395): 1–20.

IISD. 2009. Summary of the Copenhagen Climate Change Conference. *Earth Negotiations Bulletin* 12 (459): 1–30.

IISD. 2010a. Summary of the Tenth Conference of the Parties to the Convention on Biological Diversity. *Earth Negotiations Bulletin* 9 (544): 1–30.

IISD. 2010b. Summary of the Simultaneous Extraordinary COPs to the Basel, Rotterdam and Stockholm Conventions and the 11th Special Session of the UNEP Governing Council/Global Ministerial Environment Forum. *Earth Negotiations Bulletin* 16 (84): 1–15.

IISD. 2010c. Summary of the Fifteenth Conference of the Parties to the Convention on International Trade in Endangered Species of Wild Fauna and Flora. *Earth Negotiations Bulletin* 21 (67): 1–20.

IISD. 2011. Summary of the Durban Climate Change Conference. *Earth Negotiations Bulletin* 12 (534): 1–34.

IISD. 2012a. Summary of the Doha Climate Change Conference. *Earth Negotiations Bulletin* 12 (567): 1–30.

IISD. 2012b. Summary of the Eleventh Conference of the Parties to the Convention on Biological Diversity. *Earth Negotiations Bulletin* 9 (595): 1–26.

IISD. 2013. Summary of the Sixteenth Meeting of the Conference of the Parties to the Convention on International Trade in Endangered Species of Wild Fauna and Flora. *Earth Negotiations Bulletin* 21 (83): 1–29.

International Civil Service Commission. 2013. Standards of Conduct for the International Civil Service. United Nations, New York.

International Monetary Fund. N.d. About the IMF—Staff of International Civil Servants. http://www.imf.org/external/about/staff.htm. Accessed March 1, 2014.

International Monetary Fund. 1998. IMF Code of Conduct for Staff. http://www.imf.org/external/hrd/code.htm.

IPCC [Intergovernmental Panel on Climate Change]. 1998. Second Assessment Report (AR2), Working Group II, The Regional Impacts of Climate Change: An Assessment of Vulnerability.

IPCC. 2007. Fourth Assessment Report (AR4), Working Group I, Summary for Policy Makers.

Jawara, Fatoumata, and A. Kwa. 2003. *Behind the Scenes: Power Politics in the WTO.* New York: Zed Books.

Jawara, Fatoumata, and Aileen Kwa. 2004. *Behind the Scenes at the WTO: The Real World of International Trade Negotiations; The Lessons of Cancun.* London: Zed Books.

Jinnah, Sikina. 2003. Emissions Trading under the Kyoto Protocol: NAFTA and WTO Concerns. *Georgetown International Environmental Law Review* 15 (1):709–761.

Jinnah, Sikina. 2010. Overlap Management in the World Trade Organization: Secretariat Influence on Trade-Environment Politics. *Global Environmental Politics* 10 (2):64–79.

Jinnah, Sikina. 2011a. Introduction: Climate Change Bandwagoning: The Implications of Strategic Linkages for Regime Design, Maintenance, and Death. *Global Environmental Politics* 11 (3):1–9.

Jinnah, Sikina. 2011b. Marketing Linkages: Secretariat Governance of the Climate-Biodiversity Interface. *Global Environmental Politics* 11 (3):23–43.

Jinnah, Sikina. 2012. Singing the Unsung: Secretariats in Global Environmental Politics. In *The Roads from Rio: Lessons Learned from Twenty Years of*

Multilateral Environmental Negotiations, ed. Pamela Chasek and Lynn Wagner, 107–126. London: RFF Press.

Joachim, Jutta, and Birgit Locher. 2008. World Apart or Worlds Together? Transnational Activism in the US and EU. In *Transnational Activism in the US and EU: A Comparative Perspective*, ed. Jutta Joachim and Birgit Locher, 163–174. Abingdon, UK: Routledge.

Jones, Kent. 2010. *The Doha Blues: Institutional Crisis and Reform in the WTO*. Oxford: Oxford University Press.

Juma, Calestous. 1989. *The Gene Hunters: Biotechnology and the Scramble for Seeds*. Princeton: Princeton University Press.

Keohane, Robert O., and David G. Victor. 2011. The Regime Complex for Climate Change. *Perspectives on Politics* 9 (1):7–23.

Kilcullen, R. J. 1996. Modern Political Theory: Max Weber: On Bureaucracy. [Course reading guide.] Macquarie University, Department of Politics, Sydney, Australia.

Koetz, Thomas, Peter Bridgewater, Sybille van den Hove, and Bernd Siebenhüner. 2008. The Role of the Subsidiary Body on Scientific, Technical, and Technological Advice to the Convention on Biological Diversity as Science-Policy Interface. *Environmental Science & Policy* 11 (6):505–516.

Koremenos, Barbara. 2008. When, What, and Why Do States Choose to Delegate? *Law and Contemporary Problems* 71 (1):151–192.

Krasner, Stephen D., ed. 1983. *International Regimes*. Ithaca: Cornell University Press.

Lacarte, Julio A. 2004. Transparency, Public Debate and Participation by NGOs in the WTO: A WTO Perspective. *Journal of International Economic Law* 7 (3):1–4.

Lee, James. 2009. *Climate Change and Armed Conflict*. New York: Routledge.

Levi, Margaret. 1997. A Model, a Method, and a Map: Rational Choice in Comparative and Historical Analysis. In *Comparative Politics: Rationality, Culture, and Structure*, ed. Mark I. Lichbach and Alan S. Zuckerman, 19–41. Cambridge, MA: Cambridge University Press.

Litfin, Karen. 1994. *Ozone Discourses: Science and Politics in Global Environmental Cooperation*. New York: Columbia University Press.

Lukes, S. 1974. *Power: A Radical View*. London: Macmillan.

Majone, Giandomenico. 2001. Two Logics of Delegation. *European Union Politics* 2 (1):103–122.

Martin, Lisa L., and Beth A. Simmons. 1998. Theories and Empirical Studies of International Institutions. *International Organization* 52 (4):729–757.

Martinetti, Irene. 2008. Secretariat and Management Reform. In *Managing Change at the United Nations*, ed. E. Perry. New York: Center for UN Reform Education.

Martínez-Garmendia, Josué, and James Anderson. 2005. Conservation, Markets and Fisheries Policy: The North Atlantic Bluefin and the Japanese Sashimi Market. *Agribusiness* 21 (1):17–36.

Marx, Fritz Morstein. 1957. *The Administrative State: An Introduction to Bureaucracy*. Chicago: University of Chicago Press.

Mathiason, John. 2007. *Invisible Governance: International Secretariats in Global Politics*. Bloomfield, NJ: Kumarian Press.

Mavroidis, Petros C. 2005. *The General Agreement on Tariffs and Trade: A Commentary*. New York: Oxford University Press.

McConnell, Fiona. 1996. *The Biodiversity Convention—A Negotiating History: A Personal Account of Negotiating the United Nations Convention on Biological Diversity—and After*. London: Kluwer Law International.

McGraw, Desiree M. 2002a. The CBD—Key Characteristics and Implications for Implementation. *RECIEL* 11 (1):17–28.

McGraw, Desiree. 2002b. *The Story of the Biodiversity Convention*. Aldershot, UK: Ashgate.

Mearsheimer, John J. 1994. The False Promise of International Institutions. *International Security* 19 (3):5–49.

Miles, Edward L., Steinar Andresen, Elaine M. Carlin, Jon Birger Skjærseth, Arild Underdal, and Jørgen Wettestad. 2002. *Environmental Regime Effectiveness: Confronting Theory with Evidence*. Cambridge, MA: MIT Press.

Millennium Ecosystem Assessment. 2012. Guide to the Millennium Ecosystem Assessment. http://www.Millenniumassessment.org/En/History.html.

Mitchell, Ronald B. 1994. Regime Design Matters: International Oil Pollution and Treaty Compliance. *International Organization* 48 (3):425–458.

Mitchell, Ronald B. 2003. International Environmental Agreements: A Survey of Their Features, Formation, and Effects. *Annual Review of Environment and Resources* 28:429–461.

Mitchell, Ronald B. 2013. International environmental agreements database project (version 2010.2). http://iea.uoregon.edu/page.php?file=home.htm&query=static.

Moats, Helen M. 1939. *The Secretariat of the League of Nations: International Civil Service or Diplomatic Conference?* Chicago: Department of Political Science, University of Chicago.

Moberg, Fredrik, and Carl Folke. 1999. Ecological Goods and Services of Coral Reef Ecosystems. *Ecological Economics* 29 (2):215–233.

Motaal, Doaa. 2002. The Observership of Intergovernmental Organizations in the WTO Post-Doha: Is There Political Will to Bridge the Divide? *Journal of World Intellectual Property* 5 (3):477–489.

Muir, John. 1911. *My First Summer in the Sierra*. Boston: Houghton Mifflin Company.

Myers, Norman. 1993. Biodiversity and the Precautionary Principle. *Ambio* 22 (2/3):74–79.

Myers, Norman, et al. 2000. Biodiversity Hotspots for Conservation Priorities. *Nature* 403 (6772):853–858.

Nadelmann, Ethan A. 1990. Global Prohibition Regimes: The Evolution of Norms in International Society. *International Organization* 44 (4):479–526.

Najam, Adil. 2004. The View from the South: Developing Countries in Global Environmental Politics. In *The Global Environment: Institutions, Law and Policy*. 2nd ed., ed. R. Axelrod et al. Washington, DC: Congressional Quarterly Press.

National Research Council. 1992. *Conserving Biodiversity:A Research Agenda for Development Agencies*. Washington, DC: The National Academies Press.

Newell, Peter. 2000. *Climate for Change: Non-State Actors and the Global Politics of the Greenhouse*. Cambridge: Cambridge University Press.

Neumayer, Eric. 2004. The WTO and the Environment: Its Past Record Is Better Than Critics Believe, but the Future Outlook Is Bleak. *Global Environmental Politics* 4 (3):1–8.

Nielson, Daniel L., and Michael J. Tierney. 2003. Delegation to International Organizations: Agency Theory and World Bank Environmental Reform. *International Organization* 57 (2):241–276.

NOAA [National Oceanic and Atmospheric Administration]. 2012. NOAA: Carbon Dioxide Levels Reach Milestone at Arctic Sites. May 31. http://research .noaa.gov/News/NewsArchive/LatestNews/TabId/684/ArtMID/1768/ArticleID/ 10187/NOAA-Carbon-dioxide-levels-reach-milestone-at-Arctic-sites.aspx.

Oberthür, Sebastian. 2009. Interplay Management: Enhancing Environmental Policy Integration among International Institutions. *International Environmental Agreement: Politics, Law and Economics* 9 (4):371–391.

Oberthür, Sebastian, and Thomas Gehring, eds. 2006. *Institutional Interaction in Global Environmental Governance: Synergy and Conflict among International and EU Policies*. Cambridge, MA: MIT Press.

Oberthür, Sebastian, and Olav Schram Stokke, eds. 2011. *Managing Institutional Complexity: Regime Interplay and Global Environmental Change*. Cambridge, MA: MIT Press.

OECD [Organization for Economic Cooperation and Development]. 2009. *Building Blocks for Policy Coherence for Development*. Paris: OECD.

Oxfam GB Policy Department. 2000. *Institutional Reform of the WTO*. Oxford, England: Oxfam.

Parry, Martin L., et al., eds. 2007. *Contribution of Working Group II to the Fourth Assessment Report of the Intergovernmental Panel on Climate Change, 2007*. Cambridge: Cambridge University Press.

Perenti, Michael. 1970. Power and Pluralism: A View from the Bottom. *Journal of Politics* 32:501–530.

Pierson, Paul. 2000. Increasing Returns, Path Dependence, and the Study of Politics. *American Political Science Review* 94 (2):251–267.

Pollack, Mark. 1997. Delegation, Agency, and Agenda Setting in the European Community. *International Organization* 51:99–134.

Polsby, Nelson W. 1980. *Community Power and Political Theory: A Further Look at Problems of Evidence and Inference*. 2nd ed. New Haven: Yale University Press.

Purves, Chester. 1945. *The Internal Administration of an International Secretariat.* London: Royal Institute of International Affairs.

Ranshofen-Wertheimer, Egon F. 1945. *The International Secretariat: A Great Experiment in International Administration.* Washington, DC: Carnegie Endowment for International Peace.

Raustiala, Kal, and David G. Victor. 2004. The Regime Complex for Plant Genetic Resources. *International Organization* 58:277–309.

Reeve, Rosalind. 2002. *Policing Trade in Endangered Species: The CITES Treaty and Compliance.* London: Earthscan Publishers.

Rosendal, Kristin G. 2001a. Impacts of Overlapping Regimes: The Case of Biodiversity. *Global Governance* 7 (1):995.

Rosendal, Kristin G. 2001b. Overlapping International Regimes: The Case of the Intergovernmental Forum on Forests (IFF) between Climate Change and Biodiversity. *International Environmental Agreement: Politics, Law and Economics* 1:447–468.

Royal Institute for International Affairs. 1944. *The International Secretariat of the Future: Lessons from Experiences by a Group of Former Officials of the League of Nations.* London: Royal Institute for International Affairs.

Ruggie, John Gerard. 1982. International Regimes, Transactions, and Change: Embedded Liberalism in the Postwar Economic Order. *International Organization* 36 (02):379–415.

Schattschneider, E. E. 1975. *The Semisovereign People: A Realist's View of Democracy in America.* New York: Holt, Rinehart and Winston.

Schroeder, Heike, and Heather Lovell. 2012. The Role of Non-Nation-State Actors and Side Events in the International Climate Negotiations. *Climate Policy* 12 (1):23–37.

Schroeder, Michael. 2013. Executive Leadership in the Study of International Organization: A Framework for Analysis. Paper presented at the International Studies Association (ISA) Annual Meeting, April 3–7, San Francisco.

Sebenius, James K. 1992. Challenging Conventional Explanations of International Cooperation: Negotiation Analysis and the Case of Epistemic Communities. *International Organization* 46 (01):323–365.

Selin, Henrik. 2010. *Global Governance of Hazardous Chemicals: Challenges of Multilevel Governance.* Cambridge, MA: MIT Press.

Selin, Henrik, and Stacy D. VanDeveer. 2003. Mapping Institutional Linkages in European Air Politics. *Global Environmental Politics* 3 (3):14–46.

Selin, Henrik, and Stacy D. VanDeveer. 2011. Institutional Linkages and European Air Politics. In *Governing the Air: The Dynamics of Science, Policy, and Citizen Interaction*, ed. Rolf Lidskog and Göran Sundqvist, 61–92. Cambridge, MA: MIT Press.

Shaffer, Gregory. 2001. The World Trade Organization under Challenge: Democracy and the Law and Politics of the WTO's Treatment of Trade and Environment Matters. *Harvard Environmental Law Review* 25 (1):1–93.

Shaffer, Gregory. 2002a. If Only We Were Elephants: The Political Economy of the WTO's Treatment of Trade and Environment Matters. In *Political Economy of International Trade Law: Essays in Honor of Robert E. Hudec*, ed. Daniel Kennedy and James Southwick, 349–393. New York: Cambridge University Press.

Shaffer, Gregory. 2002b. The Nexus of Law and Politics: The WTO's Committee on Trade and Environment. In *The Greening of Trade Law: International Trade Organizations and Environmental Issues*, ed. Richard H. Steinberg, 81–114. Lanham, MD: Rowman & Littlefield.

Shaffer, Gregory. 2005. The Role of the WTO Director-General and Secretariat. *World Trade Review* 4 (3):429–438.

Siebenhüner, Bernd. 2009. The Biodiversity Secretariat: Lean Shark in Troubled Waters. In *Managers of Global Change: The Influence of International Bureaucracies*, ed. Frank Biermann and Bernd Siebenhüner, 265–309. Cambridge, MA: MIT Press.

Simmons, B. A., and L. L. Martin. 2002. International Organizations and Institutions. In *Handbook of International Relations*, ed. Walter Carlsnaes, Thomas Risse, and Beth A. Simmons, 192–211. Thousand Oaks, CA: Sage Publications.

Singh, J. S. 2002. The Biodiversity Crisis: A Multifaceted Review. *Current Science* 82 (6):638–647.

Slaughter, Anne-Marie. 2004. *A New World Order*. Princeton: Princeton University Press.

Speth, James Gustave. 2005. *Red Sky at Morning: America and the Crisis of the Environment*. New Haven: Yale University Press.

Stanford, Rosemary. 1994. International Environmental Treaty Secretariats: Stage-hands or Actors? In *Green Globe Yearbook of International Co-operation on Environment and Development*, ed. H. Bergesen and G. Parmann. Oxford: Oxford University Press.

Steinberg, Richard. 1997. Trade-Environment Negotiations in the EU, NAFTA, and WTO: Regional Trajectories of Rule Development. *American Journal of International Law* 91 (2):231–267.

Stokke, Olav Schram. 2000. Managing Straddling Stocks: The Interplay of Global and Regional Regimes. *Ocean and Coastal Management* 43 (102):205–234.

Stokke, Olav Schram. 2004. Trade Measures and Climate Compliance: Institutional Interplay between WTO and the Marrakesh Accords. *International Environmental Agreement: Politics, Law and Economics* 4 (4):339–357.

Strand, Jonathan R., and John P. Tuman. 2013. Japanese Foreign Aid and Voting in the Convention on International Trade in Endangered Species (CITES). Paper prepared for the 2013 Annual Meeting of the International Studies Convention, San Francisco.

Strange, Susan. 1983. Cave! Hic Dragones: A Critique of Regime Analysis. In *International Regimes*, ed. Steven Krasner, 337–354. Ithaca: Cornell University Press.

Takacs, David. 1996. *The Idea of Biodiversity: Philosophies of Paradise.* Baltimore: Johns Hopkins University Press.

Tamiotti, Ludivine, and Matthias Finger. 2001. Environmental Organizations: Changing Roles and Functions in Global Politics. *Global Environmental Politics* 1 (1):56–76.

Tollison, Robert D., and Thomas D. Willett. 1979. An Economic Theory of Mutually Advantageous Issue Linkages in International Negotiations. *International Organization* 33 (4):425–449.

UN General Assembly. 1972. 2997 (XXVII) of 15 December. Institutional and Financial Arrangements for International Environmental Cooperation.

UN General Assembly. 2001. UN Common System: Report of the International Civil Service Commission. A/RES/56/244. Adopted by the General Assembly. United Nations.

UN General Assembly. 2005. 2005 World Summit Outcome. A/RES/60/1. Adopted by the General Assembly. United Nations.

UN General Assembly. 2012. The Future We Want. A/RES/66/288. Adopted by the General Assembly. United Nations.

UN General Assembly. 2013. System-Wide Coherence—Independent Evaluation of Lessons Learned from Delivering as One. http://www.un.org/en/ga/deliver ingasone/index.shtml.

UNCEB [United Nations Chief Executive Board]. 2013. Official website. http://www.unsceb.org/.

UNEP [United Nations Environmental Programme]. 2000. UNEP Meeting on Enhancing Synergies and Mutual Supportiveness of Multilateral Agreements and the World Trade Organization, October 23, Geneva, Switzerland. UNEP, Division of Technology, Industry and Economics, Economics and Trade Unit.

UNEP. 2004. Implementing Sustainable Development: Building Capacity for Integrated Policy Design and Implementation. Workshop Report—UNEP-UNCTAD Capacity Building Task Force. UNEP, Economics and Trade Branch.

UNEP Governing Council. 1989. Decision 15/34—Preparation of an International Legal Instrument on the Biological Diversity of the Planet. May 25, Nairobi, Kenya.

UNEP World Conservation Monitoring Centre 2004. *Synergies and Cooperation: A Status Report on Activities Promoting Synergies and Cooperation between Multilateral Environmental Agreements in Particular Biodiversity-Related Conventions, and Related Mechanisms.* Cambridge, UK: United Nations Environment Programme.

UNEP World Conservation Monitoring Centre. 2013. Conventions and Policy Support—Integrated Reporting to the Rio Conventions. http://www.unep-wcmc .org/integrated-reporting-to-the-rio-conventions_675.html.

UNFCCC [United Nations Framework Convention on Climate Change]. 2008. Integrating Practices, Tools and Systems for Climate Risk Assessment and

Management and Strategies for Disaster Risk Reduction into National Policies and Programmes. Technical Paper FCCC/TP/2008/4. November 21.

United Nations. 2009. *ST/SGB/2009/6: Staff Regulations*. New York: United Nations.

United States of America. 2004. Sub-Paragraph 31(I) of the Doha Declaration: Submission by the United States. World Trade Organization Document number TN/TE/W/40.

Urpelainen, Johannes. 2012. Unilateral Influence on International Bureaucrats. *Journal of Conflict Resolution* 56 (4):704–735.

Valentini, Laura. 2005. Environmental Quality Provision and Eco-labeling: Some Issues. Working Paper No. ERSD-2005-02. World Trade Organization, Geneva.

Von Moltke, Konrad. 2001. The Organization of the Impossible. *Global Environmental Politics* 1 (1):22–28.

Waltz, Kenneth. 1979. *Theory of International Politics*. New York: Random House.

Wambaugh, Sarah. 1921. Two Accomplishments of the Existing League—The Secretariat and the Assembly. *Annals of the American Academy of Political and Social Science* 96: 16–21.

Wapner, Paul. 2011. The Challenges of Planetary Bandwagoning. *Global Environmental Politics* 11 (3):137–144.

Weber, Max. 1978. Bureaucracy. In *Economy and Society*, ed. G. Roth and C. Wittich, vol. 2. Berkeley: University of California Press.

Weber, Max. 2009. *Essays in Sociology*. London: Routledge.

Webster, D. G. 2011. The Irony and the Exclusivity of Atlantic Bluefin Tuna Management. *Marine Policy* 35 (2):249–251.

Weiler, Joseph. 2001. The Role of Lawyers and the Ethos of Diplomats: Reflections on the International and External Legitimacy of WTO Dispute Settlement. *Journal of World Trade* 35 (2):191–207.

Weiss, Edith Brown. 1993. International Environmental Issues and the Emergence of a New World Order. *Georgetown Law Journal* 81 (3):675–710.

Weiss, Thomas G., ed. 1975. *International Bureaucracy*. Lexington, MA: Lexington Books.

Weiss, Thomas G. 1982. International Bureaucracy: The Myth and Reality of the International Civil Service. *International Affairs (Royal Institute of International Affairs 1944)* 58 (2): 287–306.

Wijnstekers, Willem. 2001. *The Evolution of CITES*. Geneva, Switzerland: CITES Secretariat.

Williams, Marc. 2001. Trade and Environment in the World Trading System: A Decade of Stalemate? *Global Environmental Politics* 1 (4):1–9.

Wilson, James Q. 1967. The Bureaucracy Problem. *Public Interest* 6 (Winter): 3–9.

WTO [World Trade Organization]. 1994. Marrakesh Agreement Establishing the World Trade Organization. April 15.

WTO. 2006. Report of the Panel on European Communities—Measures Affecting the Approval and Marketing of Biotech Products. WTO, Geneva. http://wto.org/. Accessed July 21, 2009.

WTO. 2007. Understanding on Rules and Procedures Governing the Settlement of Disputes (Dispute Settlement Understanding—DSU). WTO, Geneva.

WTO Appellate Body. 1998. United States—Import Prohibition of Certain Shrimp and Shrimp Products. WT/DS58/AB/R. WTO, Geneva.

WTO CTESS. 2006a. Environmental Project Approach: Compatibility and Criteria. Proposal by India. WTO, Geneva.

WTO CTESS. 2006b. Summary Report of the Sixteenth Meeting of the Committee on Trade and Environment Special Session, July 6–7. WTO, Geneva.

WTO CTESS. 2007. Summary Report on the Eighteenth Meeting of the Committee on Trade and Environment Special Session, May 3–4. WTO, Geneva.

WTO CTESS. 2008. Summary Report on the Twenty-First Meeting of the Committee on Trade and Environment in Special Session, November 1–2, 2007. WTO, Geneva.

WTO Dispute Settlement Body. 2006. Report of the Panel: European Communities—Measures Affecting the Approval and Marketing of Biotech Products. WTO, Geneva.

WTO Secretariat. 1997. Taxes and Charges for Environmental Purposes—Border Tax Adjustment. WTO, Geneva.

WTO Secretariat. 2007a. Committee on Trade and Environment: List of Documents. WT/CTE/INF/5/Rev.8. WTO, Geneva. http://wto.org/. Accessed July 21, 2009.

WTO Secretariat. 2007b. Committee on Trade and Environment—Special Session: Existing Forms of Cooperation and Information Exchange between UNEP/MEAs and the WTO—Note by the Secretariat—Revision. TN/TE/S/2/Rev.2. WTO, Geneva. http://wto.org/. Accessed July 21, 2009.

WTO Secretariat. 2007c. Dispute Settlement: One-Page Summaries. WTO, Geneva.

WTO Secretariat. 2007d. World Trade Organization Annual Report. WTO, Geneva. http://wto.org/. Accessed July 21, 2009.

WTO Secretariat. 2012. WTO Annual Report 2012. http://www.wto.org/english/res_e/booksp_e/anrep_e/anrep12_e.pdf. Accessed May 15, 2013.

WTO Secretariat. 2013a. Committee on Trade and Environment—Special Session—Matrix on Trade Measures Pursuant to Selected Multilateral Environmental Agreements—Revision. (TN/TE/5/rev.4). www.wto.org. Accessed March 5, 2014.

WTO Secretariat. 2013b. Environment: Disputes 4. Mexico etc. versus US: "Tuna-Dolphin." http://www.wto.org/english/tratop_e/envir_e/edis04_e.htm.

WTO Secretariat. 2013c. Trade and Environment at the WTO. http://www.wto.org/english/res_e/booksp_e/trade_env_e.pdf. Accessed March 5, 2014.

Young, Margaret. 2010. Protecting Endangered Marine Species: Collaboration between the Food and Agriculture Organization and the CITES Regime. *Melbourne Journal of International Law* 11 (2):441–490.

Young, Margaret. 2011. *Trading Fish, Saving Fish*. Cambridge: Cambridge University Press.

Young, Oran R. 1991. Political Leadership and Regime Formation: On the Development of Institutions in International Society. *International Organization* 43 (3):281–308.

Young, Oran. 1994. The Effectiveness of International Governance Systems. In *International Governance: Protecting the Environment in a Stateless Society*, ed. Oran Young. Ithaca: Cornell University Press.

Young, Oran. 1996. Institutional Linkages in International Society: Polar Perspectives. *Global Governance* 2 (1):1–24.

Young, Oran. 2002. *The Institutional Dimensions of Global Change: Fit, Interplay, and Scale*. Cambridge, MA: MIT Press.

Young, Oran R., W. Bradnee Chambers, Joy A. Kim, and Claudia ten Have, eds. 2008. *Institutional Interplay: Biosafety and Trade*. Tokyo, New York, and Paris: United Nations University Press.

Young, Oran R., et al. 2006. The Globalization of Socio-Ecological Systems: An Agenda for Scientific Research. *Global Environmental Change* 16 (3):304–316.

Index